LANGUAGE HACKING

A CONVERSATION COURSE
FOR BEGINNERS

ITALIAN

Learn how to speak Italian

– with actual people –

right from the start!

BENNY LEWIS
THE IRISH POLYGLOT

First published in Great Britain in 2016 by John Murray Learning. An Hachette UK company.
First published in the US in 2016 by Quercus US

British Library Cataloguing in Publication Data: a catalogue record for this title is available
from the British Library.

Library of Congress Catalog Card Number: on file.

9781473633124
4

Cover image © Allison Hooban
Illustrations © Will McPhail
Typeset by Integra
Printed and bound by Clays Ltd, St Ives plc

John Murray Learning policy is to use papers that are natural, renewable and recyclable
products and made from wood grown in sustainable forests. The logging and manufacturing
processes are expected to conform to the environmental regulations of the country of origin.

John Murray Learning Ltd
Carmelite House
50 Victoria Embankment
London EC4Y 0DZ
www.hodder.co.uk

Also available
in ebook

YOUR MISSIONS

A NOTE FROM BENNY

It's true that some people spend years studying Italian before they finally get around to speaking the language.

But I have a better idea.

Let's skip the years of studying and jump right to the speaking part.

Sound crazy? No, it's language hacking.

#LanguageHacking is a completely different approach to learning a new language.

It's not magic. It's not something only 'other people' can do. It's simply about being smart with *how* you learn: learning what's indispensable, skipping what's not, and using what you've learned to have real conversations in Italian right away.

As a language hacker, I find shortcuts to learning new languages – tricks and techniques to crack the language code and make learning simple so I can get fluent faster. When it comes to learning new languages, I focus on getting the biggest bang for my buck.

There's no need to learn every word and grammar rule before you start using the language. You just need to know *the most common* and *the most versatile* phrases you'll need in most situations, and how to 'speak around' the problem when there's something you don't understand or know how to say yet.

#LanguageHacking isn't just a course. It's a new way of thinking about language learning. It shows you how to learn a language and gives you all the language you need – and none of what you don't. You can use it on your own or with any other book to start speaking languages faster.

I'd like to show you how it's done. See you on the inside.

Benny

Benny Lewis, Language Hacker

HOW TO USE THIS COURSE

The most common complaint I hear from language learners is:

'I studied Italian for years in school. I can understand a few words when I see them, and even sometimes when I hear them, but I still can't speak the language.'

#LanguageHacking isn't like traditional grammar-based courses. It's a *conversation* course, which means you will focus on building the language skills you need to have meaningful, real-life conversations with other people in Italian – right away.

By the end of this course, you'll be able to introduce yourself and ask and answer hundreds of typical questions in Italian. You'll know how to find and connect with other Italian speakers no matter where you live. And you will gain the skills and strategies to have countless conversations entirely in Italian – as well as the confidence to keep them going.

#LanguageHacking can be used either on its own or alongside any other language course – whether written, online, or in the classroom. Just grab your notebook and get started!

WHAT YOU'LL FIND INSIDE

This course will challenge you to **speak from day one** by completing ten missions which will grow your conversational abilities in Italian. To keep that promise, I invite you to become a part of the language hacking community, built with this course in mind, that gives you a safe and fun place to communicate with other likeminded and determined learners. You can complete the missions on your own, but you'll progress much faster if you use the language with real people, so I encourage you to submit your missions to the #LanguageHacking online community www.teachyourself.com/languagehacking for feedback (and secret mini-missions!).

SPEAKING FROM DAY 1

You can't learn to play the piano until you sit down and put your fingers on the keys. You can't play tennis until you pick up the racquet. And you can't learn a language if you don't speak it. By speaking from day one, you will:

···> pick up expressions and language from others
···> notice the expression gaps in your language you need to fill
···> become aware of how other people say things

···⟩ get feedback from others
···⟩ improve your pronunciation and fluency
···⟩ conquer the fear of speaking a new language
···⟩ feel motivated by hearing your own progress

BUILD YOUR LANGUAGE SKILLS

Build language through typical conversations

Each unit takes you through three **conversations** in Italian that show you how the language is used in common, everyday contexts. The conversations build on each other to grow your vocabulary and prepare you for your mission. Treat each conversation like a lesson, and make sure you understand everything before you move on to the next conversation.

Figure it out exercises

You'll read each conversation and listen to the audio, then I'll help you **Figure it out**. These exercises train you to start understanding Italian on your own – through context, recognizing patterns, and applying other language learning strategies – without relying on translations. By figuring out language for yourself, you'll internalize it better and recall it faster when you need it.

Notice exercises

Every conversation is followed by a **phrase list** with the key phrases, expressions, and vocab to remember from that conversation, with English translations and pronunciation to help you. **Notice** exercises get you thinking about the new language and noticing how the language works, so you're gaining an intuitive understanding of Italian.

Practice exercises

Practice exercises reinforce what you learn. You'll piece together different parts of what you know to figure out how to create new Italian phrases on your own.

Put it together

Finally, you'll take everything you've learned and **Put it Together** to create your own repertoire in Italian. I'll help you prepare 'me-specific' language you can use in real life conversations – Italian that's actually relevant to you.

SUPPORT, TECHNIQUES, AND STRATEGIES

In language hacking, your ability to have conversations in Italian is not limited by the number of words you know.

As you go along, you may develop your own shortcuts for making learning simple. If you do, share them with others and me, and use the hashtag #languagehacking.

#LanguageHacks

You'll **learn unconventional shortcuts** to boost your language abilities exponentially. I reveal the different patterns, rules and tools to help you crack the code and get fluent faster. Each of the ten hacks equips you with techniques you can use in this course and throughout the rest of your learning journey.

Conversation strategies

You'll learn essential conversation strategies, like **conversation connectors, filler words,** and **survival phrases** to strike up conversations and keep them flowing.

Grammar & pronunciation

We'll cover the foundation of the **grammar you need to know,** but I won't overload you with what's not essential to communication. I'll help you understand the important parts of Italian **pronunciation** and share techniques to help you get them right.

Side notes

I'll share more insights as we go along – like culture tips about Italian speakers and Italian-speaking countries, vocab tips on how to get creative with new phrases, and mini-hacks for better learning.

Progress you can see

You will see your progress build steadily throughout this course. Before you finish each unit, you'll **check your understanding** with audio practice that acts as a 'virtual conversation partner'. This practice gives you time to collect your thoughts and speak at your own pace.

Before you move on to your mission, you'll do a **self assessment checklist** to make sure you're prepared and to keep a visual record of the progress you're making.

MISSIONS

Each unit ends with *three tasks* that you'll complete as your final Mission.

STEP 1: build your script

To get ready for spoken practice with other people, you'll build 'me-specific' scripts with the language you need to talk about your life. These scripts make sure you're learning useful Italian phrases that are truly relevant to you.

STEP 2: speak Italian with other people... *online.*

Speaking from day one is the best way I've found to quickly reach fluency. I'll help you implement this strategy, no matter where you live, with the missions you'll complete as part of the language hacking community. You'll record yourself speaking your scripts aloud in Italian and upload them to the community where you'll get feedback from other learners and keep the conversation going. This is the best practice you can get – aside from one-to-one conversations with a native speaker. By speaking in front of others you'll become more confident using Italian in the real world.

STEP 3: learn from other learners

When you share your missions with other learners, you'll get more comfortable speaking Italian – and more importantly, you'll get comfortable speaking the imperfect beginner's Italian that everyone must use on the road to fluency. You'll gain insight into how conversations flow in Italian, and you'll learn where the 'expression gaps' are in your scripts that you need to fill to expand your conversation skills.

In other words, you'll have everything you need to genuinely start having conversations with other people in Italian. After all, isn't that the point?

Let's get started.

WHAT YOU'LL FIND ONLINE

Go to www.teachyourself.com/languagehacking to:

···⟩ Submit your missions
···⟩ Download the course audio
···⟩ Find an up-to-date list of the best free online resources to support your learning
···⟩ Review the transcripts for the audio
···⟩ Discover additional materials to help you on your learning journey
···⟩ Find out more about #LanguageHacking and Benny Lewis

Check back frequently as we add cool new language hacking features.

THE LANGUAGE HACKER CONTRACT

In this course you will:

···⟩ **get shortcuts (#languagehacks)** to learn a new *lingua* fast
···⟩ **learn the words and** *le frasi* you need to have real conversations immediately
···⟩ **gain the confidence** to start speaking *italiano* from day one
···⟩ **have access** to a *comunità* of like-minded language learners

That's my side of the bargain. It's what I'm giving you.

Now here's your side of the contract. I recommend you read it every day so it embeds in your memory and becomes part of who you are.

I will speak Italian today and every day – if only a little. It will feel awkward and uncomfortable at times. And that's okay.

I will accept that the only way to speak perfectly is to first make mistakes. The only way to overcome my fear is to face it. The only thing preventing me from speaking Italian is... speaking Italian.

I will embrace my inner Tarzan. I will say things in Italian like 'I Benny. Me writer. I Ireland.' I'll do this because I'm still learning, and because I don't take myself too seriously. I will communicate effectively instead of perfectly. Over time, I will make massive leaps.

I will build 'me-specific' scripts – mini monologues about myself. I will memorize these scripts and rely on them whenever I'm asked questions. I will discover time and time again that I can manage the most common situations I come across in a new language. I will quickly feel my confidence build as I equip myself with the language I need.

I will speak at every opportunity and be an active participant in the language hacking community. I will learn from giving and getting feedback.

I will build my skills, day by day, piece by piece.

I will learn smarter. I will be self-sufficient. I will make learning Italian part of my daily routine. I will become fluent faster than I ever imagined possible.

I am a language hacker.

Sign here: _____   Date: _____

PRONUNCIATION GUIDE

Italian is a phonetic language, which means that each single letter, or particular letter combination follows the same rule all the time.
Most letters are pronounced as you would expect them to be, but here's a quick overview of some key rules to keep in mind. Try to use the native recordings provided to train your ear and tongue to the sounds!

CONSONANTS

🔊 00.01 Most consonants in Italian are similar to those in English, but here are some exceptions.

Seen in	Explanation	Meaning
c (before 'e' or 'i')	'ch' sound, like in 'chat'	concerto, piacere, ciao
c (before 'a' or 'o' or 'u')	'k' sound, like in 'can'	con, casa, come
ch	'k' sound, like in 'chemistry'	anche, che, chi
g (before 'e' or 'i')	'j' sound, like in 'jam'	gelato, giorno, gente
g (before 'a' or 'o' or 'u')	'g' sound, like in 'go'	lingua, guidare, lungo
gh	'g' sound, like in 'go'	funghi, ghetto, spaghetti
gn	'ny' sound, like in 'canyon'	gnocchi, lasagna, bagno
r	a sound made by tapping the roof of your mouth with your tongue, like half way between an 'l' and a 'd'	artista, Irlanda, caro
sc (before 'i' or 'e')	'sh' sound, like in 'she'	capisce, uscita, pesce

VOWELS

🔊 00.02 Here are all the vowel sounds you'll hear in Italian.

Seen in	Explanation	Meaning
a	'ah' sound, like in 'apple'	casa, papà, pasta
e	'eh-' sound, like the 'e' in 'they' cut short	sera, e, me
e	open 'eh' sound, like in 'set'	presto, bello, vento
i	like the 'ee' in free	vino, amico, in
o	short 'aw' sound, like in 'pop'	nome, sole, volo
o	'oh' sound, like in 'lot'	no, cosa, otto
u	'oo' sound, like in 'room'	blu, una, Luca

You can see that there are two versions of 'e' and 'o', but you'll be understood fine if you mix them up as a beginner.

While this list doesn't cover all possible unexpected pronunciations, you should be OK saying anything else as you'd expect when reading Italian aloud.

TALKING ABOUT ME

Your mission

Imagine this – you've just arrived in Italy. You step up to get your passport checked, and the agent asks you about yourself.

Your mission is to convince the agent to let you through. Be brave and say *buongiorno*. Then have a basic exchange – entirely in Italian – for 30 seconds.

Be prepared to **say your name**, **where you're from**, **where you live**, **why you're coming to Italy**, and especially **why you're learning Italian**.

This mission will prepare you for the inevitable questions you'll be asked in any first conversation you have in Italian.

Mission prep

···⟩ Learn basic phrases for talking about yourself: *sono ...*
···⟩ Create simple sentences to talk about your likes and wants, using *voglio*, *mi piace*.
···⟩ Develop a conversation strategy: turn the tables by asking, *e tu?*
···⟩ Learn the words for countries, nationalities, professions and interests.
···⟩ Use the connector words *perché*, *e*, *ma*.

BUILDING SCRIPTS

Most first conversations in a new language are predictable. As a beginner, this is great news for you. We're going to start by building your first 'script' to help you prepare for what you'll need to say most, right away. We'll start slow and build as we move on.

If you've studied Italian before, some of the words in this unit may be familiar to you. But we'll be doing much more than just learning words in each unit: we're going to start *building scripts*. Once you learn a script, you can customize it to your needs. This will help you build your language so you can use it from the start.

#LANGUAGEHACK
get a head start with words you already know

CONVERSATION 1

The first words you'll use in every conversation

CULTURE TIP:
at the bar
In Italy, the *bar* or *caffetteria* is a place where you hang out with friends and hold casual meetings. Even the few Italians who don't drink coffee, ask their friends to meet for coffee (*prendiamo un caffè insieme*), either in a bar or at home.

Let's follow the story of Melissa, a journalist and Italian learner who has just arrived in Rome. She plans to spend the summer discovering the ancient Roman civilization, admiring Italian art, eating Italian food ... and immersing herself in Italian! She signs up for an Italian class held in a local bar, and today she's meeting her tutor, Cesco, for the first time.

🔊 01.01 This is a typical introductory conversation – one that you'll have yourself over and over. Listen to the conversation, and pay attention to the way Melissa asks *e tu?*

As a beginner, your first step is building basic, introductory conversations. After an initial greeting, a typical first conversation usually turns toward topics of where you live and what you do.

> **Cesco:** Melissa?
>
> **Melissa:** Ciao. Sì, sono Melissa. E tu?
>
> **Cesco:** Ciao e benvenuta a Roma! Sono Cesco.
>
> **Melissa:** Grazie!
>
> **Cesco:** Allora, parlami di te!
>
> **Melissa:** Allora, sono americana. E sono una giornalista. Sono qui a Roma per studiare l'italiano. E tu?
>
> **Cesco:** Sono italiano, ovviamente! Sono insegnante di italiano. E vivo qui, a Roma.

LEARNING STRATEGY:
deduce meaning from context
While you may not be able to figure out what a word means in isolation, the words around it give you clues you can combine with what you already know to deduce the meaning. This use of **context** is an essential language learning strategy.

When you see or hear new Italian words for the first time, they are going to seem like random noise. But if you train yourself to look and listen a little closer, you'll realize that there's a lot you can figure out based on the *context* of the conversation and how the words relate to English. The key is to try to notice the language for yourself.

Time to think about the conversation you just heard! Notice how Italian sentence structure differs from English. The more you actively think about the different ways Italian uses word order and expressions, the faster you'll learn.

FIGURE IT OUT

1 What do you think *sono* means? _____

2 Which two phrases does Cesco use to greet Melissa? What do you
   think they mean?

   _____   _____

3 What phrase does Melissa use to bounce the question back to Cesco?
   Underline it, then write it here. _____

4 Find the Italian word that answers each question, and write it out.

   Example: What nationality is Cesco? italiano_____

   a What's Melissa's job? _____

   b What nationality is Melissa? _____

   c Where does Cesco live? _____

You can figure out
the answers to all
these questions even
if you don't know
a word of Italian,
thanks to **context**.
Pretty cool, huh?

NOTICE

🔊 01.02 Listen to the audio and study the table.

Essential phrases for Conversation 1

CONVERSATION
STRATEGY: e tu?
If you're uncomfortable
doing a lot of talking
at first, a trick I like to
use is to simply bounce
the question back to
the other person, so I
can listen for a while. In
Italian, it's easy to do,
with a simple E tu?

Italian	Meaning
ciao	hi
sì, sono Melissa	yes, I'm Melissa
e tu?	and you?
grazie!	thanks!
allora, parlami di te!	so, tell me about yourself!
sono americana	I'm American (woman)
... italiano	... Italian (man)
sono una giornalista	I'm a journalist
sono qui a Roma ...	I'm here in Rome ...
... per studiare l'italiano.	... to study Italian.
sono italiano, ovviamente!	I'm Italian, of course!
sono insegnante di italiano	I'm an Italian teacher
vivo qui, a Roma	I live here, in Rome

VOCAB: -mente
for '-ly'
In Italian, the ending
-mente corresponds
to the English '-ly', for
example, 'obviously'
(ovviamente) or
'naturally'
(naturalmente).

1 How do you say the following in Italian?

In English we say
'I'm a dentist' and
'I'm an artist', but
in Italian the 'a/an'
is optional when
you're stating your
profession. That's
why Melissa says
Sono una giornalista
and Cesco just says
Sono insegnante di
italiano.

a I am _____ sono

b I live in (city). _____ vivo

c And you? _____ e tu

d I'm Italian. _____ sono italiano

2 Complete the Italian phrase for, 'Tell me about yourself!'

_____ parlimi _____ di te!

PRONUNCIATION: *i* and *u*

The *i* sound in Italian is always pronounced as the 'ee' in 'f**ee**l'. And the Italian *u* is always pronounced like the 'u' in 'fl**u**id'. So *tu* sounds like 'two'.

🔊 01.03 Try it yourself with these words *vivo*, *blu* and *lui*. Read the words out loud to see how you think they are pronounced, then listen to the audio and repeat to mimic the native speaker.

PRACTICE

Though some of this language may be familiar, you should still practise pronouncing these words out loud now to start building muscle memory. This will help you develop your Italian accent right away.

🔊 01.04 Here's some new vocab to help you keep building your language script. Listen to the audio and study the table.

Countries	Nationalities	Professions	Interests
Stati Uniti	americano / a	giornalista	cinema
Inghilterra	inglese	insegnante	teatro
Canada	canadese	programmatore	fotografia
Italia	italiano / italiana	farmacista	musica, danza moderna
Cina	cinese	receptionist	tennis
Australia	australiano / australiana	artista	televisione
Russia	russo / russa	medico	filosofia
Spagna	spagnolo / spagnola	segretario	bicicletta
Messico	messicano / messicana	veterinario	arti marziali
Francia	francese	architetto	computer
Irlanda	irlandese	blogger	le lingue (languages)

PRONUNCIATION: *a phonetic language*
Yes, always! While English has inconsistent spelling-to-pronunciation associations (it can be learned 'through, tough, thorough, thought, though' ...), almost every letter in Italian has a particular sound which is pronounced one way.

SPEAKING: *take a risk!*
Something I hear all the time from Italian learners is 'Benny, I've studied Italian for years, but I still can't speak it!' This happens when you spend all your time reading, listening to, or studying Italian, but not actually speaking it. Whatever you do, don't study Italian in silence. You have to use the language, even if it feels weird or silly at first. It will only get better with use!

You'll start to notice that sometimes, words are written differently depending on whether the person described is male or female. Masculine words in general end in o, and feminine words in a. More on this in Unit 3!

If you don't already have one, find a good Italian dictionary. This will help you build vocab that I call 'me-specific'. As we go along, you'll need to look up your own words that apply to your life to make your scripts more useful. Let's start now.

1 What are the professions and interests of the people in your life? What countries are they from?

   a Look for any professions, interests, country names and nationalities of people you know in the table and circle them.

   b Add three new words to each category using words that are specific to you or people close to you.

2 Now, answer these questions in Italian. How do you …

   a say your name? *Sono* … _____

   b say what nationality you are? _____

   c say your profession? _____

   d tell someone what city you live in? _____

3 Cover up the translations in the phrase list, and see if you can remember what the Italian expressions mean.

PUT IT TOGETHER

Allora, parlami di te! Let's start building your script. Throughout this course, I'll help you keep building this script. You'll draw on this again and again as you start having your first conversations in Italian with actual people.

There are lots of ways you can practise Italian in your community and online. Check out our **Resources** online for some suggestions. You'll also find suggestions for good, free online dictionaries and apps, as well as learner-friendly ink-and-paper dictionaries.

Using the conversation as a model, as well as the vocab and 'me-specific' words you just looked up, create four sentences about yourself. Write out in Italian:

⋯⟶ your name   Io Sono _____

⋯⟶ where you're from _____

⋯⟶ what you do for a living _____

⋯⟶ where you live. _____

CONVERSATION 2

Describing your interests

When you talk to someone for the first time, you'll often get a question like, 'So, what do you like to do?'. In this conversation, Cesco and Melissa talk about their interests.

🔊 01.05 Listen for familiar-sounding words to see if you can understand the gist of what the speakers are saying.

Cesco:	Allora, cosa ti piace?
Melissa:	Mi piace la pizza, ma non mi piace la bruschetta.
	Mi piace il cinema. Amo la letteratura.
	E tu? Dimmi, cosa ti piace?
Cesco:	Allora, sono molto attivo! Mi piace visitare i musei e adoro il tennis. È il mio sport preferito!
Melissa:	Dormire è il mio sport preferito!

There's so much Italian you already know thanks to **cognates** - words that are the same, or nearly the same, in both English and Italian.

PRONUNCIATION:
bruschetta
While you may be tempted to pronounce the *ch* in Italian as you would in English words like 'chat', in Italian it's actually only ever pronounced like the 'ch' in 'chemist'. Try to think of the Italian *ch* as a 'k' instead.

FIGURE IT OUT

1 What phrase does Cesco use to ask Melissa what she likes?

_____

2 Use context and words you recognize to figure out:

   a What type of food does Melissa like? _____

   b What does Melissa not like? Underline the phrase she uses to say what she doesn't like, then write it out.

   _____

   c What is Melissa's favourite "sport"? _____

3 Notice the words that look or sound familiar in the conversation. Find and highlight the Italian for these words:

   a literature   b I adore   c museums   d to visit

4 Look at the conversation again and highlight other familiar words.

NOTICE

🔊 01.06 Listen to the audio and study the table.

HACK IT: *word chunks*
It's often best to learn words in chunks rather than understanding each part. *Mi piace* is a great example. Although it translates literally as 'it pleases me', think of it as meaning '**I like**'.

Essential phrases for Conversation 2

Italian	Meaning
cosa ti piace?	what do you like?
mi piace …	I like … (to-me it-pleases)
… la pizza	… pizza
… il cinema	… cinema
… visitare i musei	… visiting museums (to-visit the museums)

ma non mi piace ...	but I don't like ...
la bruschetta	bruschetta
amo ...	I love ...
la letteratura	literature
adoro ...	I adore ...
il tennis	tennis
dormire	sleeping (to-sleep)
... è il mio sport preferito!	... is my favourite sport! (is the my sport favourite!)

GRAMMAR TIP:
word order
The word order in Italian can be different from what you're used to. Don't worry! If you use slightly incorrect word order, people will still understand you. As you read through this course, take note of the **word-for-word translations in brackets**, and you'll start to get a feel for how the language works.

1 How is the Italian phrase for 'I like' worded differently from English?

2 Notice all the familiar words. Can you fill in the translations?

a museums _____   e I don't like _____

b I like _____   f literature _____

c I love _____   g to visit _____

d I adore _____

PRACTICE

1 What is your favourite sport? Create a phrase that's true for you.

_____ *il mio sport*

preferito!

2 Now use this phrase to create new sentences about your own favourite things. What is your:

a favourite food? (*cibo*) _____ *il mio* _____ *preferito!*

b favourite film? (*film*) _____ *il mio* _____ *preferito!*

c favourite museum? (*museo*) _____ *il mio* _____ *preferito!*

3 Next, cover up the translations in the phrase list, and see if you can remember what the Italian expressions mean.

#LANGUAGEHACK:
get a head start with words you already know

I've already introduced you to a lot of cognates in this unit. Here are some simple tips to help you use them to quickly build up your vocabulary.

Can you guess the English meaning of these Italian cognates (or near cognates)?

pizza	televisione	telefono
cultura	moderno	differente
artista	situazione	

English has borrowed many words from languages related to Italian, and more recently, Italian has borrowed many words from English. Sometimes the spelling of these words is the same in both languages, and sometimes there are slight changes.

Luckily, you can follow straightforward patterns to guess when a word is likely to be a (near) cognate in Italian, so you can use something like the English word you know already. It's a safe bet to guess with cognates when you're talking about ...

professions, concepts, technical vocabulary or scientific words	pilota, trigonometria, coesione, organismo, letteratura, biologia
words ending in '-tion' in English	ammirazione , associazione, istruzione, opzione, posizione
any English nouns that end in '-tude', '-or', '-ist', '-nce', '-ty'	altitudine, attore, ottimista, arroganza, università (with slight spelling alterations)

Expert tip: Words that are formal in English are more likely to be similar in Italian. For instance, if you forget how to say 'country' in Italian, you could say *nazione* (nation) instead. This is a slightly more formal word, but you can use this cognate to get your point across, without needing to learn a new word!

Part of the unique rhythm of Italian comes from its abandonment of awkward letter combinations! Words with certain letter combinations become a repeated single letter in Italian – as in *attore* (actor), *ottimista* (optimist) and *ammira(re)* (admire). You'll also see 'h' removed from the start of words like *ospedale*.

YOUR TURN: use the hack

You'll internalize this #languagehack much better if you try it out yourself now. So let's get you using this technique right away.

1 🔊 01.07 Practise pronouncing Italian cognates and notice how different they sound to English. Repeat each word to try to mimic the speaker.

animale	*storia*	*tradizione*	*ristorante*	*politica*
dizionario	*musica*	*passione*	*nazionale*	*televisione*

2 Go back through Conversations 1 and 2 and find five cognates. Write them in the following cheat sheet.

Cognates cheat sheet

Italian cognate	English meaning	Italian cognate	English meaning
visitare	to visit	_____	_____
_____	_____	_____	_____
_____	_____	_____	_____
_____	_____	_____	_____
_____	_____	_____	_____

3 What English words can you think of that are likely to be Italian cognates? Guess four new cognates using the rules you've just learned, then use your Italian dictionary to check your answers. Write down any new cognates you discover on your cheat sheet!

Example: democracy → democrazia

You'll notice that Italian sometimes adds the word 'the' (*il*, *la*, etc.) before a noun when we wouldn't in English. We'll discuss the differences between these 'the' words later.

GRAMMAR EXPLANATION: verb + noun

The sentence structure introduced in this conversation is the verb + noun form. It uses action words (verbs) followed by a person, place or thing (noun) – the same way we do it in English. Because of this, the sentence structure will be simple for you to learn and use.

Examples: *Voglio* un cappuccino .   *Amo* la musica.   *Mi piace* la pasta.
            verb + noun   verb + noun   verb + noun

1   What things do you like, love, or dislike? Complete the sentences with the nouns from the box. Make the sentences true for you!

| la pizza | la bruschetta | il caffè | il vino | la televisione |

a   *Amo/adoro* (I love / adore) _____

b   *Mi piace* (I like) _____

c   *Non mi piace* (I don't like) _____

PUT IT TOGETHER

It's time to use this form yourself by talking about your own likes and dislikes.

1   Write out some details about your own life in Italian. Use your dictionary to look up new words that describe yourself. Be sure to:
- ⋯⟩ combine verbs you've just learned with places and things (nouns)
- ⋯⟩ create three new sentences about things you like a lot (*mi piace molto*), and two sentences about things you don't like
- ⋯⟩ describe a few of your favourite things!

     Mi piace molto l'espresso!

2   Now read your script over and over again. Try to memorize it too!

CONVERSATION 3

Why are you learning Italian?

One question you'll hear again and again is simply, 'Why are you learning Italian?'. So let's prepare your answer now.

🔊 01.08 Cesco wants to know why Melissa is learning Italian. Notice the way Melissa forms her answer. How does she say 'because'?

> **Cesco:** Dimmi, perché vuoi imparare l'italiano?
>
> **Melissa:** Be', voglio imparare l'italiano perché ... voglio parlare una bella lingua e voglio capire la cultura italiana. Poi voglio vivere e lavorare in Italia e per me la musica italiana è molto interessante!
>
> **Cesco:** Ti piace la musica classica o la musica pop?

FIGURE IT OUT

1 What words do the speakers use to ask a question (e.g. 'why?') and to give a reason (e.g. 'because'). Circle them, then write them out.

   why? _____   because _____

2 Why is Melissa learning Italian? Circle at least three of the reasons she gives in the conversation.

3 What do you think the following phrases mean in English?

   a *la cultura italiana* _____

   b *la musica classica o la musica pop* _____

   c *in Italia* _____

4 Find two cognates in this conversation, then go back and add them to your Cognates cheat sheet.

You'll definitely get this question when you have your first conversation in Italian – know how to answer it!

This filler word is technically short for *bene* (well), but strangely enough accompanied by a slight raising of the shoulders or inclination of the head...

CULTURE TIP:
become a local expert
Flattery will get you everywhere! As well as Italian culture and history, you'll find that many Italians are even prouder of the region they come from, and the traditions of their home town. Find out as much as you can about the place your Italian friends are from, and become the biggest fan of the local football team – you'll become their new best friend!

5 What do you think is the difference between *voglio* and *vuoi*?

_____

CULTURE TIP:
tu or *Lei?*
Italian has two ways
of referring to a single
'you': one is informal,
tu (with verbs ending
in *i* like *vuoi*), and the
other is formal, *Lei*.
For this course, we're
mostly sticking with the
informal form, because
honestly, that's the form
you'll use when you're
casually chatting with
people your age, or
even language partners
helping you learn.

NOTICE

🔊 01.09 Listen to the audio and study the table.

Essential phrases for Conversation 3

Italian	Meaning
perché ...	why ...
vuoi imparare l'italiano?	do you want to learn Italian?
voglio imparare l'italiano perché ...	I want to learn Italian because ...
voglio ...	I want ...
... parlare una bella lingua	... to speak a beautiful language
... capire la cultura italiana	... to understand Italian culture
e poi	and also
vivere e lavorare in Italia	to live and work in Italy
per me ...	for me ...
la musica italiana è molto interessante!	Italian music is very interesting!

Bonus 2-for-1 deal –
the words for 'why'
and 'because' are
identical in Italian:
perché.

CONVERSATION STRATEGY: smooth out your sentences with connector words

Speaking in short, simple sentences doesn't sound very natural, but when you're a beginner in Italian, it gets the job done. You can start smoothing out your Italian sentences by adding in **connector words**. Words like *e, o, ma, perché* ('and', 'or' 'but' and 'because') help you connect your thoughts to sound more natural:

'I want to learn Italian <u>because</u> I want to learn a beautiful language, <u>and</u> I want to understand Italian culture ...'

1 What words in Italian correspond to these English connector words?

a or _____ b but _____ c and _____ d because _____

2 Notice the Italian word for 'is'. Use this word to say in Italian:

a Cinema is interesting. *Il* _____ ____ _____

b The culture is different here.
   La _____ ____ *differente qui.*

3 Look at the phrase list again. Which five verbs follow the expression *voglio*? Underline the verbs then write them here.

_____ _____ _____ _____ _____

4 Write the following in Italian, and notice the similarity in the way the words are formed.

a I want to learn _____

b I love to speak _____

c I adore to live _____

5 Write out the Italian cognates:

a culture _____

b language _____

c music _____

d interesting _____

e classic _____

f pop _____

Go back and add any new words to your Cognates cheat sheet.

GRAMMAR EXPLANATION: combining two verbs

In Conversation 3, you saw a new sentence structure that combines two forms of Italian verbs – the 'I form' and the 'dictionary form'.

Here are two set phrases that use these verb types, which you can use to avoid more complicated phrases.

Voglio + verb (dictionary form)   *Mi piace* + verb (dictionary form)
'I want' + to (do something)   'I like' (It pleases me) + to (do something)

Examples: *Voglio parlare*   *Mi piace* visitare
            I want to speak   I like to visit (visiting)

You can use these combinations in nearly endless ways.

We call this the 'dictionary form' because it's the way the verb looks when you find it in a dictionary. You can also think of it as the 'to-form' (*parlare* is 'to speak'), and language buffs call it the 'infinitive'. This form will always end in *-are, -ere* or *-ire* in Italian.

In English, you might want to say 'I like visiting museums' instead of 'I like to visit museums'. In Italian, both are the same.

◀)) 01.10 Listen to the audio and study the table. Pay careful attention to the pronunciation of the words – especially their endings.

Common verbs

dictionary form	io form	dictionary form	io form
amare (to love)	amo (I love)	studiare (to study)	studio (I study)
volere (to want)	voglio (I want)	viaggiare (to travel)	viaggio (I travel)
vivere (to live)	vivo (I live)	visitare (to visit)	visito (I visit)
parlare (to speak)	parlo (I speak)	aiutare (to help)	aiuto (I help)
imparare (to learn)	imparo (I learn)	trovare (to find)	trovo (I find)

PRACTICE

1 Practise using the new sentence structure and vocabulary you've seen so far. Use the prompts given to answer the questions in Italian.

Perché studi italiano?

a _____ *questa lingua affascinante.* (**I find** this language fascinating.)

b _____ _____ *in Italia!* (**I want to live** in Italy!)

c _____ _____ _____ *nuove lingue!* (**I like learning** new languages!)

d _____ *presto l'Italia.* (**I'm visiting** Italy soon.)

Perché sei qui in Italia?

e _____ *incontrare gli italiani.* (**I want to** meet Italian people.)

f _____ _____ _____ *il cibo italiano!* (**I like eating** Italian food!)

g _____ _____ *qui.* (**I want to study** here.)

h _____ _____ *la cultura italiana.* (**I want to understand** Italian culture.)

Remember that Italian includes *il/la* before nouns – but don't worry about getting this right for now. If you're unsure, **guess** *il*, and you have a 50/50 chance of being right!

2 Use Conversation 3 and the verb list to figure out how you would say the following sentences in Italian. Write them out.

a _____ _____ *italiano.* (I love to speak Italian.)

b _____ _____ _____ _____ *i* _____. (I don't like to visit (the) museums.)

c _____ _____ _____ *le lingue.* (I like to learn languages.)

d _____ _____ *l'Italia.* (I want to visit Italy.)

3 Now practise the two sentence structures you've just learned, and combine them with the correct usage of *e, ma, o* and *perché*.

a Talk about your two favourite foods (verb + noun structure).

Mi piace _____, *e mi piace* _____.

b Say one thing you like and one thing you don't (verb + noun).

Mi piace _____, _____ *non mi piace* _____.

c Ask what someone else likes (verb + verb).

Ti piace _____, *o ti piace* _____?

d How would you begin to explain why you like something?
Mi piace _____ …

Whenever you learn new phrases, you should always supplement them with 'me-specific' language you look up yourself, to really make them your own. Always!

PUT IT TOGETHER

Now it's time for you to practise using the sentence structure yourself!

1 Create four sentences in Italian that use the sentence structures you've just learned to say things that are true for you. Look up new verbs or nouns in your dictionary. Be sure to say why you're learning Italian.

Example: <u>Voglio capire l'italiano.</u> (I want to understand Italian.)

If you're planning to visit Italy, one of your sentences should say why you're visiting or what you like about the country!

Voglio imparare l'italiano perché …

COMPLETING UNIT 1

Check your understanding

◀)) 01.11 Go back and reread the conversations. Then when you're feeling confident:

⋯⟩ listen to the audio rehearsal, which will ask you questions in Italian

⋯⟩ then pause or replay the audio as often as you need to understand the questions

⋯⟩ and repeat after the speaker until the pronunciation feels and sounds natural to you

⋯⟩ finally, answer the questions in Italian (in complete sentences).

Each unit will build on the previous one, helping you to review as you move ahead. Pause or replay the audio as often as you need to understand the questions. Do your best to answer out loud in complete sentences.

Show what you know...

Here's what you've just learned. Write or say an example for each item in the list. Then tick off the ones you know.

☑ Introduce yourself.   *Sono Benny!*
☐ Say where you're from.
☐ Talk about something you like and something you don't like.
☐ Give three Italian–English cognates.
☐ Ask the question, 'Why do you want to learn Italian?'
☐ Give a reason why you're learning Italian, 'Because ...'
☐ Give the Italian connector words for 'and', 'so', 'because' and 'but'.
☐ Give a phrase you can use to bounce a question back to someone else.
☐ Use and combine verbs in two different forms.
  ☐ I like ...
  ☐ I want to ...

LEARNING STRATEGY:
active listening
When you do a listening exercise, make sure you *actively pay attention* to the audio. A common mistake is to listen to Italian audio 'in the background', thinking it will still 'sink in'. The truth is, there's a huge difference between hearing a language and listening to a language. Make sure 100% of your attention is on the audio while it plays!

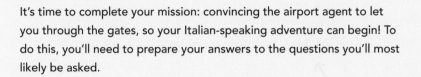

COMPLETE YOUR MISSION

It's time to complete your mission: convincing the airport agent to let you through the gates, so your Italian-speaking adventure can begin! To do this, you'll need to prepare your answers to the questions you'll most likely be asked.

STEP 1: build your script

Start your script with the phrases you've learned in this unit, combined with 'me-specific' vocabulary, to answer common questions about yourself. Be sure to:

···⟩ say your name and occupation using *sono*
···⟩ say where you're from and where you live using *sono* and *vivo*
···⟩ say why you're visiting Italy using *perché/mi piace/adoro*
···⟩ say why you're learning Italian with *voglio imparare … perché …*
···⟩ use connector words along the way to sound a bit more fluent!
···⟩ Write down your script, then repeat it until you feel confident.

LEARNING STRATEGY: *document your progress* Writing is an effective way to help **store information in your long-term memory.** Try to carefully write out each of your missions before speaking them. Keep a journal so you can see how your language develops.

STEP 2: real language hackers speak from day one … *online*

So, if you're feeling good about your script, it's time to complete your mission and share a recording of you speaking your script with the community. So, go online, find the mission for Unit 1 and give it your best shot.

You'll find some **bonus missions** too, for serious Italian hacking! Go to www.teachyourself.com/languagehacking

STEP 3: learn from other learners

How well can you understand someone else's introduction? After you've uploaded your own clip, check out what the other people in the community have to say about themselves. Would you let them past security? **Your task is to ask a follow-up question in Italian to at least three different people.**

STEP 4: reflect on what you've learned

What did you find easy or difficult about this unit? Did you learn any new words or phrases in the community space? After every script you write or conversation you have, you'll gain a lot of insight for what 'gaps' you need to fill in your script. Always write them down!

HEY, LANGUAGE HACKER, LOOK AT YOU GO!

You've only just started on the new path to #languagehacking, and you've already learned so much. You've taken the first crucial steps, and started to interact with others using Italian. This is something other students don't do even after years of studying, so you should be truly proud of yourself.

Molto bene!

2 ASKING ABOUT YOU

Your mission

Imagine this – your friend drags you to your first *scambio linguistico* (language exchange) in Rome. You want to blend in and not rely on English.

Your mission is to fool someone into thinking you speak Italian for at least 45 seconds.

Be prepared to strike up a conversation and talk about **how long you've been living** in your current location, **what you like to do**, and the **languages you speak** or want to learn. After the 45 seconds have passed, reveal how long you've been learning Italian and dazzle them! To avoid arousing suspicion, keep the other person talking by asking casual questions to show your interest.

This mission will give you the confidence to initiate conversations with new people.

Mission prep
···⟩ Use the question and answer words *da*, *da quando*.
···⟩ Ask and respond to questions using the *tu* form.
···⟩ Negate sentences using *non*.
···⟩ Develop a conversation strategy: using the filler words *allora*, *be'*, *quindi* to create conversational flow.
···⟩ Pronounce new Italian sounds (the Italian *r*).

BUILDING LANGUAGE FOR ASKING QUESTIONS

Let's build on the simple (but effective!) technique of bouncing back a question with *e tu*, and learn to form more specific questions using several new sentence structures.

#LANGUAGEHACK
learn vocab faster with memory hooks

CONVERSATION 1

Words you need to ask questions

No matter where you live in the world, there are other Italian learners who want to practise Italian with you. You can also find native speakers to help you learn. See our Resources to learn how to connect with other Italian learners and speakers.

CULTURE TIP: *scambi linguistici*
Many people in Italy want to learn English. *Scambi linguistici* is where you can meet up with locals in Italy to help you start speaking your Italian from day one. You might talk with someone for 20 minutes in Italian while he or she helps and corrects you, then 20 minutes in English. The great thing is that it's typically completely free for everyone involved!

Let's check back in with our learner, Melissa. Just a few days into her stay in Rome she has dived right into the Italian language. She has arranged a *scambio linguistico* with a local Romano, Luca, who wants to learn English.

🔊 02.01 After the initial introductions, Melissa and Luca start talking about their language skills. Pay attention to the differences between the way Luca asks questions and how Melissa answers them.

CONVERSATION STRATEGY:

anticipate common questions
When you start speaking Italian, a common conversation topic is language learning itself. It makes sense – if you're learning Italian, people will ask if you speak other languages. Have your answer prepared!

Luca:	Melissa, ti piace vivere qui a Roma?
Melissa:	Sì, certo. Amo vivere qui. Imparo tanto italiano!
Luca:	Benissimo! Parli altre lingue?
Melissa:	No, parlo solo inglese e un po' di italiano. E tu?
Luca:	Sì, io parlo bene lo spagnolo e parlo un po' di russo.
Melissa:	Davvero?
Luca:	Sì, davvero! Ma non parlo inglese!
Melissa:	Peccato!
Luca:	Non ancora … Quindi oggi spero di praticare un po' del mio inglese maccheronico.

Here, Luca says that he speaks *inglese maccheronico*, which is 'macaroni English' – an expression meaning 'broken English', since it's as messed up as macaroni.

FIGURE IT OUT

1 Use context along with what you learned in Unit 1 to figure out:

   a How many languages does Melissa speak? _____

   b Does Melissa like living in Rome?   *sì / no*

   c Does Luca speak English?   *sì / no*

2 Are these statements about the conversation *vero* (true) or *falso* (false)?

   a Melissa is not learning Italian.   *vero / falso*

   b Melissa speaks Russian.   *vero / falso*

   c Luca speaks Italian.   *vero / falso*

3 How do you say, 'yes really!' in Italian? _____

4 How do you make a sentence negative in Italian? What word makes the difference between saying 'I speak' and 'I don't speak'? _____

5 How would you negate the following statements in Italian?

   a *Voglio imparare lo spagnolo.*

   _____

   b *Vivo a Milano.*

   _____

   c *Amo l'arte moderna.*

   _____

   d *Mi piace viaggiare* (to travel).

   _____

GRAMMAR TIP:
il/lo for 'the'
You can see that sometimes in Italian, you'll say 'the' before a language name. This is usually *il*, but if the next word starts with *s* and then a non-vowel, or a *z*, *il* will change to *lo*.

NOTICE

02.02 Listen to the audio and study the table.

Essential phrases for Conversation 1

Italian	Meaning
ti piace ...	do you like ...
vivere qui?	living here?
sì, certo	yes, of course
amo vivere qui	I love living here
imparo tanto italiano!	I'm learning so much Italian
parli altre lingue?	do you speak any other languages?
no ...	no ...
parlo solo inglese	I only speak English (I-speak only English)
parlo un po' di italiano	I speak a little Italian (I-speak a little of Italian)
io parlo bene lo spagnolo	I speak Spanish well (I I-speak well the Spanish)
davvero?	really?
non parlo inglese	I don't speak English
peccato!	what a pity! (pity!)
non ancora	not yet
quindi ...	so ...
oggi spero di praticare ...	I hope to practise today ... (today I-hope of to-practise)
... un po' del mio inglese!	... a little bit of my English!

To remember that *imparo* means 'I learn', think 'I am imperfect at something until *imparo*!'

GRAMMAR TIP:
'I learn' and 'I am learning'
'I learn Italian' and 'I am learning Italian' can both be translated as *imparo l'italiano*. Nice and easy!

To remember that *non ancora* means 'not yet', imagine being on a big boat at sea having a blast with your Italian *amici*. Since you're having so much fun, when the boat pulls into port you yell 'No anchor! – (not yet!)'

1 What are the two phrases Luca uses to describe how well he speaks Spanish and Russian? Underline them in the phrase list, then write them here.

_____   _____

2 Compare *Parlo solo inglese* with 'I only speak English'. Where does the word *solo* appear? Use this word order to fill in the gaps in Italian.

a _____ _____ _____ (I only speak Italian.)

b _____ _____ _____ _____ _____
(I only love classical music.)

GRAMMAR TIP:
word order
You'll notice that word order can sometimes be different in Italian. If you use a slightly incorrect word order, people will understand you fine. For now, whenever you see a sentence translated again in parentheses like this, you can get a glimpse into how the language works without worrying about why.

GRAMMAR EXPLANATION: asking questions and giving answers

The structure of question sentences doesn't differ from the structure of simple statements. Asking yes / no questions in Italian couldn't be simpler: you just need to raise your intonation at the end of a sentence.

🔊 02.03 Listen to the audio and notice how the intonation makes it clear whether it's a questions or a statement.

a Ti piace vivere qui a Roma? ↗   (Do you like living here in Rome?)

b Ti piace vivere qui a Roma. ↘   (You like living here in Rome.)

c Non parli altre lingue? ↗   (Don't you speak any other languages?)

d Non parli altre lingue. ↘   (You don't speak other languages.)

GRAMMAR EXPLANATION: 'don't'

To make a negative statement in Italian, just add *non* before the verb. So, the negation of the sentence *Amo il tennis* is simply *Non amo il tennis* (lit. 'not I-like the tennis').
– The 'do' in 'I do not like ...' isn't translated.

Examples:
Non ti piace il teatro.   →   You don't like theatre.
Parli inglese? No, non parlo inglese.
→   Do you speak English? No, I don't speak English.

You'll notice the slight difference between *no* (no) and *non* (not) in Italian. So when answering a question negatively, you may say: No, non vivo a Milano (No, I don't live in Milan).

1 Practise using question and answer forms. Use the forms given below to answer the questions first in the affirmative, then in the negative.

> *mangio* (I eat)   *lavoro* (I work)   *voglio* (I want)

a *Mangi carne?* (Do you eat meat?)

Sì _____   No _____

b *Lavori in ospedale?* (Do you work in the hospital?)

Sì _____   No _____

c *Vuoi venire alla festa?* (Do you want to come to the party?)

Sì _____   No _____

PRACTICE

1 Fill in these sentences with the missing word(s) in Italian.

a *Parlo* _____ *inglese.* (I speak **only** English.)

b _____ _____ _____ _____ *russo.*
   (**I'm learning a little bit of** Russian.)

c *Imparo* _____ *italiano qui a Roma.*
   (I'm learning **so much** Italian here in Rome.)

d _____! _____ *parlo* _____! (**Really! I don't** speak Italian!)

e _____, _____ *spagnolo!* (**Today, I'm studying** Spanish!)

2 🔊 02.04 Practise recognizing the difference in sound between questions and statements in Italian. Listen to the audio. Choose 'D' if you hear a *domanda* (question), and 'R' if you hear a *risposta* (reply).

a D / R	c D / R	e D / R
b D / R	d D / R	f D / R

3 Change these statements to questions. Then say them out loud (use question intonation!)

a *Alessandro vive a Roma.* _____

b *Parli spagnolo.* _____

c *Marco impara l'italiano.* _____

PUT IT TOGETHER

1 Practise learning new words for languages on your own. Use your
  dictionary to look up the Italian translations for the languages given.
  Then add, in Italian, two more languages that you would like to learn.

  a German ＿＿＿＿＿＿＿   d ＿＿＿＿＿＿＿＿＿＿＿

  b French ＿＿＿＿＿＿＿   e ＿＿＿＿＿＿＿＿＿＿＿

  c Chinese ＿＿＿＿＿＿＿

2 Time to create sentences that are true for you! How would you
  answer the questions? If you speak other languages, say whether you
  speak them 'well' or 'only a little bit', and if you want to learn other
  languages, say which ones. Write out your answers here in Italian. Then
  repeat them out loud.

  a *Parli altre lingue?*

     Sì, parlo ＿＿＿＿＿＿＿＿＿＿＿＿＿＿＿＿＿＿＿＿

     No, ＿＿＿＿＿ *parlo* ＿＿＿＿＿＿＿＿＿＿＿＿＿＿＿＿

  b *Vuoi imparare altre lingue?*

     Sì, voglio ＿＿＿＿＿＿＿＿＿＿＿＿＿＿＿＿＿＿＿＿

     No, ＿＿＿＿＿ *voglio* ＿＿＿＿＿＿＿＿＿＿＿＿＿＿＿＿

#LANGUAGEHACK:
learn vocab faster with memory hooks

You may think you don't have the memory to learn lots of new words. But you absolutely can! The trick I use for remembering vocab is **mnemonics**, or memory hooks.

A mnemonic is a learning tool that helps you remember a lot more words and phrases. I've already given you two mnemonics in Conversation 1. Remember:

> ⋯⟫ *Non ancora* ('No anchor!') means 'not yet'?
> ⋯⟫ *Imparo* ('I'm imperfect until I learn') means 'I learn'?

These associations act like glue for your memory. The key to a good mnemonic is to think about an image or sound that connects the word to its meaning, then try to make it silly, dramatic, or shocking – make it memorable!

The easiest way to do this is through **sound association**. Simply say the Italian word out loud until you can think of an English word that sounds like it. It may even be similar in meaning.

Examples:

> ⋯⟫ the word for 'light', *la luce*, starts with the same sound as 'Lucy', so think of the Beatles song 'Lucy in the sky with diamonds' and how much light shines through diamonds.
> ⋯⟫ the word for 'book' *il libro*, sounds like 'library'.

If you can't think of a similar-sounding word, then try to use a **powerful image** to hook the Italian word and its meaning to a familiar word in an interesting or ridiculous (to go with the example) way.

Example:

> ⋯⟫ to remember that *sole* means 'sun', imagine looking up at the sky and seeing the 'sole' of a giant foot shining there.

YOUR TURN: use the hack

I'll occasionally hint at tricks you can use to remember new vocab. For now, you should get used to creating new mnemonics yourself!

🔊 **02.05** Listen to the audio to hear the pronunciation of each word. Then use sound or image association to create your own mnemonics for each. Repeat the words to mimic the speakers.

a *la strada* = 'the street'
b *caro* = 'expensive'
c *la cosa* = 'thing'

CONVERSATION 2

How long have you been learning Italian?

Another 'first question' you can expect when you speak Italian with someone new is 'How long have you been learning Italian?' Let's learn to recognize and respond to that question now.

🔊 02.06 Can you identify the Italian phrase for 'how long ...?'

> Luca: Da quando studi italiano?
>
> Melissa: Studio italiano da due settimane.
>
> Luca: Solo due settimane!? Parli molto bene italiano!
>
> Melissa: No, non è vero ... sei molto gentile. Grazie.
>
> Luca: Prego. Adoro imparare nuove lingue!
>
> Melissa: Interessante! Quante lingue vuoi imparare ancora?
>
> Luca: Be', un giorno spero di imparare tre lingue: l'inglese, il giapponese e l'arabo. Specialmente il giapponese, perché mi piace la cultura giapponese.
>
> Melissa: Oh! Il giapponese è molto difficile.
>
> Luca: Macché! È come bere un bicchiere d'acqua!

It's quite common to receive complimenti (compliments) in Italy. A good way of responding is to say *Sei molto gentile*, as Melissa does here. But if you hear somebody saying Non fare complimenti! (Don't make compliments!), they mean 'don't stand on ceremony', to put you at ease!

FIGURE IT OUT

1 Use context along with what you learned in Unit 1 to figure out the following details. Highlight the relevant phrases in the conversation, then write your answers in Italian.

a How long has Melissa been studying Italian? _____

b How many languages does Luca hope to learn? _____

c Which language does Luca most want to learn and why?

_____

CULTURE TIP:
quirky expressions
One of the best things about studying a foreign language is all the new expressions you'll encounter. This one literally translates as 'It's like drinking a glass of water'. In English, the more common translation is 'It's as easy as pie'. Just like with *inglese maccheronico* earlier, don't expect to be able to translate such phrases literally, but do look for the fun equivalents!

2 Match the Italian words with their meanings in English.

a	*solo*	1	yet / still
b	*vero*	2	true
c	*lingue*	3	only
d	*ancora*	4	languages

3 What is the meaning of these words?

a specialmente _____   b difficile _____

4 Complete the phrase in Italian.

Parli _____ _____ *italiano!* (You speak Italian very well!)

5 Write out the Italian phrases that are used in Conversation 2 to:

a say 'you're welcome' _____

b ask 'how long?' (lit. 'since when?') _____

c ask 'how many?' _____

NOTICE

◀)) 02.07 Listen to the audio and study the table.

Essential phrases for Conversation 2

Italian	Meaning
da quando …	how long … (since when)
studi italiano?	have you been studying Italian? (you-study Italian)
studio italiano …	I've been learning Italian … (I-learn Italian)
da due settimane	for two weeks
parli molto bene italiano!	you speak Italian very well!
no, non è vero …	no, that's not true …
sei molto gentile	you're very nice
grazie	thank you
prego	you're welcome
quante lingue … ancora?	how many more languages …?
un giorno spero di imparare	one day I hope to learn
tre lingue	three languages
… è molto difficile	… is very difficult

VOCAB: *da* –
'since' (or 'for')
English uses the phrase 'have been' in expressions like 'I have been learning Italian for two weeks,' whereas Italians would say 'I learn Italian "since" two weeks'. Use the word *da* in situations like this. It's a useful word for asking and answering the question 'since when?' In questions, *da quando* can mean 'since when?' or 'for how long?'. In answers, *da* by itself means 'since/for'.

GRAMMAR TIP:
quanti or quante?
The word you use for 'how many' changes depending on whether the object you're talking about is masculine (*quanti* – *quanti giorni* 'how many days') or feminine (*quante* – *quante volte* 'how many times'). We'll cover which is which in the next unit.

1 Highlight the phrase that means 'since when' in the phrase list. What does the word *quando* means on its own? _____

2 Use the phrase list to write out details about the conversation in Italian.

    a How long has Melissa been learning Italian?

       Melissa studia _____

    b Which languages does Luca hope to learn?

       Luca spera _____

3 How would you say these phrases in Italian?

    a it's true _____   b culture is interesting _____

4 Notice how the speakers form their answers to questions starting with *Quante* and *Da quando*. Fill in the gaps with the corresponding question / answer words.

    a _____ *lingue parli?* → *Parlo due lingue.*

    b *Da quando studi italiano?* → *Studio la lingua* _____ *febbraio* (February).

    c *Quante lingue parli?* → *Parlo due* _____.

    d _____ _____ *parli italiano?* → *Parlo la lingua da due anni.*

To remember **settimana**, imagine someone who finds cities so overwhelming that he only visits them once a 'week', because he's not a 'city man'. For **mese**, think of a field of maize (corn) that grows so fast, it's ready to pick every 'month'. For **anno**, think of the word 'annual'.

PRACTICE

Here's some new vocab to help you add to your 'me-specific' script.

🔊 **02.08 Listen to the audio and study the table.**

Numbers (0–10) and time periods

Italian	Meaning	Italian	Meaning
un/una	one	nove	nine
due	two	dieci	ten
tre	three	zero	zero
quattro	four		
cinque	five	un giorno	a day
sei	six	una settimana	a week
sette	seven	un mese	a month
otto	eight	un anno	a year

GRAMMAR EXPLANATION: plurals

To make a word plural in Italian, follow these simple steps:

⋯⋗ If a word (singular) ends in -o or -e, the last vowel **changes to -i** in the plural.

Examples: *un giorno* → *due giorni*   *un mese* → *tre mesi*

⋯⋗ If a word (singular) ends in -a the last vowel changes to -e in the plural.

Examples: *una settimana* → *quattro settimane*
una lingua → *sette lingue*

⋯⋗ The word for 'the' also changes between genders:

Examples: *i ragazzi* **(the boys)**   *le ragazze* **(the girls)**

And that's it. You're done!

1 Complete with the missing Italian words.

Da _____ giorni sei _____?
(How many days have you been here?)

2 Translate the following phrases into Italian.

a five days _____   c eight months _____
b three years _____   d four weeks _____
e I have been living in Italy since New Year's Day. (*da Capodanno*)

_____

f I have been learning Italian for nine weeks.

_____

Capodanno is the *capo* ('head') of the *anno*, which is basically what New Year's Day is, isn't it?

3 Now create a sentence that's true for you. Respond to the question by saying how many days, weeks, months or years you've been learning Italian.
Da quando studi italiano? _____

4 Think of some interesting mnemonics for the following words (focus on the pronunciation, rather than the spelling): *quattro, cinque, sette.*

PRONUNCIATION EXPLANATION: the Italian *r*

If you try to pronounce the Italian 'r' based on an English 'r', you'll get nowhere fast because they are simply too different. The Italian *r* is actually more like a sound halfway between an English 'l' and 'd'.

Here's a #languagehack to learn it almost instantly: try to say 'la, da, la, da, la, da ...' in succession. Pay attention to where your tongue is and see if you can move it between the two. So if you try to say 'calo, cado, calo, cado, calo, cado ...' and average them out, you would be saying something very close to *caro* (expensive). Try it!

🔊 02.09 Here are some words you've already seen that use the *r* sound. Listen to the audio and repeat, trying your best to mimic the speaker.
a *vero* (true)   c *imparo* (I learn)   e *cultura* (culture)
b *per* (for)   d *interessante* (interesting) f *praticare* (to practise)

PUT IT TOGETHER

Create a cheat sheet with vocab that's immediately relevant to you.

Numbers and times of year cheat sheet

_____	(your phone number)
_____	(your age)
_____	(your birth month)
_____	(the month you started learning Italian)
_____	_____
_____	_____

Look up other important numbers in your life – the ages of your children, how many cats you have – and add them to your cheat sheet! Make sure to write out the number to refer to, not the digits!

VOCAB: ho – 'I have'
In Italian, to say your age, you literally say 'I have (number) years.' Remember – a lot of the time you can't translate word-for-word from English!

HACK IT: learn vocab strategically
Remember, you don't need to memorize all of the numbers or other types of vocab in Italian right away. Start by thinking about what you'll need to say most often, and learn that first. The rest will come with time, and conversation!

1 How old are you? Look up the number that corresponds to your age, and add it to the cheat sheet. Then use the following phrase to say how old you are.

Example: Ho <u>ventisette</u> anni → I'm 27 years old.

Ho _____ anni.

2 Look up your birth month, as well as the month (or year!) you started learning Italian. Add them to your cheat sheet. Then, use *da* to answer the question: *Da quando studi italiano?*

Example: Studio italiano <u>da ieri</u> (yesterday)

Studio italiano _____ _____ _____!

3 How do you say your phone number in Italian? Add yours to the cheat sheet.

4 *Da quando studi italiano?* Someone asks you how long you've been learning Italian. You answer, then you want to continue the conversation by asking your own question. Use the phrases you've learned to ask, in Italian:

a How long have you been living in Italy ? (*vivi*)

_____

b How long have you been teaching Italian? (*insegni*)

_____

CONVERSATION 3

Sharing your opinions

After chatting for a bit, Melissa and Luca start to share ideas about how best to learn a new language.

🔊 02.10 Can you understand Melissa's method of learning Italian?

> **Luca:** Melissa, cosa fai per imparare l'italiano?
>
> **Melissa:** Allora, studio i vocaboli e vado a lezione ogni settimana.
>
> **Luca:** Ah, be'… non mi sembra una buona idea.
>
> **Melissa:** Perché?
>
> **Luca:** Perché per imparare lo spagnolo mi piace andare a lezione ogni giorno.
>
> **Melissa:** Mamma mia! Come fai?
>
> **Luca:** Semplice … Faccio le lezioni a casa, su Internet. È facile, sai?
>
> **Melissa:** Molto interessante. Devo fare così anch'io!
>
> **Luca:** Ti piace leggere molti libri, no? Quello aiuta!
>
> **Melissa:** Sì, è vero, sono d'accordo.

Yes, Italians really do say *mamma mia* (my mother!) to express surprise or dismay!

PRONUNCIATION: *aiuta*
Because each letter typically has a single sound, if you sound this word out, it's like 'ah-ee-oo-tah', or 'ah-yoo-tah'. Try it with *lingua*, 'leengwah', *qui* 'kwee' and *Europa* 'ew-roh-pah'. When multiple vowels are connected like this, you can imagine the *i* to be like a 'y' and the *u* to be like a 'w' and it will be easier to sound out!

FIGURE IT OUT

CONVERSATION STRATEGY: *filler words*
You will see some occasional 'filler words' used in these conversations. While they don't add meaning to the conversation, just like how we say 'well...', 'so...' and 'y'know ...', in English, in Italian you will hear filler words like *allora, be', quindi, bene* and *comunque* in natural conversations. When you need to hesitate, use filler words and it will make your conversation feel more natural!

1 What does *cosa fai* mean? What about *come fai*?

_____   _____

2 Underline the phrases meaning 'every week' and 'every day'.

3 Answer these two questions in Italian.

   a How often does Melissa have an Italian class? _____

   b How often does Luca have a Spanish class? _____

4 Find and circle:

   a two uses of 'it's'   b at least two filler words
   c at least three cognates or near cognates in the conversation

5 *Vero o falso?* Select the correct answer.

   a Luca likes to have his Spanish classes on the internet.   *vero / falso*
   b Luca thinks it's a good idea to go to class every week.   *vero / falso*
   c Melissa studies vocabulary to learn Italian.   *vero / falso*
   d Luca thinks reading books is a bad idea.   *vero / falso*

NOTICE

🔊 02.11 Listen to the audio and study the table.

Essential phrases for Conversation 3

Italian	Meaning
cosa fai ...	what are you doing ...
per imparare l'italiano?	to learn Italian? (for to-learn Italian)
studio i vocaboli	I study vocabulary
vado a lezione ogni settimana	I go to class every week
... ogni giorno	... every day
non mi sembra una buona idea	I don't think it's a good idea (not to-me it-seems a good idea)
mi piace andare ...	I like to go ...
come fai?	how do you do that?
a casa, su Internet	at home, on the Internet
è facile, sai?	it's easy, you know?

LEARNING STRATEGY: *learn in opposites*
Since you've already learned the word *non*, you've practically doubled your vocabulary with a shortcut to saying opposites. Imagine that you want to say, 'this is hard', but you haven't learned the word 'hard' yet. You can simply say it's 'not easy'. *Non è facile.*

faccio le lezioni a casa	I have class at home
devo fare così anch'io!	I should do it too! (I-should to-do so also-I)
ti piace leggere molti libri?	you like to read a lot of books?
quello aiuta!	that helps!
è vero, sono d'accordo!	that's true, I agree!

VOCAB: devo 'I should'
Devo will always be followed immediately by another dictionary form verb:
Devo mangiare bene. 'I should eat well'.
Devo studiare più vocaboli. I should study more vocabulary.

1 In the phrase list there are several phrases the speakers use to give their opinions. Find them and write them out.

a I think _____

b I agree _____

c I should _____

d Simple! _____

e That helps! _____

**VOCAB: così
'like this/that'**
You'll hear the word *così* often in Italian, meaning 'like this/that', 'this way' 'so', 'thus', as in *Devi fare così la pizza ...* (You have to make a pizza like this).

PRONUNCIATION EXPLANATION: *g, c* and *h*

Italian is a phonetic language, with each letter usually leading to a single sound. It makes it quite easy to pronounce new words as you see them! One exception though is how you will see *g, c,* and *h* used.

🔊 **02.12 Read each of the Italian words and attempt to pronounce them yourself. Then, listen to the audio and repeat to mimic the speaker.**

g ⸱⸱⸱⸢ Before nearly all letters, g sounds just like in 'go': *gatto, guida, lingua, grande.*
⸱⸱⸱⸢ But before *e* and *i*, it sounds like the 'j' in 'jam': *giorno, viaggiare, oggi, gente, generalmente, giapponese, gelato.*

c ⸱⸱⸱⸢ Before nearly all letters, c sounds just like in 'cat': *casa, carta, clima, commento.*
⸱⸱⸱⸢ But before *e* and *i* it's like the 'ch' in 'chat': *città, ciao, certo, celeste, arancia.*

h ⸱⸱⸱⸢ At the start of words, h is silent. So, *ho, hai* (I have, you have) are pronounced 'oh' and 'eye'.
⸱⸱⸱⸢ The combinations *gh* or *ch* are pronounced like 'g' in 'go' or 'c' in 'cat' (despite the *e/i*): *colleghe, funghi, chi, perché, chiedere, chiamata.*

Interestingly, this lack of an 'h' sound leads to Italians pronouncing English loan words or names in a funny way, like 'Arry Potter', 'Acker', 'Ip op' or 'Amburger'.

GRAMMAR EXPLANATION: verb forms

In Conversation 3, you met a lot of new verbs used in different ways. Now you need to know how to conjugate them into different forms.

Let's start with the most common regular verbs for now. The 'I' and 'you' forms of regular verbs, regardless of their endings in the dictionary form (*-are*, *-ere* and often *-ire*), are created in the same way.

Step 1: Drop the *-are/-ere/-ire*
Step 2: Add *-o* for *io*; add *-i* for *tu*

imparare	→	*imparo*	*seguire*	→	*seguo*
(to learn)		*impari*	(to follow)		*segui*
vivere	→	*vivo*	*studiare*	→	*studio*
(to live)		*vivi*	(to study)		*studi*

io and tu

You'll notice that the words *io* (I) or *tu* (you) don't actually come up that much in Italian. This is because they are implied by the spelling of the verb forms: *imparo* (**I** learn) vs. *impari* (**you** learn). Pretty handy, huh?

You'll see *io* and *tu* included sometimes to add emphasis, as in *io parlo* for '*I* speak' or contrast – *io parlo italiano, ma tu parli inglese* (I speak Italian, but *you* speak English).

Irregular verbs

In this course, we don't have a lot of verbs that don't fit these patterns, but one you've seen so far is 'to go', which has the dictionary form *andare*, but the very different *io* form of *vado* and the *tu* form of *vai*. Other verbs like these are *fare, volere, dovere*. Learn these top irregular verbs for now:

andare - 'to go'	fare - 'to do / make'	volere - 'to want'	dovere - 'must'
(io) vado	(io) faccio	(io) voglio	(io) devo
(tu) vai	(tu) fai	(tu) vuoi	(tu) devi

PRACTICE

1 Practise changing verbs into the *tu* form.

a *parlare* (to speak) → *parlo* → _____
b *visitare* (to visit) → *visito* → _____
c *vedere* (to see) → *vedo* → _____
d *rispondere* (to answer) → *rispondo* → _____
e *sentire* (to hear) → *sento* → _____

Changing a verb from its dictionary form – like 'to learn' (*imparare*) – to other forms like 'I learn' (*imparo*) or 'you learn' (*impari*), is what language teachers typically refer to as conjugating the verb.

If the dictionary form ends in *-iare*, you won't put two 'i's together in the *tu* form. Saying 'studii' would just be weird, wouldn't it?

2 Complete the table to practise changing verbs into *io* and *tu* forms.

Common verbs

dictionary form	*io* form	*tu* form
amare (to love)		
imparare (to learn)		
mangiare (to eat)		
dormire (to sleep)		
scrivere (to write)		
lavorare (to work) ←		
decidere (to decide)		

GRAMMAR TIP:
*boost your vocab –
add an o!*
Lavoro (I work) can
also be used as a noun
meaning 'work' or
'job'. In fact, there are
many times when you
can change the ending
of a verb you know to
create a related noun,
just by adding an o.
For example:

⇢ *ricordo* = I remember/
a memory

⇢ *gioco* = I play/a
game

⇢ *invito* = I invite/
an invitation

⇢ *disegno* = I draw/
a drawing

3 Now fill in the blanks with the correct forms.

a _____ *qui a Venezia, no?* (You live here in Venice, right?)

b _____ *parlare italiano stasera.* (I want to speak Italian tonight.)

c _____ *russo.* (I'm studying Russian.)

d _____ *la pizza.* (I make pizza.)

e _____ *un cappuccino.* (I want a cappuccino.)

4 Fill in the blanks with the missing word(s) in Italian.

a _____ *ti piace* _____? (What do you like to do?)

b _____ *i* _____ *di italiano ogni giorno?*
(Are you studying Italian vocabulary every day?)

c *Sai che* _____ *il tiramisù?* (Do you know that I'm making tiramisù?)

d _____ *tre giorni alla* _____. (I work three days each week.)

e _____ *un po'* _____ _____. (I learn a little every day.)

5 Practise what you know by translating these full sentences in Italian.

a I like to speak Italian. _____

b You should eat here. _____

c You know that I've been learning Italian for (I learn since) two weeks.

_____

d You love to speak Italian. _____

PUT IT TOGETHER

Cosa fai per... ? Use what you've just learned, along with any new 'me-specific' vocabulary you've looked up, to write four sentences about yourself.

···⟩ Use *voglio* to say something you want to do one day.
···⟩ Use *vado* to describe somewhere you like to go every so often.
···⟩ Use *devo* to say something you should do.
···⟩ Use *studio* to say something you are learning.

COMPLETING UNIT 2

Check your understanding

🔊 02.13 Go back and reread the conversations. When you're feeling confident:
···⟩ listen to the audio rehearsal, which will ask questions in Italian
···⟩ pause or replay the audio as often as you need to understand the questions
···⟩ repeat after the speaker until the pronunciation feels natural to you
···⟩ answer the questions in Italian (in complete sentences).

Show what you know ...

Here's what you've just learned. Write or say an example for each item in the list. Then tick off the ones you know.

- ☑ Ask a 'yes' or 'no' question.   *Vivi qui a Roma?*
- ☐ Create *io* and *tu* verb forms (e.g. from *imparare*).
- ☐ Use the opinion phrase, 'I think'.
- ☐ Ask the question, 'How long have you been learning Italian?'
- ☐ Say since when you've been learning Italian.
- ☐ Say what other languages you speak or want to learn.
- ☐ Negate a sentence using *non* (e.g. *mi piace viaggiare*).
- ☐ Give three filler words.
- ☐ Pronounce the Italian *r*:
  - ☐ Studi italiano?
  - ☐ Certo! Mi piace la cultura italiana!

COMPLETE YOUR MISSION

It's time to complete your mission: fool someone into thinking you speak Italian for at least 45 seconds. To do this, you'll need to prepare to initiate a conversation by asking questions and replying with your own answers.

STEP 1: build your script

Keep building your script by writing out some 'me-specific' sentences along with common questions you might ask someone else. Be sure to:

···> ask a question using *da quando?*
···> ask a question using *cosa ti piace?* or *cosa fai?*
···> say whether or not you speak other languages (and how well)
···> say what other languages you want/hope to learn
···> say how long you've been learning Italian using *da*.
···> write down your script, then repeat it until you feel confident.

STEP 2: all the cool kids are doing it ... *online*

You've put the time into preparing your script, now it's time to complete your mission and share your recording with the community. Go online to find the mission for Unit 2, and use the Italian you've learned right now!

Momentum is a powerful tool. Once you get started, it's so much easier to keep going.

STEP 3: learn from other learners

How well can you understand someone else's script? **Your task is to listen to at least two clips uploaded by other learners.** How long have they been learning Italian? Do they speak any other languages? Leave a comment in Italian saying which words you were able to understand and answering a question they ask at the end of their video. And ask them one of the questions you've prepared.

STEP 4: reflect on what you've learned

What new phrases did you learn in the online community? Always write them down!

HEY, LANGUAGE HACKER, DO YOU REALIZE HOW MUCH YOU CAN ALREADY SAY?

After only two missions, you've learned so many words and phrases you can use in real conversations. Don't forget that you can mix and match words and sentences to create endless combinations. Get creative!

In the next few units, you'll learn more about how to have conversations in Italian – even if you have a limited vocabulary or haven't been learning for very long.

È facile, sai?

3 SOLVING COMMUNICATION PROBLEMS

Your mission

Imagine this – you're having a great time at your *festa* when someone decides it's time to play a party game – describe something without saying the word itself!

Your mission is to use your limited language and win the game. Be prepared to **use 'Tarzan Italian'** and other conversation strategies to **describe a person, place or thing** of your choosing in Italian.

This mission will help you overcome the fear of imperfection and show you how, with just a few words and a powerful technique, you can make yourself understood.

Mission prep

⋯⋗ Use phrases for meeting new people: *piacere, Come ti chiami?*
⋯⋗ Use survival phrases to ask for help with your Italian: *più piano, non capisco, Puoi ripetere?*
⋯⋗ Make direct requests: *dimmi, Puoi aiutarmi?*
⋯⋗ Talk about what you have and what you need to do with *ho* and *devo*.
⋯⋗ Develop a new conversation strategy: use 'Tarzan Italian'.

BUILDING LANGUAGE FOR MEETING SOMEONE NEW

Practising your Italian with a tutor or teacher online, especially when you don't live in Italy, is one of the most effective (and affordable) ways to learn more Italian in a shorter amount of time. You can do this right away, even if you don't know many phrases yet.

In this unit you'll learn strategic survival phrases you can use whenever there's something you don't understand, and you'll use 'Tarzan Italian' to communicate with limited language or grammar. Strategies like these help you become comfortable making mistakes when speaking, and help you have meaningful conversations despite being a beginner.

#LANGUAGEHACK
power-learn word genders with the word-endings trick

It's easy to have conversations with other Italian speakers online. I've done this for all the languages I've learned. These days I schedule online chats from home to maintain my strongest languages, including Italian. See our Resources to learn how.

PRONUNCIATION: *gn, gl*
If you've ever enjoyed some delicious Italian *gnocchi* or dug into a delectable *lasagne* then you know all about the *gn* pronunciation! Whenever you see this, simply pronounce it as an 'ny' sound. Similarly, think of *tagliatelle* and how *gl* is like a 'ly' sound as you say *voglio* [voh-lyoh].

CONVERSATION 1

Your first online chat

◀)) 03.01 Melissa has decided to take Luca's advice and have an online Italian lesson from home. She's about to have her first online conversation with Daniele, her new Italian teacher. Since this is Melissa's first time meeting Daniele, how does she introduce herself?

Daniele: Ciao! Come va?

Melissa: Ciao! Tutto bene. Grazie mille che mi insegni l'italiano! Come ti chiami?

Daniele: Prego. Nessun problema. Mi chiamo Daniele. E tu?

Melissa: Mi chiamo Melissa.

Daniele: Che bel nome! È un piacere conoscerti, Melissa.

Melissa: Grazie, molto gentile. Anche per me è un piacere.

Daniele: Allora, dove ti trovi?

Melissa: Ehm … più piano, per favore?

Daniele: In che città sei?

Melissa: Ah, sì. Adesso sono a Roma.

FIGURE IT OUT

1 Find the one false statement from the following:

   a Melissa asks Daniele to repeat himself more slowly.

   b Daniele wants to know why Melissa is learning Italian.

   c Daniele asks where Melissa is.

2 How do you say the following in Italian?

   a thank you _____   c please _____

   b you're welcome _____

3 What do you think the following phrases mean in English?

   a nessun problema _____   b Come ti chiami? _____

4 Can you guess the question (in English) that Daniele asks Melissa at the end of the conversation?

_____

NOTICE

🔊 **03.02** Listen to the audio and study the table.

Notice that **Come ti chiami?** isn't exactly the same as 'What's your name', but more like 'How do you call yourself?' when you look at it word for word. Think of it as a **sentence chunk** to remember for now and it will be easier!

PRONUNCIATION: sce
If you've got experience playing a musical instrument, you'll know what a *crescendo* is. This word shows that another interesting way of representing a familiar sound in Italian is to use *sce* or *sci* for what English speakers write as 'sh', so this gives *conoscerti* as 'koh-noh-sher-tee'.

Essential phrases for Conversation 1

Italian	Meaning
ciao! Come va?	hi! How are you?
tutto bene!	everything is good!
grazie mille	thank you very much (thanks thousand)
che mi insegni l'italiano	for teaching me Italian (that to-me you-teach the-Italian)
come ti chiami?	what's your name? (how yourself you-call?)
prego	you're welcome
nessun problema	no problem
mi chiamo	my name is (myself I-call)
che bel nome!	what a pretty name!
è un piacere conoscerti	nice to meet you it's a pleasure to-know-you
molto gentile	that's nice (very kind)
allora, dove ti trovi?	so, where are you? (where yourself you-find)
più piano, per favore	slower, please
in che città sei?	which city are you in?
adesso sono a Roma	now, I'm in Rome

1 What phrase can you use when someone is speaking too fast?

_____

2 How do you say the following in Italian?

    a Nice to meet you. _____

    b Everything's good. _____

    c I'm in London right now. (London = *Londra*) _____

    d Where are you? _____

3 Write the literal English meaning of the Italian verb forms:

   a *conoscerti* _____

   b *ti trovi* _____

   c *mi chiamo* _____

> You've also seen this sentence structure used in *mi piace* (I like), *ti piace* (you like), and *mi chiamo,* (my name is – but literally, 'I myself call').

PRACTICE

1 🔊 03.03 Look again at the phrase list. Replay the audio to check your pronunciation of the words:

grazie   *conoscerti*   *Roma*   *dove ti trovi*   *per favore*

2 Match the English question with its correct form in Italian.

   a *Vivi in Italia?*
   b *Cosa fai per imparare l'italiano?*
   c *Come studi l'italiano?*
   d *Come ti chiami?*
   e *Devo parlare più piano?*
   f *Dove ti trovi?*

   1 What's your name?
   2 Where are you?
   3 Do you live in Italy?
   4 How do you study Italian?
   5 Should I speak slower?
   6 What are you doing to learn Italian?

> Remember, questions like 'Do you want to eat now?' simply translate as *Vuoi mangiare adesso?* (literally, '*You-want to-eat now?*'). The question word 'do' is almost never directly translated to Italian.

3 Fill in the blanks with the missing word(s) in Italian.

   a *Ho* _____ *lavoro* _____.   (I have **a lot** of work **today**.)

   b *Luca* _____ *occupato* _____ *il tempo!*
      (Luca **is** busy **all** the time!)

   c _____ *lavori* _____?   (**Where** are you working **now**?)

   d _____ _____*mi a cucinare.*   (You **should teach** me to cook.)

4 The Italian verb 'to teach', *insegnare*, is a bit tricky. Come up with a creative mnemonic to help you remember it.

GRAMMAR EXPLANATION: word order with objects

When Melissa said, *Come ti chiami?*, you saw a new sentence structure in action:

Example: you teach me ··⟶ *mi insegni* (me you-teach)

Simply put, the person or thing being talked about in a sentence (the object), will appear before the verb in Italian, instead of after the verb, as in English. These are words like 'me', 'you', 'it', 'him', 'her' and 'them'.

ti do = I give you   *mi dai* = you give me

If there are two verbs, you'll hear the object word after the second, in place of the final *e*:

voglio darti = I want to give you   *Posso darlo?* = Can I give it?

Here's some new vocab that will help you better understand this sentence structure.

GRAMMAR TIP: *dammi!*
– adding *mi*, *ti* or *lo*
There are cases where *mi/ti/lo* comes after the verb, such as when it's in the dictionary form or when it's a command, like *fammi* (*fammi pensare* 'let me think'), *dammi* (*dammi il libro* 'give me the book'), and *dimmi* (say/tell me). It's also possible to use the object before the first verb, as in: *ti voglio dire*, or *lo posso dare* – but we'll use the former version in this course.

◀)) 03.04 Listen to the audio and study the table.

Some of these verbs don't follow the pattern you've learned already. You may have seen *dai* and thought 'Wait, shouldn't that also be 'di'?'. These are irregular verbs, i.e. verbs that don't follow normal rules. Don't worry about them for now, just learn the forms you see here and you'll get to the rest with time!

Dictionary form	Phrase with object	Meaning	Dictionary form	Meaning
amare	ti amo	I love you (you I-love)	amarti	to love you
insegnare	mi insegni	you teach me (me you-teach)	insegnarmi	to teach me
sentire	non ti sento	I can't hear you	sentirti	to hear you
vedere	lo vedo	I see it	vederlo	to see it
dire	mi dici	you tell me		to tell me
aiutare	mi aiuti	you help me		to help you
dare	mi dai	you give me		to give you
inviare	lo invio	I send it		to send it
scrivere	mi scrivi	you write to me		to write to you
chiamare	ti chiamo	I call you		to call you
mangiare	non lo mangio	I don't eat it		not to eat it

1 There are some missing words in the table. Fill in the empty spaces using the correct sentence structure.

2 Complete these sentences with the correct object word in Italian.

    a _____ do.   (I'm giving **you**.)

    b Non _____ vedo.   (I don't see **it**.)

    c Puoi aiutar_____?   (Can you help **me**?)

    d Non _____ sento!   (I can't hear **you**!)

3 Complete these sentences by writing the correct verb form in Italian.

Example: *Puoi* insegnarmi?   (Can you **teach** me?)

    a *Lo* _____   (I **understand** it.)

    b *Puoi* _____?   (Can you **write** it?)

    c *Mi* _____?   ((Do) you **see** me?)

    d *Voglio* _____ ...   (I want to **tell** you ...)

4 Now put the words in the correct order to make complete sentences.

    a *ti/disturbare/voglio non* (I don't want to disturb you.)

    _____

    b *dire/mi/puoi* (Can you tell me?) _____

    c *inviare/lo/voglio* (I want to send it.) _____

    d *posso/ti/chiamare/non* (I can't call you.) _____

> Remember that whenever you use two verbs together, the second will be in dictionary form – Puoi (Can you) + dirmi (to-tell-me).

PUT IT TOGETHER

⋯⟩ Use *adesso* to write two sentences about where you are or what you're doing now.

⋯⟩ Use standard Italian verbs to write two sentences about what you're doing or where you're going today.

⋯⟩ Use your dictionary to look up new words that you need.

    Dove ti trovi?

CONVERSATION 2

I don't understand

If **capisco** is 'I understand' (or 'I see what you mean'), then **capisci** (pronounced 'kahpee-shee') is 'you understand'. A version of this word has become infamous in Italian gangster movies and cheesy TV shows. 'Capeesh?'

How can you remember that the verb **sentire** means 'to hear'? Well, it's pronounced something like 'sen tear-ray'. So a good mnemonic might be something like how when you hear a beautiful and familiar sound, your ear feels **sentimental** for it (and sheds a tear for it).

As Melissa continues her online class, she has trouble understanding Daniele.

🔊 **03.05** How does Daniele rephrase his sentences when Melissa asks for help?

Daniele: Perché dici che 'adesso' sei a Roma? Vivi in un'altra città?

Melissa: Mi dispiace. Non capisco.

Daniele: Perché – per quale ragione – sei a Roma?

Melissa: Ah, ho capito. Sono qui per imparare l'italiano!

Daniele: Davvero? Molto interessante!

Melissa: E tu? Dove sei?

Daniele: Sono in Italia, a Napoli. Vivo e lavoro qui.

Melissa: Puoi ripetere, per favore?

Daniele: Mi senti? Vivo a Napoli, quindi sono in Italia.

Melissa: Un momento … Non ti sento bene.

- Mi dispiace.
- Non capisco.
- ho capito
- Puoi ripetere, per favore?
- Un momento…Non ti sento bene.

FIGURE IT OUT

1 *Vero o falso?* Select the correct answer.

   a Daniele asks Melissa why she is in Rome.   *vero / falso*

   b Melissa says she is in Rome for work.   *vero / falso*

   c Daniele lives in Rome.   *vero / falso*

2 There are several Italian words in the conversation that sound similar to their English counterparts. Can you guess their meaning?

   a *interessante*   b *ripetere*   c *ragione*   d *momento*

3 What is the meaning of these phrases?

   a *Vivi in un'altra città?* _____

   b *Puoi ripetere?* _____

   c *Non ti sento bene.* _____

   d *Mi senti?* _____

LEARNING STRATEGY:
infer the meaning
Find one word in the conversation that you don't understand and circle it. Now take a closer look to see if you can **infer the word's meaning**. When you think you may know what it means, look the word up in a dictionary to see if you're right!

NOTICE

GRAMMAR TIP: *-isco*
You saw in Unit 2 how most regular verbs work. One final point worth noting is that you'll see many *-ire* verbs replace the *-ire* with *-isco* for the *io* form, and *-isci* for the *tu* form. If in doubt, use the more common *-isco* form when you have an *-ire* verb. You'll see the same thing in *finire*, *finisco*, *finisci* (to finish, I finish, you finish).

VOCAB: *per 'in order to'*
Per followed by a dictionary form of the verb in Italian means something like 'in order to', as in *Sono qui per parlare con gli italiani!* (I'm here (in order) to speak with Italian people)!

🔊 **03.06** Listen to the audio and study the table. Repeat the phrases to try to mimic the speakers.

Essential phrases for Conversation 2

Italian	Meaning
perché dici che ...?	why do you say ...?
vivi in un'altra città?	do you live in another city?
mi dispiace	I'm sorry
non capisco	I don't understand
per quale ragione sei a Roma?	for what reason are you in Rome?
ho capito	I understand (I've understood)
sono qui per imparare l'italiano	I'm here (in order) to learn Italian
dove sei?	where are you?
sono in Italia	I'm in Italy
vivo e lavoro qui	I live and I work here
puoi ripetere?	can you repeat that?
mi senti?	do you hear me?
un momento …	one moment …
non ti sento bene	I can't hear you well

1 Find examples of the following forms in the phrase list, and write them out.

a the *io* and *tu* forms of *vivere* (to live)

_____   _____

b the *io* and *tu* forms of *essere* (to be)

_____   _____

c the *tu* forms of *potere* (to be able to/can) and *dire* (to say)

_____   _____

d the *io* forms of *lavorare* (to work) and *sentire* (to hear)

_____   _____

e the *io* form of *capire* (to understand) and its negative form

_____   _____

CONVERSATION STRATEGY 1: survival phrases

In Conversations 1 and 2, you've seen several 'survival phrases' that Melissa used to tell Daniele she's having trouble with her Italian. Survival phrases are your secret weapon for 'surviving' any conversation in Italian, even when you're having trouble understanding. Learn these phrases, and you'll never have an excuse to switch back to English.

1 Add to the cheat sheet with the survival phrases you've learned so far.

2 Create two new survival phrases by combining *puoi* (can you) with dictionary forms of verbs, and add them into your cheat sheet.

   Example: Can you write it, please? <u>Puoi scriverlo, per favore?</u>

   a I don't understand. **Can you help me?** _____

   b I have only been learning Italian for a month. **Can you speak slower?**
   _____

Your survival phrases cheat sheet

Italian	Meaning
Come si dice ...?	How do you say ... ?
_____	Slower please.
_____	I'm sorry.
_____	I don't understand.
_____	Can you repeat that?
_____	One moment.
_____	I can't hear you.

GRAMMAR EXPLANATION: 'listen', 'look', 'tell me' – the 'command' form

When you want to tell someone to 'watch', 'repeat' or 'go', you'll need to use the 'command' (or imperative) form. You saw this used in Unit 1, when Mario told Melissa, *Parlami di te!* You'll hear a handful of words used this way again and again, such as:

Guarda! (Look!)	*Ascolta!* (Listen!)	*Vieni!* (Come!)
Dimmi! (Tell me!)	*Ascoltami!* (Listen to me!)	*Aiutami!* (Help me!)

Using the command form is usually quite simple:

⋯⋗ For verbs like *parlare* and *imparare* (*-are* verbs), just change the ending to -a: (*parla*, *impara*).

⋯⋗ For verbs like *dormire* and *leggere* (*-ire* and *-ere* verbs), use the same ending as the *tu* form – usually *-i*: (*dormi*, *leggi*).

You can also attach *mi, ti, lo / la* to the end as an object – but keep in mind that it changes slightly for *dire* (*dimmi*), *dare* (*dammi*) and *fare* (*fammi*):

Examples: *ascolti* (you listen) → *Ascoltalo!* (Listen to him!)
guardi (you look) → *Guardami!* (Look at me!)

It's good to know a few of the most common verbs in the command form, but you can easily get by without using this form if you just add 'can you' before any dictionary verb you know.

Examples: *Guarda!* (Look!) → *Puoi guardare?* (Can you + to look)
Parla! → *Puoi parlare? Vieni!* → *Puoi venire?*
Aiutami! → *Mi puoi aiutare?*   *Ascolta!* → *Puoi ascoltare?*

PRACTICE

1 Combine words you know to practise creating new sentences in Italian.

a Where do you live?_____

b What are you saying? (What you-say?) _____

c In which other city do you want to live?

_____

d Why do you want to work in Rome?

_____

e Do you work in a university? Have I understood well?

_____

2 You have now seen all of the main question words used in Italian!

a Use the phrase lists from Conversations 1 and 2 to add to the table the Italian question words you've seen.

b Next, use your dictionary to look up how to ask 'who?' in Italian. Add the Italian translations to the table.

Question words cheat sheet

Meaning	Italian	Meaning	Italian
Why?	_____	When?	_____
What?	Che?/Cosa?	Who?	_____
How?	Come?	How many?	_____
Where?	_____	Can you?	_____
Which?	Quale?		

3 What question words would you ask in Italian to get the following answers?

a *Sabato.* _____

b *14.* _____

c *Paolo.* _____

d *Alla stazione* _____

e *Perché voglio.* _____

PUT IT TOGETHER

Let's keep building your script. Use new 'me-specific' vocab to create new sentences about yourself in Italian. Be sure to include:

⋯⊱ where you're from, and where you live now (use *ma* and *adesso*)
⋯⊱ how long you've lived there (use *da*) and why you live there
⋯⊱ where you work (use *lavorare + in un/una*)
⋯⊱ how long you've worked there (use *da*).

VOCAB: *che* and *cosa* as 'what' You can say either *che* or *cosa* to mean 'what'. *Che* is used more the further south you go, with *cosa* more likely in the north of Italy. *Che cosa* is also possible, and on its own *cosa* also means 'thing'.

I've had wonderful experiences learning Italian with native speakers. They'll often compliment you for doing such a good job, even if you're a beginner.

CONVERSATION 3

A bad connection

You'll find people in Italy to be extremely patient and friendly. Rest assured that you can speak broken Italian with native speakers and they will be happy to help you. Try it!

🔊 03.07 Melissa and Daniele are having Internet connection problems. Which word does Melissa use to tell Daniele that her connection is bad?

VOCAB: ouch! hey! ugh!
As in English, Italian has different interjections that are great for expressing emotion, to make even your reactions more Italian. These are some of the most common:

ehi!	hey!
ahi!/ahia!	ouch!
bleah!	ugh!
boh ...	I have no idea!
eh?	what?/right?
uffa!	what a bore!
mah ...	who knows?

GRAMMAR TIP: *credo che - 'I think that'* Opinion verbs like *credo che/penso che* normally require a special verb form (called the subjunctive), which suggests uncertainty. Mastering this isn't usually for beginners, but the great news is that you really don't have to worry much about it for now, and can avoid it by simply adding in a hesitation to 'reset' your sentence. Italians use it less and less when speaking, so it's OK if you don't too, at least at this stage.

Melissa: Credo che la mia connessione ... non funziona bene. Mi dispiace!

Daniele: Nessun problema. Vuoi disattivare la tua webcam?

Melissa: Non è la mia webcam. Ho un problema con ... sai ... ehm ... non ricordo la parola! La mia cosa di internet!

Daniele: Il tuo wifi? Il tuo portatile?

Melissa: Ecco! Il mio portatile. Devo installare un software. Aspetta un momento.

Daniele: Va bene, aspetto ...

Melissa: Forse ... mi senti adesso?

Daniele: Non bene.

Melissa: Mi dispiace, ho bisogno di un computer nuovo ... Posso chiamarti la prossima settimana?

Daniele: Certo, tranquilla! Quando vuoi parlare di nuovo? Sabato?

Melissa: D'accordo. A presto!

Daniele: Alla prossima!

FIGURE IT OUT

1 There are several Italian words in the conversation that are the same or similar to their English counterparts. Can you guess their meaning?

a disattivare.　　b installare.　　c connessione.

2 Use words you know along with context to figure out which one of the following statements is not true.

    a Melissa thinks she doesn't have a good connection.

    b Daniele can't hear Melissa well.

    c The problem is with Melissa's webcam.

    d Melissa and Daniele agree to talk another time.

3 Answer the questions about the conversation.

    a What are the words Melissa uses to describe the kind of computer she needs? *un computer* _____

    b How do you apologize in Italian? *Mi* _____

    c What are two ways of saying goodbye in Italian?

    _____ _____

    d How do you express 'I need' in Italian? _____ ...

4 Write out the following phrases in Italian:

    a no worries _____   **d** maybe _____

    b that's fine _____   **e** you know _____

    c it's not my _____

5 Highlight the word meaning 'week'. Is the word masculine or feminine? How do you know? _____

6 What do you think the word *la mia* means? _____

CONVERSATION STRATEGY 1: use 'Tarzan Italian' to communicate with limited words

As a beginner, you won't always know how to say exactly what you want to say. Instead of feeling frustrated about it, focus on getting your point across, rather than speaking eloquently. This means getting comfortable making mistakes.

That's why I recommend you embrace 'Tarzan Italian'. Find ways to convey your ideas that are understandable, even if your grammar or word choice isn't beautiful. You can still get your meaning across if you know just the key words. For example, if you want to ask 'Could you tell me where the bank is?' you could convey the same meaning with only two words, 'Bank ... where?' Just like Tarzan:

Mi puoi dire dove si trova la banca? → ***Banca ... dove?***

Mistakes are a necessary part of the process – you can't learn Italian without making lots of them. Mistakes aren't just inevitable, they are important for making progress. In games like chess, players are advised to lose 50 games as soon as possible. Why not take this philosophy to the extreme and aim to make 200 mistakes a day in Italian? Get them out of your system sooner, and you can improve so much faster.

Being able to think up simpler ways to convey an idea is a key skill for reaching fluency. As a beginner, producing simple, even non-grammatical Italian will allow you to contribute to more conversations, which will actually boost your progress!

1 Try out your 'Tarzan Italian'. Look at these common sentences. Isolate the key words, then use 'Tarzan Italian' to convey the same meaning.

Example: *Non capisco. Puoi ripetere, per favore?*
→ Ripetere, per favore?

a *Ti dispiace parlare più piano?* _____

b *Mi puoi dire quanto costa questo?* _____

c *Scusa, sai dove si trova il supermercato?* _____

CONVERSATION STRATEGY 2: memorize the power nouns: *persona, luogo, cosa*

persona (person)   *luogo* (place)   *cosa* (thing)

These words are power nouns by definition, so they encapsulate pretty much all other nouns. You can use them in a huge number of situations when you want to describe something but don't know the Italian word.

In Italian, many things are named in the form of:
(something) **of** (something else)

Examples: *la stazione dei treni* train station (lit. 'station of the trains')
la fermata dell'autobus bus stop (lit. 'stop of the bus')
la torta di cioccolato chocolate cake (lit. 'cake of chocolate')

We can use this to our advantage. Any time you don't know the word for something you can simply use this formula:
(power noun) + *di* + (any word related to the thing in question)

For example. If you can't remember the words for:
⋯▸ bed   (*il letto*)   ... try 'thing of sleep'   → **cosa** di dormire
⋯▸ teacher   (*l'insegnante*) ... try 'person of teaching' → **persona** di insegnare
⋯▸ train station (*la stazione dei treni*) ... try 'place of trains'   → **luogo** di treni

1 Try it out. How could you convey your meaning using power nouns?

Example: pen? → 'thing of writing' cosa di scrivere

a library?   → 'place of books'   _____
b waitress? → 'person of restaurant' _____

NOTICE

🔊 03.08 Listen to the audio and study the table.

Essential phrases for Conversation 3

Italian	Meaning
la mia connessione non funziona bene	my connection is not working well
nessun problema	no problem!
non è la mia webcam	it's not my webcam
ho un problema con ...	I have a problem with ...
sai ...	you know ...
non ricordo la parola!	I forget the word!
il tuo ... wifi? portatile?	your ... wifi? laptop?
ecco!	that's it!
devo ...	I have to ...
aspetta un momento	wait a minute
va bene	alright
forse	maybe
mi senti?	do you hear me?
ho bisogno di ...	I need ... (I've need of)
posso chiamarti ...	can I call you ...
la settimana prossima	next week
certo, tranquilla!	of course, no worries!
quando vuoi parlare ... di nuovo?	when do you want to speak ... again? (of new)
d'accordo, a presto!	OK, see you later!
alla prossima!	see you next time! (to the next)

If you need to access someone's **wifi**, just ask for their **password** – *Qual è la password del wifi?* (What's the wifi password?)

There are many ways to **sign off** or say **goodbye** to someone. You could say *ciao, ci vediamo* (see you), *alla prossima* (until the next (time)), *a dopo* (until later), *a presto* (until soon) or just a day (like *a domani!* for 'see you tomorrow!' or a *lunedì* for 'see you Monday').

GRAMMAR TIP: *potere* – 'to be able to' 'I can' and 'you can' are translated as *posso* and *puoi*, from the dictionary form *potere*. As you can see, this doesn't fit our regular pattern for verb forms. Certain verbs like this just need to be learned as you see them, but luckily there aren't that many that are so different to the norm.

1 Use the phrase list to fill in the gaps with the missing verb forms:

a *avere* (to have) → _____ (I have) → *hai* (you have)

b *potere* (to be able to) → _____ (I can) → *puoi* (you can)

c *sentire* (to hear) → *ti sento* (I hear you) → _____ (you hear me)

d _____ (to call) → *mi chiamo* (I call myself) → *ti chiami* (you call yourself)

e *credere* (to think) → _____ (I think) → *credi* (you think)

2 Notice the connector words in the phrase list. If someone says, *mi dispiace*, and you want to tell them 'it's OK', you could use two phrases from the phrase list. Here is one. Find the other and write it out.

nessun problema _____

3 In this conversation, Melissa uses the new survival phrase, 'I don't remember the word!'. Find it in the phrase list, then add it to your survival phrases cheat sheet.

VOCAB EXPLANATION: *la tecnologia in italiano*

The most frequently used term for 'laptop' in Italy is *portatile*, but you may also hear the term *laptop*. In fact, many technology terms used in Italian are taken from English and used popularly instead of the Italian equivalent:

With all this help, *perché non* open your *cellulare, portatile o computer*, look for *configurazione in the menu*, and change all your *interfacce digitali* to *italiano*?

webcam	e-mail	internet	(doppio) clic
hardware	software	computer	display/schermo
hard disk	homepage/home		web (also la rete)
fare il log in	fare il download/scaricare		wifi

as well as words that follow our cognates pattern. Some have even morphed into verbs, like, *disattivare, installare, connettere,* and *copiare*.

PRACTICE

1 Practise creating new phrases by combining the verbs from this conversation with other words you know.

a I think that + it works _____
b you think that + I can _____
c I can + to say _____
d you can + to call _____
e I have to + to work _____
f I have to + to have _____
g you have to + speak _____

2 Fill in the missing words in Italian.

a _____ _____ un software _____?
(Can you install a new software (application)?)

b _____ _____, io ti _____ _____.
(If you want, I can help you.)

c La _____ volta, _____ _____ _____ una
connessione migliore.
(Next time, I hope to have a better connection.)

d _____ ricordo _____ _____!
(I don't remember where it is!)

e Ora _____ _____! _____ _____?
(I hear you now! Can you say it again?)

GRAMMAR EXPLANATION: *mio/mia/miei/mie* (my)

The way you say 'my, your, his / her' in Italian is more than a single word translation – you need to know the gender and number of what comes next. As you can see in this conversation, 'your laptop' is *il tuo portatile* and 'my thing' is *la mia cosa* You'll get used to it but here's an overview:

English	Masculine singular	Feminine singular	Masculine plural	Feminine plural
my	*il mio*	*la mia*	*i miei*	*le mie*
your	*il tuo*	*la tua*	*i tuoi*	*le tue*

As you can see, Italians say 'the my' (adjusting the form of 'the' appropriately), but the translation is just 'my'.

Now fill in the blanks with the missing possessives in Italian.

a *Il* _____ *migliore amico si chiama Daniele.* (My best friend's name is Daniele.)

b *La* _____ *casa è molto grande.* (Your house is very big.)

c *Adoro le* _____ *scarpe!* (I love your shoes!)

#LANGUAGEHACK:
power-learn word genders with the word-endings trick

As you'll have seen, Italian words are divided into masculine or feminine. The gender affects whether the word is prefaced with *il* or *la* (both meaning 'the'), *un* or *una* (both meaning 'a / an'):

Feminine: *la conversazione*   (the conversation)   *una donna* (a woman)
Masculine: *il treno*   (the train)   *un uomo* (a man)

When you first start learning Italian, it can seem like genders are assigned at random. For instance the word *mascolinità* is feminine, and *femminismo* is masculine!

But word gender has nothing to do with whether the concept of the word is masculine or feminine. It's actually the *spelling* of the word, in particular the word's ending, that determines its gender. Here's the general rule for how to guess a word's gender based on its spelling:

If a word ends in *-o*, always guess masculine.

> Examples: *il pollo* (the chicken), *un bacio* (a kiss), *il profumo* (the perfume/cologne), *un gatto* (a cat)

If a word ends in *-a/à* always guess feminine.

> Examples: *un'idea* (an idea), *la differenza* (the difference), *la cultura* (the culture), *la manica* (the sleeve), *l'università* (the university), *la felicità* (happiness)

If it ends in *-ma*, *-tore/-sore*, or most consonants, it's also usually masculine. Loanwords from other languages not ending in *-a* are also masculine.

> Examples: *il programma* (schedule), *l'autore* (author), *il cursore* (cursor), *il film*, *il software*

If it ends in *-ione* or *-tudine* it's feminine. Female roles ending in *-trice* are also feminine.

> Examples: *l'educazione* (education), *l'altitudine* (the altitude), *l'attrice* (the actress)

Words with *-ista* endings are masculine when referring to a male, but feminine when referring to a female!

> Examples: *il turista* and *la turista*, *il pianista* and *la pianista*, *il giornalista* and *la giornalista*

GRAMMAR TIP: 'the' and 'a/an'

The Italian words for 'the' and 'a/an' usually change according to the first letter(s) of the next word. You've seen that instead of *il*, you say *lo* before s and another non-vowel, or before z: *lo spagnolo*, *lo spazio* (the space), *lo zio* (the uncle). The same thing happens with *uno* instead of *un*: *uno svizzero* (a Swiss man). And in the plural, these words use *gli* instead of *i*: *gli studi*. Finally, before vowels these articles change:

una → *un'*: *un'amica* (but not *un'amico*)   *il* → *l'*: *l'amico*, *l'albergo*
la → *l'*: *l'amica*, *l'indicazione*, *l'agendina*   *i* → *gli*: *gli amici*, *gli animali*

YOUR TURN: use the hack

1 Guess the genders of the following words. Fill in the gap with either *un, un'* or *una*.

a _____ *popolo*

b _____ *città*

c _____ *commedia*

d _____ *organismo*

e _____ *appartamento*

f _____ *differenza*

g _____ *teatro*

h _____ *pace*

i _____ *religione*

j _____ *telefono*

k _____ *vino*

l _____ *libreria*

m _____ *peperone*

n _____ *poema*

o _____ *azione*

> This is another one of those situations where guessing is your friend. And it would almost never cause a communication problem! There are always exceptions, but this hack will help you guess it right most of the time.

2 Now fill the gaps for those same words with *il, la* or *l'*.

a _____ *popolo*

b _____ *città*

c _____ *commedia*

d _____ *organismo*

e _____ *appartamento*

f _____ *differenza*

g _____ *teatro*

h _____ *pace*

i _____ *religione*

j _____ *telefono*

k _____ *vino*

l _____ *libreria*

m _____ *peperone*

n _____ *poema*

o _____ *azione*

3 Now, you should be able to answer the question: Why is *mascolinità* feminine, and *femminismo* masculine? _____

PUT IT TOGETHER

forse... ho ... ho bisogno di ...

Now let's keep building on your script. Use the new phrases you've just learned to create two sentences about yourself in Italian. Be sure to look up new 'me-specific' words in your dictionary so that you're practising phrases that you'd use in a real conversation. Describe in Italian:

···⟫ your opinion of the newest smartphone on the market (use *forse*)

···⟫ what technology you have now (use *ho*)

···⟫ some things you have to buy (use *ho bisogno di*).

COMPLETING UNIT 3

Check your understanding

🔊 03.09 Review the conversations from this unit, and when you're feeling confident:

⋯⋗ listen to the audio and write down what you hear.

⋯⋗ feel free to pause or replay the audio as often as you need.

Show what you know ...

Here's what you've just learned. Write or say an example for each item in the list. Then tick off the ones you know.

☐ Say 'hello' and 'nice to meet you'.
☐ Give two phrases for saying goodbye.
☐ Say 'I understand' and 'I don't understand'.
☐ Say something that you have and something that you need.
☐ Use the survival phrases, 'Can you repeat that?' and 'Slower, please?'.
☐ Use Italian object words in the right word order, e.g. 'Can you help me?'.
☐ Give the Italian words for 'person' 'place' and 'thing'.

COMPLETE YOUR MISSION

It's time to complete your mission: using 'Tarzan Italian' to play (and win!) the word game. To do this, you'll need to prepare phrases for describing an Italian person, place or thing that other people could guess – without knowing the word itself.

STEP 1: build your script

Let's practise embracing 'imperfectionism' with today's script. Underline the key words you need to convey your point, then look them up in your dictionary – but don't try to have perfect grammar! If you come across a complex expression, try to think of simpler words to convey the same idea.

Keep building your script using 'Tarzan Italian' and the unit conversation strategies. Be sure to:

···⟩ say whether you're describing a person, place or thing
···⟩ for a person, describe him/her with any words you know (what is his/her *lavoro*? Where is he/she *adesso*?)
···⟩ for a thing, describe whether it's something you have (*ho*), need (*ho bisogno di*), like or dislike
···⟩ for a place, describe what types of people live there or things associated with it.

For example, you could say:

> C'è ... persona ... lavoro ... al cinema ...
> Molto famoso ... è un uomo ... pirata pazzo ... dire sempre
> ... dove rum?

Write down your script, then repeat it until you feel confident.

STEP 2: practice makes perfect ... *online*

Getting over the embarrassment of 'looking silly' is part of language learning. Use your 'Tarzan Italian' to help you overcome these fears! Upload your clip to the community area, and you'll be surprised at how much encouragement you get.

It's time to complete your mission and share a recording with the community. Go online to find your mission for Unit 3 and see how far you can get with your 'Tarzan Italian'.

If you get stuck, you're probably struggling with perfectionist paralysis. Take a step back, and remind yourself that your script is supposed to be imperfect today!

Really! The more time you spend on a task, the better you will get! (Studies show that you will be 30% better than your peers who don't practise their speaking regularly.)

HACK IT:
change your search preferences to italiano
Did you know that many major websites automatically detect your language from your browser settings, and adjust accordingly? You can change these settings to *italiano*, and you'll instantly notice your search engine, social networking sites and video searches will automatically change to Italian! You can also simply go to *google.it* (and click *italiano*) to search Italian language websites around the world ... then be sure to type your key words in Italian!

STEP 3: learn from other learners

Can you guess the words? After you've uploaded your own clip, get inspiration from how others use 'Tarzan Italian'. **Your task is to play the game and try to guess the words other people describe.** Take note of the clever ways they use the conversation strategies from the unit, and stash them into a mental note to try later on your own.

STEP 4: reflect on what you've learned

Did you learn about new places and people from the community? Write down anything interesting that you might want to look into later – a famous actor you might want to look up, or a film you may want to see. What gaps did you identify in your own language when doing your mission? What words do you reach for over and over? Are there any words you hear frequently, but don't understand? Keep note of them!

HEY, LANGUAGE HACKER, YOU'RE ON A ROLL!

By learning to work around a limited vocabulary, you really can start speaking Italian with other people in no time. It's not about learning all the words and grammar. It's about communicating – sometimes creatively. By finishing this mission, you've learned valuable skills that you'll use again and again in the real world.

Next, you'll learn to talk about your plans for the future.

Continua così!

4 DESCRIBING YOUR FUTURE PLANS

Your mission

Imagine this – you want to spend a few weeks exploring Europe, but you can only afford the trip if your Italian-speaking friend comes with you and you split the cost.

Your mission is to make an offer they can't refuse! **Describe the trip of your dreams** and convince a friend to take the trip with you. Use *andiamo ...* to draw the person in and say all the wonderful things you'll do together. Be prepared to **explain how you'll get there** and **how you'll spend your time**.

This mission will help you expand your conversation skills so you can talk about your future plans and combine new phrases for better Italian flow.

Mission prep

⋯⋗ Develop a conversation strategy for breaking the ice: *ti dispiace se ...*
⋯⋗ Talk about your future travel plans using *voglio/devo* or simply the present form.
⋯⋗ Describe your plans in a sequence: *per cominciare, poi, quindi ...*
⋯⋗ Learn essential travel vocabulary: *puoi prendere un treno*.
⋯⋗ Memorize a script that you are likely to say often.

BUILDING LANGUAGE FOR STRIKING UP A CONVERSATION

When you want to practise Italian, it takes a bit of courage to get started. But preparing phrases in advance to break the ice helps a lot. In this unit, you'll build a ready-made script you can use for the start of any conversations. You'll discover how to make a conversation with a new Italian speaker more casual, and hopefully even make a new friend or two!

#LANGUAGEHACK
say exponentially more with these four booster verbs

CONVERSATION 1

Excuse me, do you speak Italian?

Melissa is back at her local language group. She's been practising her Italian for a few weeks now, and she wants to build up her confidence to approach a stranger and strike up a conversation.

🔊 04.01 What phrases does Melissa use to approach someone new?

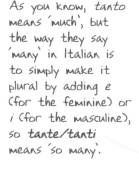

As you know, *tanto* means 'much', but the way they say 'many' in Italian is to simply make it plural by adding *e* (for the feminine) or *i* (for the masculine), so *tante/tanti* means 'so many'.

Melissa: Scusa, parli italiano?

Paola: Sì! Sono di Milano.

Melissa: Benissimo! Ti dispiace se pratico il mio italiano con te?

Paola: Perché no? Vieni! Puoi sederti qui.

Melissa: Grazie e piacere di conoscerti!

Paola: Piacere mio! Sono Paola. Come ti chiami?

Melissa: Mi chiamo Melissa. Devi sapere che sono ancora principiante.

Paola: Ma sai già dire tante cose!

Melissa: Grazie, ma ho bisogno di praticare molto di più con italiani.

Paola: Bene, non ti preoccupare, sono molto paziente! Quindi, parliamo!

FIGURE IT OUT

1 *Vero o falso?* Select the correct answer.

   a Paola is from Milan.   *vero / falso*

   b Melissa asks Paola to go to a café with her.   *vero / falso*

   c Paola is impatient.   *vero / falso*

2 Find and underline the phrases in the conversation where:

   a Paola tells Melissa where she's from.   c Melissa asks to practise Italian with Paola.

   b Melissa asks Paola if she speaks Italian.   d Paola says she is still a beginner

3 Now find these three words in the conversation and circle them.

   a Italians   b patient   c beginner

4 Give the Italian equivalent of the phrases:

   a Let's talk! _____   b Don't worry! _____

NOTICE

🔊 04.02 Listen to the audio and study the table.

Essential phrases for Conversation 1

Italian	Meaning
scusa	excuse me
parli italiano?	do you speak Italian? (you-speak Italian?)
benissimo!	great!
ti dispiace se …	do you mind if … (you it-displeases if)
… pratico il mio italiano con te?	… I practise my Italian with you?
perché no?	why not?
vieni! puoi sederti qui	come! you can sit here
piacere mio!	my pleasure! (pleasure mine)
devi sapere che …	you should know that …
sono ancora principiante	I'm still a beginner
sai già dire tante cose!	you can already say so many things!
ho bisogno di …	I need to … (I-have need of)
praticare molto di più	practise much more
non ti preoccupare	don't worry (not yourself to-worry)
sono molto paziente!	I am very patient!
quindi, parliamo!	so let's talk!

1 Find the following in the phrase list, and write them out in Italian.

   a two phrases you can use to approach someone to practise Italian with

   _____   _____

   b the expression you should use to ask someone if they mind something

   _____

2 Complete the sentences using *già*, *ancora*, or *tanto*.

   a I'm still speaking.   *Parlo* _____.

   b I'm already speaking.   *Parlo* _____.

   c I'm speaking so much.   *Parlo* _____.

   d I still know the address.   *So* _____ *l'indirizzo.*

   e I already know where to go.   *So* _____ *dove andare.*

   f I know so much Italian.   *So* _____ *italiano.*

GRAMMAR EXPLANATION: saying 'we' with *-iamo*

To form a verb with 'we', simply take the dictionary form of the verb, knock off the *-are/-ere/-ire* part and replace it with *-iamo*.

Examples: parlare → *Parliamo italiano ogni giorno.* (We speak Italian every day.)

vedere → *Vediamo molti film.*   (We watch a lot of films.)

You can also make 'let's ...' suggestions by simply using this *-iamo* form!

Andiamo al parco!   Let's go to the park!

PRACTICE

1 Fill in these sentences with the missing word(s) in Italian.

   a _____ *parole* _____ *ogni* _____.
      (We learn new words every day.)

   b _____ *più* _____ *con i principianti.*
      (We talk slower with beginners.)

   c _____ *insieme lo spettacolo.* (We watch the show together.)

   d _____ *la radio.* (Let's listen to the radio!)

CONVERSATION STRATEGY: memorize regularly-used scripts

A lot of people get nervous speaking to someone new for the first time – especially in another language. But when you plan out what you'll say in advance, you have less to worry about. Luckily, many conversations take a similar pattern, and you can use this to your advantage.

Learn set phrases

Just because you don't know the grammar behind a phrase, it doesn't mean you can't use it. You can simply memorize full phrases as chunks, so you can use them whenever you need to.

Try this with the very useful power phrase, *Ti dispiace se* ... (Do you mind if ...), which can be used in a variety of situations and conversation topics.

Memorize a script

When you learn set phrases that are specific to you and combine them together, you create a personal 'script' you can use over and over again.

For instance, over the course of my travels I'm frequently asked, 'Why are you learning this language?' and I'm often asked about my work as a writer, which isn't easy to explain as a beginner. But because I know these questions are coming, I don't need to answer spontaneously every time. I craft a solid response in advance so I can speak confidently when the question inevitably comes up.

For you, it may be your upcoming travels to Italy or your interest in Italian culture, or the personal reasons why you're learning the language. Ultimately, if you know you'll need to give an explanation or mini-story frequently, memorize it to have ready when it's time to produce.

⋯▸ **Decide what you want to say**, make it personal to you.

⋯▸ Then simplify it as much as possible to **remove complicated expressions**. If possible, do this in Italian from the start by jotting down key words and phrases – you can fill in the script later. If you find this tricky, start your script in English and then try to translate it in to Italian.

⋯▸ Finally, **when you have your final script**, recite it as often as you can until you commit it to memory.

You can ride a bike without understanding aerodynamics, you can use a computer even if you don't know the physics of how circuits work ... and you can use Italian phrases at the right time, **even if you don't understand each word** and why they go together the way they do!

This is fine in casual environments, but if you are talking to someone older than you, a stranger in passing, or in formal situations, you'd say *Le dispiace se* ... instead.

HACK IT: *have your script native-approved* You can even have a native speaker review your scripts and refine them to good Italian. It's fine to speak spontaneously with mistakes, but you may as well get it right if you're memorizing it in advance. It's easy and free when you know where to look. See our Resources section to find out how to get free online help.

PUT IT TOGETHER

1 If you were planning to visit Italy, in what situations might you ask the question, *ti* (or *Le*) *dispiace se ...?* Use this phrase along with your dictionary to create sentences you could imagine yourself using:

⋯⋗ at a social event (e.g. '... if I speak with you?')

⋯⋗ in a park (e.g. '... if I touch your dog?)

⋯⋗ at a café (e.g. '... if I take this seat?')

⋯⋗ at someone's house (e.g. '... if I open the window?').

2 Pick one of the following situations, then prepare a few phrases ahead of time you can use without having to think on the spot.

⋯⋗ Situation 1: Someone finds out that you're learning Italian ... and they also happen to speak Italian. For this, I like to prepare some phrases like: 'Ah, you speak Italian!' 'I'm still a beginner.' 'I've only been learning since ...'

This is a great memorized script to have in your back pocket. You'll use it loads. You may know a few phrases already, but it's good to know a go-to answer for this question.

⋯⋗ Situation 2: Someone asks you to give a mini life story, or asks why you are learning Italian. For this, you might say something like: 'I think the language is beautiful!' 'And one day I hope to go to Italy.'

⋯⋗ Situation 3: You need to interrupt a young person on the street to ask a question in Italian. Politeness goes a long way here, so for this I like to memorize a script like: 'excuse me' 'I'm sorry' 'Do you mind if I ask you something?'

CONVERSATION 2

Talking about travel plans

Since Melissa and Paola are both visitors to Rome, travel is a natural conversation topic. In fact, as you learn any new language, you'll likely be asked (or want to ask someone) about travelling to different places.

🔊 04.03 What phrase does Paola use to ask, 'Do you travel a lot?'

> **Paola:** Allora, quanto tempo resti a Roma? Vuoi viaggiare molto?
>
> **Melissa:** Non molto … resto qui a Roma per alcuni mesi, poi vado a Firenze.
>
> **Paola:** Perché non visiti Milano, la mia città? Puoi prendere un treno da qui durante il weekend per conoscere la città.
>
> **Melissa:** È un'idea fantastica! Forse il prossimo weekend. Questo weekend non avere tempo.
>
> **Paola:** Vuoi dire 'non ho tempo'?
>
> **Melissa:** Sì, esattamente. Scusa!
>
> **Paola:** Non fa niente! Anch'io voglio viaggiare di più. Voglio vedere altre città in Italia, come Assisi. Ora o mai più!
>
> **Melissa:** Vero, ma c'è tanto da fare qui a Roma!

In Italian, the way to say 'you mean ...' is **vuoi dire** ... (literally 'you want to-say'). You may hear this as you're learning and getting corrections from others. You can also say *voglio dire* to clarify something you've said.

A common expression in Italy to say 'don't worry about it' is **non fa niente** (literally, 'it doesn't make anything'). You could also say *figurati!* meaning 'not at all!' (literally, something like 'imagine it').

FIGURE IT OUT

1 Use context along with words you know to figure out:

a Where does Paola suggest that Melissa visit? _____

b What other cities does Paola want to see? _____

c Which word does Melissa use incorrectly? _____

2 Underline the following phrases, then write them out here in Italian.

a you're in Rome for how long? _____

b for a few months _____

3 Is the word *weekend* masculine or feminine? How do you know?

VOCAB: 'there is' / 'there are'
The Italian phrase c'è (pronounced like 'che' in 'chest' in English) means 'there is'. The plural ('there are') is ci sono. Examples: *c'è un libro*; *ci sono tre libri* ('there is a book'; 'there are three books').

4 Can you work out the meaning of these phrases?

    a *forse il prossimo mese* _____

    b *vuoi dire* _____   c *c'è tanto da fare* _____

5 Match the words from the conversation with their meanings.

    a *altre*   1 like

    b *poi*   2 never

    c *durante*   3 then

    d *come*   4 during

    e *mai*   5 more

    f *più*   6 other

NOTICE

◀)) 04.04 Listen to the audio and study the table.

Essential phrases for Conversation 2

Italian	Meaning
resti a Roma?	are you staying in Rome? (you-remain at Rome)
vuoi viaggiare molto?	do you want to travel a lot?
resto qui …	I'm staying here … (I-remain here)
per alcuni mesi	for a few months (for some months)
poi vado a …	then I'm going to …
perché non …	why not …
visiti la mia città?	visit my city (you-visit the my city)
puoi prendere un treno da qui	you can take a train from here
durante il weekend	during the weekend
per conoscere la città	to get to know the city
forse il prossimo weekend	maybe next weekend
questo weekend	this weekend
vuoi dire …	you mean … (you-want to-say …)
non ho tempo	I don't have time
non fa niente!	don't worry!
anch'io voglio viaggiare di più	I want to travel more myself (me-too I-want to-travel of more)
voglio vedere altre città, come …	I want to see other cities, like …
ora o mai più!	it's now or never!
vero, ma c'è tanto da fare!	true, but there's a lot to do!

HACK IT:

use simpler phrases to avoid complicated sentences

The Italian phrase for 'I plan to …' uses tricky grammar that we won't talk about just yet, but you'll still need to talk about your plans! For now, here's a simple #languagehack to get around it. Use a different phrase that gets the job done – in this case, *voglio* (I want) or *vuoi* (Do you want?). To top it off, although it sounds odd in English, in Italian it's perfectly natural to use *vuoi* to ask someone about their upcoming plans.

We've seen the word *adesso* used for 'now', but another alternative is *ora* (which also means 'hour'). You'll hear both words used interchangeably.

1 What phrases could you use to:

    a recommend a place someone should visit _____

    b correct yourself in Italian by saying 'I mean …' _____

    c ask, 'Do you mean …?' _____

2 Take a closer look at the following expression from the phrase list.

    for a few months = _____ *alcuni* _____

3 Match up the Italian phrases with the correct English translations.

    a *lavori*   **1** why not visit

    b *perché non visiti*   **2** you can take

    c *voglio vedere*   **3** you travel

    d *viaggi*   **4** you work

    e *voglio viaggiare di più*   **5** I want to see

    f *puoi prendere*   **6** I want to travel more

4 For each sentence, choose the correct form of the Italian verb, then write out the rest of the sentence yourself.

    a *Viaggio / Viaggi / Viaggiare* _____? (Do you travel much?)

    b *Vediamo / Vedi / Vedere la Cappella Sistina* _____.
    (Let's see the Sistine Chapel tomorrow.)

    c _____ *visito / visiti / visitare* _____. (I want to visit Milan.)

    d *Prendo / Prendi / Prendere un taxi* _____. (I take a taxi in the city.)

Here's some additional vocab you can use to talk about your own travel plans.

GRAMMAR TIP: abbreviations

There are certain Italian words that end in o, which you'd expect to be masculine, but are feminine. This is because they are shortened versions of longer words, so *la metro(politana)*, *la moto(cicletta)* and *l'info(rmazione)*.

The word **macchina**, as you'd expect, means 'the machine', but is also the most common way to refer to a car in Italian!

Travel vocab

Italian	Meaning
prendere ...	to take ...
il treno	the train
l'autobus	the bus
la metro	the metro
un taxi	a taxi
andare in ...	to go by ...
aereo	plane
treno	train
macchina	car
bici	bicycle

PRACTICE

Vocab: *volare*

In Italian, usually you only use the verb *volare* (to fly) when emphasis is on the mode of transport itself, rather than on getting from A to B, such as *Non mi piace volare* (I don't like flying). The rest of the time, you say "to go by plane", such as: *Vado a Milano in aereo. Per andare a Berlino prendo l'aereo.*

1 Notice the verb meaning 'to take' in Italian. How would you say 'I take' and 'you take'?

   a to take _____   c you take _____

   b I take _____

2 Now practise using this vocabulary in different ways.

   a I'm taking the train. _____

   b I'm driving (going by car) _____

   c I'm flying (going by plane) to London (Londra). _____

3 Fill in the correct forms for each of the following phrases:

   a the weekend   _____ weekend

   b this weekend   _____ weekend

   c next weekend   il _____ weekend

   d each / every weekend _____ weekend

You should remember this word from Unit 2.

4 Fill in the blanks with the missing words in Italian.

a *Perché non* _____ *al belvedere del Gianicolo* _____
_____ *tutta la città di Roma.* (You should **go to** the belvedere of
Gianicolo **in order to see** all of Rome.)

b *Voglio* _____ *altre città* _____ *Venezia* _____ *Napoli!*
(I want **to visit** other cities like Venice **and** Naples!)

c _____ _____ *in Italia,* _____ *andare in aereo.*
(**In order to go** to Italy, **you should** fly.)

d *Devo* _____ _____ _____ *o è meglio* _____ _____ _____?
(Should I **go by train**, or is it better to **go by car**?)

e _____ _____ *tante* _____ *per andare in macchina.*
(**There are** so many **reasons** to drive.)

PUT IT TOGETHER

1 Read and respond to the following questions in Italian. Use your
dictionary to look up the 'me-specific' vocab you'll need.

a *Dove vai per il tuo prossimo viaggio?*
Vado a _____

b *Per quanto tempo? Per quanti giorni? Per quante settimane? Per
quanti mesi?*
Per _____

c *Quando vai? Questo mese? Il prossimo mese? Quest'anno? Il
prossimo anno?*
Vado _____

d *Come vai? Vai in auto / in macchina/ in aereo ? O prendi il treno?*
_____

CONVERSATION 3

Talking about weekend plans

Melissa and Paola continue talking and start making plans for the weekend.

🔊 **04.05** Notice how the phrases *voglio* and *vuoi* are used to talk about future plans. How does Paola ask, 'What do you want to do?'

VOCAB: *posto* and *luogo* for 'place'
We've seen previously that the word for 'place' is *luogo*, but you can also use *posto* interchangeably most of the time.

CULTURE TIP: *squillo*
Squillo simply means a 'ring' or a 'missed call' that you intentionally give someone so that their number shows up on your phone and you can save it. But the word is even more versatile than that! You can use that missed call to mean simply 'I'm thinking of you', 'hey, what's up?', 'I'm at your door, come down to let me in' and even 'I know I'm late, but I'm almost there!'

Paola:	Quindi, cosa vuoi fare qui a Roma?
Melissa:	Dunque, per cominciare voglio vedere il Colosseo. Poi voglio bere qualcosa all'Antico Caffè Greco, il posto preferito di D'Annunzio, un poeta italiano. E per finire visito Trastevere per i suoi fantastici ristoranti! E voglio parlare italiano con tutti, chiaramente.
Paola:	Incredibile! Hai molto da fare! Voglio fare le stesse cose – posso venire con te?
Melissa:	Sì, perfetto! Sono contenta di avere una nuova amica! Possiamo scoprire la città insieme!
Paola:	Penso di essere libera domani, ma non lo so ancora. Posso chiamarti?
Melissa:	Sì. Ecco il mio numero. Mi fai uno squillo? Vuoi anche il mio indirizzo email?
Paola:	Sì, per piacere. Ti chiamo stasera.
Melissa:	Perfetto! Ci vediamo!

FIGURE IT OUT

1 *Vero o falso?* Select the right answer, then correct the false statement.

    a The first thing Melissa will do is visit Trastevere.   *vero / falso*

    b Then she is going to Antico Caffè Greco.   *vero / falso*

    c Next she is going to look for restaurants.   *vero / falso*

    d Melissa thinks she is free tomorrow, but she is not sure yet.   *vero / falso*

    e Paola is going to call Melissa tonight.   *vero / falso*

2 Give the answers to the following questions in Italian, starting with the prompted phrase.

    a Why is Melissa going to Trastevere?

       Per _____

    b Why is Melissa going to Antico Caffè Greco?

       Per _____

3 What is the meaning of these phrases?

    a *il posto preferito di D'Annunzio* _____

    b *Hai molto da fare!* _____

4 Highlight the translations of these phrases in the conversation. Then write them out.

    a What are you going to do in Rome?

       _____

    b I want to do the same things.

       _____

NOTICE

Essential phrases for Conversation 3

Italian	Meaning
cosa vuoi fare?	what are you going to do?
per cominciare, voglio vedere ...	first, I am going to see ...
poi voglio bere qualcosa ...	next, I'll have a drink ... (I want to-drink something)
posto preferito	favourite place
e per finire ...	and finally ... (and for to-finish)
voglio parlare italiano con tutti	I will (want to) speak Italian with everyone!
hai molto da fare!	you will be busy! (you've a-lot from to-do)
voglio fare le stesse cose	I want to do the same things
posso venire con te?	can I join you? (can-I to-come with you)
possiamo scoprire la città insieme!	we can discover the city together!
penso di essere libera domani	I think I am free tomorrow
non lo so ancora	I don't know (it) yet
posso chiamarti?	can I call you?
ecco .. il mio numero	here's ... my number
... il mio indirizzo email	... my email address
ti chiamo stasera	I'll call you tonight

1 Find the Italian phrases for 'first', 'then' and 'finally' in the phrase list and circle them. Write them out.

a first _____   b next _____   c finally _____

2 Take a closer look at some of the language in the phrase list to determine how you could say in Italian:

a I'm going to see _____

b you are going to do _____

3 What phrase could you use to:

a give someone your (phone) number? Your email address? _____

_____

b ask someone for their (phone) number or email address? _____

_____

PRACTICE

CONVERSATION STRATEGY: **talking about the future**

1 Match the correct Italian phrases with the English translations.

   a *Puoi mandarmi un messaggio?*   1 Can you email me?

   b *Puoi chiamarmi?*   2 Can I text you?

   c *Posso mandarti un'email?*   3 Can I call you?

   d *Posso mandarti un messaggio?*   4 Can you text me?

   e *Posso chiamarti?*   5 Can I email you?

   f *Puoi mandarmi un'email?*   6 Can you call me?

2 Fill in the blanks with the missing words in Italian.

   a _____ _____, ti _____ il mio _____ _____
      _____. (One moment, I'm going to give you my **phone number**.)

   b _____ _____ molto da fare, ma _____ _____
      libero! (**Tonight** I'm going to be busy, but **I am free tomorrow**!)

   c *Non lo* _____ _____ ... *aspetta* ... _____ !
      (I don't **see** it **yet** ... wait ... **here it is**!)

   d *Non* _____ *se* _____. (I don't **know** if **I'm going to be able**.)

   e *Vado al bar* _____ *tutti! Vuoi* _____ _____ _____ ?
      (I'm going to the bar **with** everyone! Do you want **to come with me**?)

   f _____ *in treno* _____, _____ ?
      (We'll **go** by train **together, OK**?)

3 Practise creating new sentences in Italian about travel.

   a I want to travel to Italy. _____

   b Where should I spend time? _____

   c You don't know already? _____

   d No ... Do you think that you can help me?
   _____

   e Of course! First, you can sit with me.
   _____

   f Let's eat, and I'll tell you how to discover my favourite place!
   _____

CONVERSATION STRATEGY: **talking about the future**
Italian has a future verb form, but its use is more restricted than 'I will ...', and you can't use *andare* (to go) like you would in English (as in 'I'm going to eat ...'). Instead things are actually much simpler in Italian!

All you need to do is **add in a time factor that implies the future** and use the normal present form that you've seen up to now. This is a common way to say what your plans are. For instance, Melissa says: *Ti chiamo stasera* (I'll call you tonight), even though it's literally just 'I call you tonight'. In this case, adding in *stasera* makes it the *future*.

E basta! (and that's that!)

#LANGUAGEHACK:
say exponentially more with these four booster verbs

You can start to see that saying things right in Italian means learning how to form verbs differently between *tu, io, noi* and so on. And that's even before you start changing from present tense to future or past ... which is when things can really start to get messy! Sometimes – especially when you're just starting out – this can feel overwhelming.

But don't panic! You will eventually learn to handle even the messiest of those verb forms, but for now, here's a handy trick you can use to press the snooze button on learning conjugations. Learn these four 'booster' verbs and their forms, and they can do the heavy lifting for you. Simply follow them up with the dictionary form of any other verb you may want to use.

booster verb + dictionary form

Mi piace for interests

If you wanted to say 'I go out every weekend', you'd need to know the *io* form of the verb *uscire* (to go out). Or, you could use *mi piace* or *ti piace* as a booster verb.

Back in your first mission, you used *mi piace* + verb to describe your interests. In this case, if you know that 'to go out' in its dictionary form is *uscire*, you can combine it with *mi pace* to express the same idea:

Mi piace	+ *uscire*	→	*ogni weekend.*
Booster verb	+ **dictionary form**		
(I like)	+ (to go out)	→	(every weekend)

Voglio for intentions – 'going to'/'want to'

You can talk about your intentions using *voglio*. This is also a useful alternative to suggest your future plans, if you don't want to use the present form of a verb. To use this 'future' form on your own, again simply put the dictionary form of the verb after *voglio, vuoi* or *vogliamo*:

Voglio vedere il film domani.	I want to see the film tomorrow.
Vogliamo andare a Roma domani.	We'd like to go to Rome tomorrow.
Non vuoi studiare.	You don't want to study.

Devo for obligations

This very handy verb can be used to say you 'have to', 'should', or 'must' do something. For example, instead of 'I'm working tomorrow', why not say:

Devo lavorare domani.   I have to work tomorrow.

or use it to give a recommendation:

Devi prendere il treno.   You must take the train.

Posso for possibilities

Finally, to help express yourself better, use this verb to clarify that you 'can' or 'are able to' do something. For instance, if you don't remember how to say 'I tell' (*dico*), you could say 'I can tell':

Ti posso dire la password, se vuoi? I can tell you the password if you want?
Mi puoi chiamare dopo?   Can you call me later?

YOUR TURN: use the hack

1 Use *voglio* + verb or the present form to create sentences in the future tense.

a I will be busy tomorrow! _____
b I'm going to do a lot tonight. _____
c Will you call me tomorrow? _____
d Are you going to eat in the restaurant this weekend?

_____

e I'm not going to go to Venice next week. _____

2 Fill in the gaps using a booster verb and the verbs provided.
a _____ _____ *nel mare.* (I swim in the sea.) (*nuotare* = to swim)
b _____ _____ *italiano insieme.* (We learn Italian together.)
c _____ _____ *il caffè?* (Do you drink coffee?) (*bere* = to drink)

3 Translate the following into Italian:

a You are not very busy. _____
b You are going to be very busy. _____
c Will you speak Italian tonight? _____
d We are going to go to Rome. _____

PUT IT TOGETHER

1 You've already learned to talk about the next trip you're planning (or dreaming of!). Now go even more in depth to describe what you're going to do when you get there. Try to include:

⋯⋗ what you think you'll do first (*Per cominciare, voglio …*)
⋯⋗ what you'll do next (*Poi …*)
⋯⋗ which sites you are going to visit (*Visito …*)
⋯⋗ where do you plan to go to eat or to drink?
  (*Per mangiare/bere vado …*)
⋯⋗ something you want to see (*Voglio vedere …*).

Per cominciare …

2 Now imagine that you've met someone you'd like to hang out with later.

⋯⋗ give them your contact details (*Ecco qui …*)
⋯⋗ ask them to call, text, or email tomorrow (*Puoi …?*).

COMPLETING UNIT 4

Check your understanding

🔊 **04.07** You know the drill! Listen to the audio rehearsal, which will ask you questions in Italian. Use what you've learned to answer the questions in Italian with details about yourself.

To check that you're understanding the audio, don't forget that you can always look at the transcript online.

Show what you know ...

Here's what you've just learned. Write or say an example for each item in the list. Then tick off the ones you know.

- ☐ Ask a question using 'Do you mind if …'?
- ☐ Use *voglio* + dictionary form or simply the present tense to say something you will do tomorrow, this weekend or next year.
- ☐ Give one sentence each using 'still' and 'already'.
- ☐ Use *per* to say how long you'll do something.
- ☐ Give three methods of travel in Italian.
- ☐ Give the Italian words to say 'first', 'next' and 'finally'.

COMPLETE YOUR MISSION

It's time to complete your mission: convince your friend to go with you on your adventure. To do this, you'll need to describe the trip of your dreams, using *io* forms and *tu* forms to say how you and your friend would spend your trip.

Travel is a popular topic among language learners, so this is a script you'll want to make sure you have down solid.

STEP 1: build your script

Che vuoi fare in Italia?

Create a script you can use to tell other language hackers about your travel plans. Incorporate as many new words or phrases from this unit as possible – *già, sempre, poi*, etc. Be sure to say:

- ⋯⟩ where you're going
- ⋯⟩ what you plan to do when you get there (for example, you could name popular monuments or tourist attractions, what you will eat or drink, etc.)
- ⋯⟩ what you want to see first (what are you most excited to explore?)
- ⋯⟩ when you'd like to go and how long you'd like to be there
- ⋯⟩ how you'll get there and how you'll get around once you're there
- ⋯⟩ who you plan to travel with.

Give recommendations to other language hackers for things to do at this destination! Write down your script, then repeat it until you feel confident.

STEP 2: feedback promotes learning ... *online*

Give and get feedback from other learners – it will massively improve your Italian!

When the opportunity presents itself in real life, you won't always have notes at the ready, so let's emulate this by having you speak your script from memory. Make sure to revise it well!

This time, when you make your recording, you're not allowed to read your script! Instead, speak your phrases to the camera, relying on very brief notes, or even better, say your script from memory.

STEP 3: learn from other learners

How do other language hackers describe their travel plans and dreams? After you've uploaded your clip, **your task is to give and get feedback by voting for the holiday you'd most like to join in on**. Or say whether or not you'd like to join and why.

STEP 4: reflect on what you've learned

After this mission, you'll have seen and heard so many useful new words and phrases and you'll know more about new and different places to visit. What would you like to add to your script next? Your travel plans?

Your language partners can be a great resource for tips and stories on travel and culture! Plus, travel aspirations are a great conversation starter.

HEY, LANGUAGE HACKER, LOOK AT EVERYTHING YOU'VE JUST SAID!

Isn't it so much easier when you already know what you want to say? A lot of language learning involves repeatable and sometimes predictable conversations. If you take advantage of this and prepare answers you typically give you can be extremely confident in what you say!

Now, let's build new phrases in your script that you can use to talk about your friends and family.

Fantastico!

5 TALKING ABOUT FAMILY AND FRIENDS

Your mission

Imagine this – your good friend develops a serious crush on your Italian *amico* and asks you to play matchmaker.

Your mission is to casually talk up your friend and spark the interest of *il tuo amico italiano* to get those two out on a date! Be prepared to **describe your relationship with your friend – how you met, where he or she lives and works**, and the kinds of **things he or she likes to do**.

This mission will get you comfortable talking about other people and using new verb forms as well as descriptive language.

Mission prep

⋯⟩ Talk about 'he' / 'she' using the *lui / lei* forms.
⋯⟩ Talk about 'they' using the *loro* forms.
⋯⟩ Use phrases to describe things you do with other people: *passo il tempo, noi, insieme* …
⋯⟩ Learn essential family vocabulary: *il marito, la sorella* …
⋯⟩ Use the two forms of 'to know': *sapere* and *conoscere*.

BUILDING LANGUAGE FOR DESCRIBING YOUR RELATIONSHIPS

Until now, our conversations have focused mostly on describing *io, tu* and *noi*. We'll build on that now with vocabulary you can use to talk about anyone else.

#LANGUAGEHACK
use clues and context to understand much more than you think

You could also say the Italian equivalent of 'What do you (both) have planned?', which we'll get to later, but it's just as easy to say 'What do you have planned with her?' – Cosa hai in programma con lei? – as we did here. You can often find a way to rephrase what you don't know into something that uses words/grammar you do know!

VOCAB: conosco
for who you 'know'
This is another way to say 'I know' in Italian. In this case, it means 'knew a person'. More on this in Conversation 2!

la sua can mean 'his' or 'her', but which one will always be clear based on the context.

CONVERSATION 1

What do you have planned?

Melissa has been taking online Italian classes for a few weeks. Today she's practising with Giulia, an Italian tutor from Sicily. Melissa is excited to talk about the new friend she made at her language group.

🔊 05.01 Notice how Giulia greets Melissa. Which phrase means 'What's new?'

Giulia:	Ciao Melissa, la mia studentessa preferita! Cosa mi dici di nuovo?
Melissa:	Tutto bene! Infatti questa settimana esco con una nuova amica.
Giulia:	Sono contenta di questa novità. Chi è? Come si chiama?
Melissa:	Si chiama Paola. È di Milano. È ingegnere e la conosco da una settimana. Frequentiamo lo stesso gruppo di scambio linguistico.
Giulia:	OK, e quanto tempo resta in città? Cosa hai in programma di fare con lei?
Melissa:	Resta qui a Roma solo una settimana. Domani vogliamo andare a un ristorante. Poi passiamo la settimana insieme a esplorare Roma. E il prossimo weekend credo che ci vediamo a Milano.
Giulia:	Mio marito è di Milano! Adoro la sua città natale – la visitiamo ogni estate.

FIGURE IT OUT

1 What is the meaning of the following?

a Chi è? _____   b Come si chiama? _____

2 Three of the following statements about the conversation are *falso*.
Underline the incorrect parts, and write the correct words in Italian.

a Melissa is spending time with a new friend next week.

_____

b Paola works as a lawyer. _____

c Paola has been in Rome for only a week.

_____

d Tomorrow, Melissa and Paola are going to a restaurant.

_____

e This weekend, Melissa is going to see Paola in Milan.

_____

3 You've learned a lot of words that tell you *when* something is
happening. Find these words in the conversation and write out the
Italian translations.

a this _____   d after that _____

b next _____   e every summer _____

c tomorrow _____

4 Write out these phrases in Italian:

a What's new? _____   d in fact _____

b Who is it? _____   e I'm happy to _____

c my favourite student _____

NOTICE

🔊 **05.02** Listen to the audio and study the table. Notice and highlight any phrases you think you could use in your own life.

Essential phrases for Conversation 1

Italian	Meaning
la mia studentessa preferita!	my favourite student!
cosa mi dici di nuovo?	what's new? (what me you-say of new)
infatti	in fact
questa settimana ...	this week ...
esco con una nuova amica	I'm going out with a new friend (f)
sono contenta di questa novità	I'm happy to hear that (I'm happy about this news)
chi è? come si chiama?	who is she? what is her name?
è di Milano	she's from Milan
è ingegnere	she's an engineer
la conosco da una settimana	I've known her for a week
quanto tempo ... resta in città?	how long ... is she in town? (she-remains in city)
resta qui solo una settimana	she's only here for a week
cosa hai in programma di fare con lei?	what are you planning to do with her?
domani ...	tomorrow ...
vogliamo andare a un ristorante	we want to go to a restaurant
poi, passiamo la settimana insieme ...	after that, we'll spend the week together ...
a esplorare Roma	exploring Rome (in-order to-explore Rome)
il prossimo weekend ...	next weekend …
credo che ci vediamo a Milano	I think I'll visit her in Milan (I-think that us we-see at Milan)
mio marito è di Milano!	my husband is from Milan!
adoro la sua città natale	I love his hometown
la visitiamo ogni estate	we visit it every summer

1 *Sono contento / contenta di* (I am happy to / about) is another power expression. Use this expression in different ways by combining it with the verbs and nouns given.

Examples: I'm happy ...   *Sono contento / contenta ...*

about this news.   *di queste novità.*

to talk with you   *di parlare con te.*

a to watch the film _____.

b to be here _____.

c to say that I can travel _____.

d about this job _____.

e about this restaurant _____.

2 This conversation introduces verb forms for talking about 'he' and 'she' in Italian. Find six of the 'he' / 'she' verb forms in the phrase list.

3 Notice the new verb forms used in this conversation. Find the following sets of related verbs, and write them out here.

a he is _____   e she is _____

b we visit _____   f we plan to go _____

c I'm going out _____

d we'll spend _____

4 This conversation uses new phrases you can use to talk about your plans with other people. Write out in Italian:

a I'm spending time _____

b we're planning to _____

c we'll spend the weekend _____

5 Look at the phrase *la conosco* in the phrase list.

a How is the word order different from English?

_____

b Using the same sentence structure, how would you say in Italian, 'I see her'? _____

> **GRAMMAR TIP:** *lo, la, li/le* 'him', 'her' and 'them'
> In Unit 3 you learned to use *mi* and *ti* as objects of a sentence in Italian. The same works with *lo* (him), *la* (her) and *li / le* (them m/f). As well as to replace people, they can also replace objects and things (you've already seen *lo* used for 'it'). Remember to put these object words in front of your verb. So you can say:
> *lo adoro*   'I adore **him / it**'
> *la mangia* 'he's eating **it**'
>   (e.g. *la pizza*)
> *li vedo*   'I'm going to see **them**'

PRACTICE

🔊 **05.03** Here's some new vocab you can use to talk about your family. Listen to the audio and follow along with the table. Repeat the words to mimic the speakers.

Famiglia e amici

Italian	Meaning	Italian	Meaning
(migliore) amico/a	(best) friend (m/f)	zio/zia	uncle/aunt
marito/moglie	husband/wife	figlio/figlia	son/daughter
ragazzo/a	boyfriend/girlfriend	figli	children
compagno/a il/la partner	partner (m/f)	coinquilino/a	roommate/flatmate
genitori	parents	cugino/a	cousin (m/f)
padre/madre	father/mother	Sono single	I'm single
papà/mamma	dad/mum	È complicato	It's complicated
fratello/sorella	brother/sister	gatto/cane	cat/dog
nonno/nonna	granddad/grandma	elefante	elephant

1 Use your dictionary to fill in the last few rows of the family members vocab list with words for family members (or pets!) you have.

2 Fill in the blanks with the missing words in Italian.

a _____ _____ o _____?
(Do you have brothers or sisters?)

b _____ vicino? (Is he close (nearby)?)

c Io e il mio _____ Jim _____ _____ un'attività _____.
(My friend Jim and I, we are going to start a business together.)

Usually you add 'the' in Italian before a possessive, but this isn't the case with family members: *mio padre, mia sorella, mio cugino* etc. Note that this applies only to the singular. So, we say *mio figlio* but *i miei figli*, *mia sorella* but *le mie sorelle*.

d Mia _____ è _____ dottoressa. _____ in un ospedale.
   (My **mum works** as a doctor. **She works** at a hospital.)

e Amo_____ il_____ con i miei_____. (I love **spending the weekend** with my **children**.)

f Parlo con _____ _____ tutto il tempo e _____ _____ spesso.
   (I talk to **my brother** all the time, and I **see him** often.)

g Io e _____ _____ _____ _____ sempre l'estate _____.
   (**My family** and I, we always **spend** the summer **together**.)

h Dove _____? (Where does **he work**?)

i _____ _____ _____ fa jogging _____ _____. (**My girlfriend jogs every day**.)

3 Use the phrase list from Conversation 1 to answer the questions and practise creating
sentences about your friends and family members.

   a Come si chiama il tuo migliore amico? _____

   b Da quando lo conosci? _____

   c Che lavoro fa? _____

GRAMMAR EXPLANATION: *lui* (he), *lei* (she)

So far your scripts have relied mostly on the *io* and *tu* forms of verbs.
Now let's look at the forms for *lui / lei* (he / she).

lui / lei – he / she
Forming verbs for 'he' and 'she' is very easy. Simply take the dictionary
form of the verb and replace:

-are with -a	(parlare → lui / lei parla)
-ere with -e	(leggere → lui / lei legge)
-ire with -e or -isce	(sentire → lui / lei sente,
	finire → lui / lei finisce).

Examples: *Melissa visita Cosenza.* **Melissa is visiting** Cosenza.
          Finisce oggi? **Is he finishing** today?
          Ha ventianni. **He / she is** twenty years old.

The exceptions
There are very few verbs that don't follow this pattern. The important
ones to know are:

···▷ *Lorenzo va a lezione ogni giorno.* (Lorenzo **goes** to class every day –
   from *andare* 'to go')
···▷ *Sara è medico.* (Sara **is** a doctor – from *essere* 'to be')
···▷ *Lui vuole andare a Venezia lunedì.* (He **wants** to go to Venice on
   Monday – from *volere* 'to want')
···▷ *Lei può correre per ore.* (She **can** run for hours – from *potere* 'can')
···▷ *Maria deve andare dal dentista.* (Maria **has to** go to the dentist – from
   dovere 'must / have to')

You'll typically know who's being talked about from context, so you usually won't even have to bother saying *lui* or *lei*. For example, if we know we're talking about Melissa and you wanted to say 'she is working tomorrow', you don't need to say 'lei lavora domani', you could just say lavora domani.

While it may look like a translation mistake, Italian actually says 'he has 20 years' to express age, while in English we'd say it with a version of 'to be'.

#LANGUAGEHACK: use clues and context to understand much more than you think

Getting into Italian may feel overwhelming when you think there are so many words and sentence structures you don't know yet. But even as an absolute beginner, you have a huge head start. Here are five strategies you can use to help you understand when you are spoken to, even when a dictionary is nowhere in sight:

1 Get clues from the **category** of the conversation

It's highly unlikely that you'll find yourself in an Italian conversation where you have no idea what the subject is. Chances are, you were the one who asked the other person a question, such as *Cosa fai nel tuo tempo libero?* (What do you do in your spare time?), and now it's your turn to listen to the reply.

Simply knowing what **word category** to expect can make a huge difference. For instance, if you aren't sure whether a person said *pesca* (peach) or *pesce* (fish), then the fact that you're talking in a restaurant should make it obvious!

A conversation is almost never about 'anything'. There are topics people are more likely to discuss in a given conversation.

2 Use **visual markers** to infer the meaning of words

Suppose you don't know the Italian word for 'water'. You're at a restaurant on your first day in Italy, the waiter arrives and you hear '&%$## @@[]ç / &?'.

If you pay attention to the additional context you're getting from **visual markers**, then you can infer the meaning of new words and phrases.

⋯⋗ Where is the person looking? Is the waiter looking at your glass?
⋯⋗ Where are their hands or body pointing?
⋯⋗ What facial expression do they have? What kind of reply is he expecting?
⋯⋗ Is he looking to see if you're satisfied? Or is he waiting for some specific information from you?

As well as visual markers, intonation will also tell you whether something is a question, a request, a command or a casual comment.

3 Look for **signpost words** at the beginnings and ends of sentences

The same way that you'll see signs alerting you when you're *entering* and *leaving* certain areas, conversations often work the same way! For instance, if you hear phrases along the lines of:

Dove.... smartphone	('Where... smartphone')
stasera.... libro	('This evening... book')
venerdì... cinema	('Friday... cinema')

... you can get a pretty good idea of the gist of the phrase as a whole. Each word brings you closer to the truth, – even if you only recognize the beginning and ends!

Some common **signpost words** to look out for are:

⋯⋗ **question words**: *chi, quando, dove* (who, when, where)
⋯⋗ **time indicators**: *questa settimana, stasera* (this week, this evening)
⋯⋗ **booster verbs**: *Vuoi? Posso?* (Do you want? Can I?)

4 Rely on **connector words** for hints about where the sentence is headed

Can you deduce how the following sentences will end?

Bevo caffè con latte ma senza ...	*Se succede questo di nuovo ...*
I drink coffee with milk but without ...	If that happens again ...

Connector words function to connect one part of a sentence with another. This makes them very reliable signposts for what type of information is to come!

In the examples above, **ma** ('but') is a big hint that the speaker doesn't drink coffee with sugar, and **se** ('if') most likely indicates a threat of some consequence. When you hear these words you can very confidently infer that:

⋯⋗ *ma*: there's a contradiction of what was previously said. If you understood either statement, you can guess the other one is opposing in some way
⋯⋗ *se*: something unsure may happen, and you could hear a positive / negative consequence of it
⋯⋗ *perché*: the first statement happened as a result of the second.

YOUR TURN: use the hack

1 🔊 05.04 Listen to the audio, and use signpost words or connector words to help you guess which of the two options suggested is the most likely translation, and circle it.

    a *Non ... gelato qui ... posto?*
        I don't like the ice cream here. Do you want to go to another place? /
        I don't like ice cream, and you?

    b *... il film ... e tu?*
        I want to watch the film tonight, and you? / Did you see the film?

You might be tempted to talk about where you 'met' someone, but we haven't learned how to talk about things that happened (in the past) yet. It's coming up in Unit 7. In the meantime, practise rephrasing sentences so you can convey the same idea using phrases you know now. This is an invaluable skill in language learning.

PRACTICE

1 Think about which 'me-specific' verbs you would need to talk about the people close to you. You might include verbs you can use to talk about:

⋯⋗ where specific members of my family live
    Example: *mia sorella vive ...*

⋯⋗ what my partner (boyfriend / girlfriend / husband / wife) does for work
    Example: *mio marito scrive ...*

⋯⋗ what a friend does to relax
    Example: *la mia amica, Paola, guarda la televisione ...*

PUT IT TOGETHER

1 Using what you learned in Conversations 1-3, create a script that answers the following questions about *la tua persona preferita*:

⋯⋗ What is his / her name?
⋯⋗ Where does he / she live?
⋯⋗ Who does he / she live with?
⋯⋗ What does he / she do for work?
⋯⋗ How long have you known him / her?
⋯⋗ What does he / she like to do?

CONVERSATION 2

Who do you live with?

Let's build on the language you can use to talk about people in your life. The conversation continues as Melissa and Giulia talk about their families.

🔊 05.05 How does Melissa ask 'how long' Giulia has been married?

Melissa: Sei sposata?

Giulia: Sì! Mio marito si chiama Davide.

Melissa: Da quanto tempo stai con lui?

Giulia: Stiamo insieme da molto tempo. Conosco la sua famiglia da 20 anni. E tu?

Melissa: Per il momento sono single.

Giulia: Con chi vivi?

Melissa: Vivo a casa di Giacomo, il mio coinquilino. Mio padre conosce suo zio. Ha un cagnolino adorabile, Giotto!

Giulia: Mmm … Non mi piacciono i cani. Rompono sempre tutto.

Melissa: Assolutamente no! Il cane di Giacomo non rompe mai niente. Giotto è buonissimo.

Giulia: Vedo che andate d'amore e d'accordo!

> To describe a person's possessions in Italian, rephrase your sentences to use 'of,' in this case: *casa di Giacomo* (house of Giacomo)

GRAMMAR EXPLANATION: *piccolo / piccola / piccoli / piccole*

In Italian, descriptive words tend to 'agree' with what they describe, following the same endings we've seen for genders and plurals. For example:

Adoro la sua sedia rossa. E guarda, ha anche un tavolo rosso! Perché ha tante cose rosse?

(I love her red chair. And look, she also has a red table! Why does she have so many red things?)

If the descriptive word ends in *-e* in its singular form, then it stays the same regardless of gender, and changes to *-i* in the plural. For example:

Mario è gentile, Daniela è intelligente. Sono persone interessanti.

FIGURE IT OUT

1 Complete or answer these questions in Italian about the conversation.

    a How long does Giulia say she's been married?
      Giulia sta insieme a suo marito da _____ _____.

    b At whose house does Melissa live?
      Vive a _____ ____ _____.

    c Is Melissa married or single? _____ _____.

2 Find these words in the conversation and write them in Italian.

    a married _____

    b single _____

    c flatmate _____

3 Is the word *famiglia* masculine or feminine? _____

4 How do you say the following in Italian?

    a when I go back _____

    b Do you mean to say … _____

    c for example … _____

NOTICE

◀)) 05.06 Listen to the audio and study the table.

Essential phrases for Conversation 2

Italian	Meaning
sei sposata?	are you married?
mio marito si chiama ...	my husband's name is ...
da quanto tempo stai con lui?	how long have you been with him?
stiamo insieme da molto tempo	we have been together for a long time
conosco la sua famiglia da venti anni	I've known his family for twenty years
sono single	I'm single
con chi vivi?	who do you live with?
vivo a casa di Giacomo	I live at Giacomo's place
è il mio coinquilino	he's my flatmate / roommate
mio padre conosce suo zio	my father knows his uncle
ha un cagnolino adorabile	he has an adorable little dog
non mi piacciono i cani	I don't like dogs!
rompono sempre tutto	they always break everything (they-break always everything)
assolutamente no!	not at all!
non rompe mai niente!	(he) never breaks anything!
è buonissimo!	(he) is very good!
vedo che andate d'amore e d'accordo!	I see that you are getting along!

LEARNING STRATEGY:
pairs of Opposites
It helps to **learn words in pairs of opposites**, like *mai* and *sempre*. Or you can learn them in clusters. For instance, if something is between *un po'* and *molto*, then try *abbastanza*, which can mean 'enough', 'rather' or 'quite'.

One great thing about studying foreign languages is the new expressions you'll encounter. This one translates as 'getting along like a house on fire!'. Don't try to translate these phrases literally, but look for the fun equivalents!

1 Find the three he / she verb forms in Italian and highlight them.

2 Using the Italian phrase for 'Giacomo's place' as a model, how would you say 'my brother's dog' in Italian?

VOCAB EXPLANATION: *sapere* and *conoscere* (to know)

Italian has two ways of saying 'to know'. Most of the time you'll use *sapere*, which implies that you know a piece of information, or how to do something:

> *so* (I know), *sai* (you know), *sa* (he / she knows)

The other form, *conoscere* implies that you are familiar with something, or that you know a person:

> *conosco* (I know), *conosci* (you know), *conosce* (he / she knows)

Generally, you'll use *conoscere* instead of *sapere* if you can replace the word 'know' with 'know of' or 'be familiar with'. For example, you can't really say 'I know of how to drive,' but you can say 'I *am familiar with* Rome' (*conosco* Roma) or 'I *know of* Mario' (*conosco* Mario).

Conoscere is an especially useful verb because it also means 'to meet', as in *ho conosciuto molta gente ieri* (I met lots of people yesterday).

Examples: *So che parli italiano.*   (I know that you speak Italian.)
Conosco questa canzone!   (I know this song!)

1 Choose between *sapere* and *conoscere* based on the context. Think 'know of / be familiar with' or 'know how'.

a *Conosco / So questo libro.*
b *Conosci / Sai a che ora inizia il concerto?*
c *Conosciamo / Sappiamo Pietro.*
d *Lei conosce / sa nuotare?* (to swim)

PRACTICE

1 Practise answering questions about your relationships with other people. If your answer is yes, fill in the answer. If the answer is no, write in a 'no' reply.

a *Sei sposato / a, single o hai la ragazza / il ragazzo?*

_____

b *Hai figli? Quanti?*

Sì, ho _____ / *No,* _____

c *Con chi vivi?*

Vivo _____ / *Vivo da solo.* (I live alone.)

2 To ask 'who do you live with?' Giulia says *con chi vivi?* which uses a different word order from English. Practise using this word order to form questions.

Example: Who are you giving it to? → <u>A chi lo dai?</u>

a Where are you coming from (*da*)? _____

b Who are you going with? (*con*) _____

c What time (*ora*) does the class start (*a*)?

_____

GRAMMAR TIP:
prepositions at the start
Italian sentences can't end in prepositions (words like *a, di, dopo, con, in*). But it's easy to change your word order if you imagine a more formal way of saying the sentence in English: 'with whom do you live?'

3 A useful phrase to know is *voglio dire* (literally 'I want to say'), which translates as 'I mean'. Use this phrase to say the following:

a Do you mean …? _____

b He / she means … _____

c It means … _____

d We mean … _____

4 Fill in the blanks with the missing words in Italian.

a _____ *il mio migliore* _____ *da cinque anni.* _____
_____ _____.
(**I have known** my best **friend** for five years. **We're a lot alike.**)

Use the present tense with the word *da* – so you'd say 'I know …' rather than 'I have known'.

b *Oggi è il compleanno* _____ _____ _____.
(Today is **my mother's** birthday.)

PUT IT TOGETHER

Use the new vocab you've learned to build on the script you wrote in Conversation 1. Write four sentences about someone close to you, in which you describe things like:

···› how long you've known him/her (*conosco + da*)
···› how long you've been together or married (*stare insieme + da*)
···› what you're going to do together (*vogliamo + infinitive*).

La conosco da …

_____
_____
_____

CONVERSATION 3

There are four of us

You can use the phrase **siamo in** for 'there are (number) of us' to talk about a group you're in. It's a useful phrase in a lot of scenarios, from describing your family to telling a waiter how big a table you need.

The conversation gets a bit more detailed now, as Melissa tries to describe the people she has met.

🔊 **05.07** How do you say in Italian, 'they are not …'?

Melissa:	Hai figli?
Giulia:	Sì, siamo in quattro. Abbiamo due figli. Si chiamano Cesare e Massimiliano.
Melissa:	Oh, che nomi splendidi! Mi piacciono molto.
Giulia:	Tu intendi avere una famiglia?
Melissa:	Non lo so … Ho una vita pienissima. Ho tanto da fare!
Giulia:	E se incontri a Roma un italiano carino ed è colpo di fulmine? Resti là per sempre?
Melissa:	Che spiritosa! Conosco molti italiani, ma di solito non sono … come si dice in italiano, 'my type'?
Giulia:	Non sono il tuo tipo, sì, ho capito. Ma non si sa mai … tutto è possibile!

VOCAB: *ho capito*
We've seen capisco used for 'I understand/ I see what you mean', but you can also use *ho capito*, which is literally 'I've understood'.

FIGURE IT OUT

1 Find the answers to these questions in the conversation. Write them out.

    a How many people are in Giulia's family? _____

    b Does Melissa ever want to have a family? _____

    c How do you say in Italian 'they're not … "my type"?

    _____

2 Look at the conversation. What do the following phrases mean?

    a *Abbiamo due figli.* _____

    b *Come si dice in italiano …?* _____

    c *italiani* _____

3 Highlight these phrases in the conversation.

    a their names are
    b such beautiful names!
    c you never know

NOTICE

🔊 05.08 Listen to the audio and study the table.

Essential phrases for Conversation 3

Italian	Meaning
hai figli?	do you have children?
sì, siamo in quattro	yes, there are four of us (yes, we-are in four)
abbiamo due figli	we have two children
si chiamano ...	their names are …
che nomi splendidi	such gorgeous names!
mi piacciono molto	I like them a lot (me they-like a lot)
tu intendi avere una famiglia?	do you want to have a family?
non lo so ...	I don't know …
e se incontri un italiano carino?	what if you meet a charming Italian?
resti là … per sempre?	will you stay there … forever? (for always)
che spiritosa!	you are funny!
di solito non sono ...	they are usually not …
come si dice in italiano …?	how do you say in Italian …?
non si sa mai! tutto è possibile!	you never know! anything is possible!

GRAMMAR EXPLANATION: *loro* (they)

VOCAB: *si as 'one' or 'they'*
When you want to say 'you', in the sense of 'people in general', in many cases you can use the he/she form of the verb with *si*. *A Milano si parla italiano* – this is like the formal English of 'In Milan one speaks Italian'.

When you want to talk about *Melissa e Giulia* and what they are doing, you'll need to use a new form: **loro**. To make the 'they' form, take the dictionary form of the verb and replace:

⋯⟩ -are with -ano   (*parlare* → *loro parlano*, *imparare* → *loro imparano*)

⋯⟩ -ere with -ono   (*leggere* → *loro leggono*)

⋯⟩ -ire with -ono or -iscono   (*sentire* → *loro sentono*, *capire* → *loro capiscono*).

In a similar way to what you've seen already, some verbs don't follow this pattern:

⋯⋟ andare (to go): *loro vanno*

⋯⋟ essere (to be): *loro sono*

⋯⋟ volere (to want): *loro vogliono*

⋯⋟ potere (can): *loro possono*

⋯⋟ fare (to do): *loro fanno*

1 Fill in the gaps with the correct form of the verb given.

a *Loro* _____ *andare al cinema.* (volere)

b *Le sorelle* _____ *delle notizie.* (parlare)

c *Giulia e Melissa* _____ *insieme a pranzo.* (mangiare)

d *Loro* _____ *di visitare presto la Toscana.* (sperare)

e *Melissa e Giulia* _____ *molto.* (viaggiare)

2 Fill in the irregular verb forms in the table. They're extremely useful, so when you've finished, close your eyes and randomly point at one of the forms and make a sentence with it. Do this five times.

dictionary form	io form	tu form	lui / lei form	noi form	loro form
volere					
essere					
andare					
conoscere					
capire					

PRACTICE

1 How would you say 'It's not possible!' in Italian? _____

2 Match the correct Italian phrases with the English translations.

a *andiamo*   1 they are

b *vanno*   2 we know

c *siamo*   3 they are going

d *sanno*   4 we are

e *sono*   5 they know

f *sappiamo*   6 we are going

3 Use the verb forms you've learned to fill in the gaps for each question-answer pair.

  a *Tuo fratello è uno studente? No, _____ ingegnere!*

  b *I tuoi genitori sono al lavoro? No, _____ in vacanza!*

  c *Il tuo amico vuole viaggiare con te?*
    No, _____ _____ con mio cugino!

  d *Le tue sorelle vogliono leggere il tuo libro?*
    No, _____ vedere la televisione.

PUT IT TOGETHER

Siamo in quattro! You should now have most of the 'me-specific' vocab you need to talk about your family or group of friends. Create a script of between four and six sentences about:

···⟩ your parents or family – their names, ages, or where they live
    (*loro* + verb)
···⟩ your children, nephews, or cousins – their names, ages, what they're doing or what they
    like (*lui / lei / loro* + verb)
···⟩ your friends – how you know them, what they do or what they like
    (*lui / lei / loro* + verb)
···⟩ your co-workers – what they say, what you're working on together
    (*lui / lei / loro* + verb)
···⟩ your pets, people you admire, or anyone else you want to describe!

COMPLETING UNIT 5

Check your understanding

🔊 **05.09** Listen to this audio rehearsal, which asks questions in Italian, followed by a short answer.

Combine the answer with the verb in the question to give the full answer. Feel free to pause or replay the audio as often as you need.

> Example: *Con chi vive Giovanni? (con sua madre)*
>   → Lui vive con sua madre.

Show what you know ...

Here's what you've just learned. Write or say an example for each item in the list. Then tick off the ones you know.

- ☐ Give the Italian phrases for:
    - ☐ 'my mother' and 'my father'
    - ☐ 'your sister' and 'your brother'
    - ☐ another family member of your choice.
- ☐ Give two phrases you can use to express how you 'spend time' or what you 'plan' to do.
- ☐ Give one sentence each using:
    - ☐ the *lui* verb form to describe what someone (m) you know works as
    - ☐ the *loro* verb form to describe what some friends of yours are doing right now.
- ☐ Say something you plan to do with another person using *noi* and *insieme*.
- ☐ Use *conoscere* to say something or someone you 'know' (are familiar with).

COMPLETE YOUR MISSION

It's time to complete your mission: talk up your friend to spark an interest in *il tuo amico italiano*. To do this, you'll need to prepare a description of your friend and explain the story of how you met and all the good things about him or her.

STEP 1: build your script

Chi è la persona più importante della tua vita? Use the phrases you've learned and 'me-specific' vocab to build scripts about your favourite person. Be sure to:

···⟩ say who it is (*il mio amico, mio fratello, mia sorella*)
···⟩ explain why the person is so important to you (*lui, lei*)
···⟩ say how long you've known each other (*conoscere + da*)
···⟩ describe their characteristics, jobs, family, etc. (*il suo / la sua*)
···⟩ describe things you do together (*noi* and *insieme*)

Write down your script, then rehearse it until you feel confident.

STEP 2: keep it real ... *online*

This is a script you'll use and build on over and over when you talk about your nearest and dearest in Italian in real life. Start using it right away to fill the gaps in your script as soon as you can! So, go online, find the mission for Unit 5, and share your recording with the community.

STEP 3: learn from other learners

Your task is to ask a follow-up question in Italian to at least three different people, to inspire them to build on their scripts just a little bit more.

STEP 4: reflect on what you've learned

What new words or phrases did you realize you need to start filling your gaps?

Use your language to communicate with real people! You need to speak and use a language for it to start to take hold in your long-term memory. And it's the best way to see and feel your progress.

Remember, your missions help you, but also help others expand their vocabulary.

HEY, LANGUAGE HACKER, YOU'RE OVER HALFWAY THERE!

You have successfully overcome one of the biggest challenges in language learning: getting started and then keeping it up. Momentum will take you a long way in learning Italian quickly, so you should feel good about how far you've come. Always focus on what you can do today that you couldn't do yesterday. Next up: you'll apply what you know to prepare for conversations at the Italian dinner table.

Continua così!

110 ···⟩ 5 TALKING ABOUT FAMILY AND FRIENDS

6 HAVING SOME FOOD, DRINK AND CONVERSATION

Your mission

Imagine this – you've discovered an incredible restaurant near *casa tua*, so you invite a new Roman friend to join you there. You feel *molto elegante*. But it turns out (to your horror) that your friend has heard bad things about it. *Bleah*, he says, *é un mortorio ...*

Your mission is to **convince your friend to come with you** to the restaurant. Be prepared to **give your opinion** and **say why you disagree**. Back it up with details of why the place is so *alla moda* – **describe food you like** and **why you like it**.

This mission will help you become comfortable agreeing, disagreeing and explaining your point of view, as well as talking about food and restaurants – a very important topic.

Mission prep

- ⋯⟩ Learn phrases and etiquette for dining out: *per me*, *prendo*, *mi può portare*, *vorrei*.
- ⋯⟩ Use food and drink vocabulary: *(dell') acqua naturale o frizzante*, *un bicchiere di vino rosso / bianco*.
- ⋯⟩ Use expressions for giving opinions and recommendations: *secondo me*.
- ⋯⟩ Make comparisons using *più*, *meglio*, *peggio*.

BUILDING LANGUAGE FOR ITALIAN DINNER CONVERSATION

Here's where your conversations can start to get more interesting. Having a long meal filled with fun discussion is a key part of Italian culture – and sharing both agreements and disagreements makes for much more interesting conversations.

#LANGUAGEHACK
sound more fluent with conversation connectors

CONVERSATION 1

For me, I'll have …

🔊 06.01 Melissa and her friend Paola sit down to eat at a restaurant in Rome. What phrase does the waiter use to ask, 'Are you ready?'

Melissa: Ho fame. Ah – ecco il cameriere qui!

Waiter: Buonasera, quanti siete?

Melissa: Siamo in due.

Waiter: Va bene, questo tavolo è libero. Ecco il menu.

Paola: Molto bene. Per ora ci porta dell'acqua frizzante e due spritz? Grazie!

Waiter: Prego, fate con comodo!

Waiter: Avete deciso?

Paola: Sì! Abbiamo già deciso.

Waiter: Prego!

Melissa: Ehm … per me gli gnocchi, per piacere.

Waiter: *E per Lei?*

Paola: Io prendo i ravioli.

Waiter: E da bere?

Paola: Vuoi bere qualcosa?

Melissa: Vorrei un bicchiere di vino bianco. E tu, Paola? Cosa prendi?

Paola: Mi può portare del vino rosso e ancora un po' d'acqua?

Waiter: Arrivo subito!

FIGURE IT OUT

Look back at the conversation and answer the questions.

1 What does Melissa order to eat? And to drink? Find each in the conversation and underline them.

2 What does the phrase *Avete deciso* mean? _____

3 Can you see any uses of 'you'-plural in the conversation? What about formal 'you'? Circle them.

4 Underline the phrases Melissa and Paola use to order:
  a gnocchi   b ravioli   c bicchiere di vino

5 Use what you find in the conversation to write out the following phrases in Italian.

  a And to drink? _____

  b What will you have? _____

  c We already know. _____

CULTURE TIP: *mangia!*

Italians have a passion for food and love spending time at the table. Just have a look at the menu and you'll understand. Start with an *antipasto* (meaning 'before the meal' – starter). After that choose a *primo* (first course, usually pasta), then indulge in a *secondo* (second course, such as meat or fish) but don't forget to order a *contorno* (side dish). Then delight yourself with a *dolce* (dessert). A coffee (*espresso* of course!) generally ends the Italian eating experience, but don't be surprised if the waiter asks if you fancy *un liquorino*!

acqua

When you order water in a bar or restaurant in Italy, the waiter will ask if you would like mineral (*acqua naturale*) or sparkling water (*acqua frizzante*), unless you specify. Sparkling water is very common in Italy and probably one out of two or three Italians drink it!

aperitivo

The Italian *aperitivo* is a very popular social event. After work and just before dinner, people often meet in a bar to have drinks (usually a cocktail – *spritz* being a favourite) and eat some snacks, while they socialize. The type and amount of food offered with the drinks depends on the city, so you could end up with a full stomach before dinner even starts! It's a fun tradition all over the country.

NOTICE

🔊 06.02 Listen to the audio and study the table.

Essential phrases for Conversation 1

<table>
<tr><td colspan="2"></td></tr>
</table>

Italian	Meaning
ho fame!	I'm hungry! (I have hunger)
ecco il cameriere qui	here's the waiter (here-is the waiter here)
buonasera!	good evening!
quanti siete?	how many? (how-many you-are?)
siamo in due	there are two of us (we-are in two)
va bene, questo tavolo è libero	OK, this table is free
ecco il menu	here's the menu
per ora, ci porta dell'acqua frizzante e due spritz?	for now, will you bring us some sparkling water and two spritz?
prego, fate con comodo!	you're welcome, take your time!
avete deciso?	are you (pl) ready? (have-you (pl) decided?)
abbiamo già deciso	we know already (we've already decided)
prego!	what would you like?
per me, gli gnocchi, per piacere	for me, the gnocchi, please
e per Lei?	and for you? (formal)
io prendo i ravioli	I'll take the ravioli
e da bere?	and to drink?
Vuoi bere qualcosa?	Do you want something to drink?
vorrei …	I'd like …
un bicchiere di vino bianco	a glass of white wine
mi può portare …	can you bring me …
e ancora un po' d'acqua?	and another water?
arrivo subito!	right away!

VOCAB: prego!
Prego is one of the most versatile words in Italian. In this conversation, the waiter encourages the customers to order with a simple *Prego!*, meaning 'What would you like?'. But *prego* can be translated differently depending on the situation:
- as a common answer to 'thank you': *Grazie mille!* (Thanks a million!) – *Prego* (You're welcome)
- to encourage someone to do something: *Posso entrare?* (May I come in?) – *Prego!* (Sure!)
- to ask somebody to repeat what they said: *Prego? Non ho capito!* (Sorry? I don't understand).

VOCAB: vorrei – 'I would like'
You know how to use *voglio* for 'I want,' but another, less direct option is *vorrei* or 'I would like', which works better in formal situations.

1 Look at *ho fame* in the phrase list. How does Italian express this feeling differently? _____

2 Underline the phrases which are used to:
   a order some water   b order a wine

3 Highlight the five phrases used to place an order. Then replay the audio to practise your pronunciation of the phrases:

a I'll take ...　　c we'll have　　　　　　　　e I would like ...

b For me ...　　d Can you bring me ...?

4 Match the verbs with their corresponding meaning in English.

a *voglio*　　　　　　　　　　1 You want?

b *Vuoi?*　　　　　　　　　　　2 Are you going to drink?

c *Vuoi bere?*　　　　　　　　3 I'm going to drink

d *bevo*　　　　　　　　　　　4 I want

PRACTICE

1 *Vuoi ... qualcosa?* (Are you going to ... something?) is a power phrase. You can modify it in endless ways. Practise using it with different verbs. Use the answer given to figure out which verb works best.

a *Vuoi* _____ *qualcosa?* → *Sì, sushi!*

b *Vuoi* _____ *qualcosa?* → *Sì, vino!*

c *Vuoi* _____ *qualcosa?* → *Sì, un libro!*

2 Fill in the blanks with the missing words in Italian.

a _____ *deciso.* (**We've** decided.)

b *Ancora* _____ _____ *di gnocchi, per favore!*
   (**Some** more gnocchi, please!)

c *Io prendo del* _____ *rosso e* _____ _____ *un*
   _____ *d'acqua.*　.
   (I'll have red **wine**, and **she'll have a glass** of water.)

d _____ _____ *mangiare?*
   (**What would you like** to eat?) (*desiderare*)

e *Hai* _____ _____? (Are you **already hungry**?)

3 Which words do the speakers use to say how much of their drinks they want. Circle the correct answer, then add the missing Italian word.

a _____ *vino rosso*　　　　　　(a / some)

b _____ *bicchiere di vino bianco*　(a / some)

c _____ *acqua frizzante*　　　　(a / some)

Here's some important vocab related to eating and drinking to give you a solid base.

Eating and drinking vocab

Italian	Meaning	Italian	Meaning
cibo	food	prendo	I'll have (I take)
avere fame (ho fame)	to be hungry (I'm hungry)	(fare) colazione	(to have) breakfast
avere sete (ho sete)	to be thirsty (I'm thirsty)	pranzo / pranzare	lunch / to have lunch
mangiare	to eat	cena / cenare	dinner / to have dinner
bere (io bevo)	to drink (I drink)	carne	meat
bibita	(soft) drink	pollo	chicken
cucinare	to cook / to prepare	manzo	beef
vegetariano	vegetarian	maiale	pork
con / senza	with / without	pesce	fish
Sono allergico/a alle nocciole …	I'm allergic to nuts	verdure	vegetables
Cosa mi può consigliare?	What can you recommend?	frutta	fruit
Ancora un/una …	One more …	succo d'arancia	orange juice

I'd suggest you also **take a pocket dictionary** or use one of the dictionary apps/sites recommended in our Resources, on your phone. You may want to try something on the specials board!

Before you head to an Italian restaurant, it's a good idea to learn the names of your favourite dishes in advance to save you the trouble.

4 What food or drink do you usually order? Add them to the table in Italian.

PUT IT TOGETHER

1 *Buonasera!* Role-play a conversation in which you order your favourite food and drink in Italian at a restaurant. Respond to the questions by ordering anything you like (as long as it's in Italian!). Take inspiration from what you've learned in this unit, or use your dictionary.

You'll order a starter, a first course, two drinks and a dessert – *Oggi hai fame e sete!* (You've already seen *il menù* and it conveniently has all your favourite foods on it!)

Cameriere:	Ha già deciso?
Tu:	_____
Cameriere:	Ah, buona scelta! E come primo?
Tu:	_____
Cameriere:	Lei è proprio un buongustaio! E da bere?
Tu:	_____ e _____
Cameriere:	Arrivo subito!
	(30 minuti dopo ...)
Tu:	(Call the waiter over.) _____
Cameriere:	Ha finito?
Tu:	(Say yes, and that you have already chosen your dessert.)
	_____
Cameriere:	Cosa prende?
Tu:	_____
Cameriere:	... Ecco qui! Buon appetito!

2 Imagine that you're going to cook a meal and are planning your shopping list. Create three 'me-specific' phrases to describe your normal mealtime routine. Use the vocab you've learned in this unit, as well as any new words you need from your dictionary. Try to include:

⋯⟩ what you're planning to eat or drink (*mangiare / bere*)
⋯⟩ whether you normally cook at home (*cucinare a casa*), have dinner in a restaurant (*cenare fuori / cenare in un ristorante*), etc.

CONVERSATION 2

In my opinion …

CULTURE TIP: *debate!* Italian speakers aren't afraid to raise controversial subjects in conversations. After a heated debate, people get back to being the best of friends. If a tricky-to-discuss topic comes up, this means that the other person is interested in hearing your opinion! If you aren't comfortable talking about the topic, feel free to mention this – but why not try to offer a basic opinion, to get some interesting practice time!

Dinner conversation is very important to Italians. A meal is meant to be enjoyed with friends, with interesting discussions, and sometimes debates!

🔊 06.03 Melissa and Paola discover they don't see eye to eye on where they should go in Rome. Listen to determine which phrases mean 'I agree' and 'I disagree'.

Paola:	Allora, domani a che museo andiamo?
Melissa:	Ovviamente dobbiamo vedere la Cappella Sistina!
Paola:	No, ci sono così tanti musei a Roma e tu scegli quello con più turisti!
Melissa:	So che ci sono molti turisti, ma bisogna vederla!
Paola:	Non sono d'accordo! Secondo me è meglio il Pantheon, e poi c'è meno gente.
Melissa:	Hai ragione, ci sono meno turisti ma non è così interessante!
Paola:	Non è vero! Ha un'architettura incredibile! È unico!
Melissa:	Sono d'accordo. L'architettura è interessante, ma non lo trovo bello.
Paola:	Sai che molti romani trovano la Cappella Sistina noiosa e tu la vuoi visitare.
Melissa:	Mmm, troviamo un compromesso. Se per te il Pantheon è meglio della Cappella Sistina, possiamo andare al Pantheon domani per l'architettura. Ma lunedì, quando ci sono meno turisti, possiamo andare alla Cappella Sistina, per l'arte!
Paola:	Ci sto!

FIGURE IT OUT

1 Find the following details in the conversation and underline them.

    a What are the names of the two *luoghi di interesse* (places of interest) being discussed?

    b Where does Melissa think they should visit?

    c What is Melissa's opinion of the Pantheon?

    d What phrases show that Melissa and Paola will make a compromise?

2 Now find these phrases in the conversation and circle them:

    a the most touristy   d there are less tourists

    b there are a lot of tourists   e if you think that

    c there are fewer people

3 Answer the questions in Italian using the English responses provided.

    a *Cosa dobbiamo vedere?* _____

       (We need to see the Mediterranean Sea.)

    b *Perché vuoi andare in spiaggia?* _____

       (Because the beach is more relaxing.)

4 Write out the Italian phrases for:

    a obviously _____   c I don't agree _____

    b I agree _____   d That's not true! _____

5 Use context to deduce the meaning of the words in bold.

    Paola dice che ...

    a *il Pantheon è* **meglio** *della Cappella Sistina* _____

    b *nel Pantheon c'è* **meno** *gente che alla Cappella Sistina* _____

    c *molti romani* **trovano** *la Cappella Sistina noiosa* _____

NOTICE

GRAMMAR TIP: *dovere*
Dovere is a verb with irregular forms. So far you've seen: *devo, devi, deve, devono* (I / you / he / they have to) Here we have the completely different 'we' form, *dobbiamo*.

🔊 **06.04** Listen to the audio and study the table.

Essential phrases for Conversation 2

Italian	Meaning
a che museo andiamo?	which museum are we going to?
ovviamente dobbiamo vedere ...	obviously we need to see ...
no, ci sono così tanti musei …	there are so many museums ...
tu scegli quello con più turisti!	you choose the one with the most tourists!
so che ci sono molti ...	I know there are a lot of ...
ma bisogna vederla!	but it has to be seen!
non sono d'accordo!	I disagree!
secondo me ...	in my opinion …
è meglio il Pantheon	the Pantheon is better (it's better the Pantheon)
e c'è meno gente!	and there are fewer people!
hai ragione	you're right (you-have reason)
ma non è così interessante!	but it's not as interesting!
ha un'architettura incredibile!	it has amazing architecture!
è unico!	there's nothing like it!
sono d'accordo	I agree
non lo trovo ...	I don't find it ...
troviamo un compromesso	let's make a compromise
se per te ...	if you think that ...
è meglio di	it's better than
possiamo andare ... per l'arte	we can go ... for the art!
ci sto!	deal!

VOCAB: *bisogna*
Here's a very useful expression, which means that whatever follows must be done. In this conversation, *bisogna vederla* means 'it must be seen!' or 'I have to see it!'. Since the next word (verb) will be in the dictionary form, you can use it to express anything that 'needs' to happen. For example: *Bisogna bere il vino italiano!* You really should drink Italian wine!

1 Find the phrase for 'you're right' in the phrase list. What expression from Conversation 1 also uses *avere* (to have) in Italian instead of 'to be' as you would in English? _____

2 Find the words used for comparison and circle them in the phrase list. Then write them out.

a the most ⎯⎯⎯⎯   b better ⎯⎯⎯⎯   c less / fewer ⎯⎯⎯⎯

3 How would you write the following in Italian?

a I find it ⎯⎯⎯⎯⎯⎯⎯⎯

b I know that ⎯⎯⎯⎯⎯⎯⎯⎯

c you know that ⎯⎯⎯⎯⎯⎯⎯⎯

d I know that there are ⎯⎯⎯⎯⎯⎯⎯⎯⎯⎯⎯⎯⎯⎯

e you know that there are ⎯⎯⎯⎯⎯⎯⎯⎯⎯⎯⎯⎯⎯⎯

f there is nothing like it ⎯⎯⎯⎯⎯⎯⎯⎯⎯⎯⎯⎯⎯⎯

4 Each of these phrases is useful for expressing your opinion in Italian. Match the Italian phrase to its English counterpart.

a *secondo me*   1 I agree
b *non sono d'accordo*   2 you're right
c *hai ragione*   3 in my opinion
d *sono d'accordo*   4 I don't agree
e *trovo*   5 I would like
f *vorrei*   6 I find

VOCAB: *c'è / ci sono* 'there is' / 'there are'
Do you remember *c'è / ci sono* from previous conversations? When you're walking around a big city in Italy, you can use *ci sono* to exclaim *Ci sono così tanti ...!* (There are so many ...!) or *Ci sono troppi ...!* (There are too many ...!). Both *tanti* and *troppi* change their endings to match the word that follows. So you can also have *tante ragioni* or *troppe persone*. Similarly, *così tanto* is 'so much' and *troppo* is 'too much'.

CULTURE EXPLANATION: Italian slang

Italian slang changes a little from place to place and is notoriously difficult to translate, but here are some of my favourites with approximations!

Bello / bella – used to address someone in a nice way, similar to 'buddy' or 'mate', even though the word literally means 'beautiful'.

Occhio – 'careful / watch out!' used in everyday situations – if you're about to cross the street when you shouldn't, your friend may yell *occhio!*

Allora – 'so ...' a great phrase and filler for adding emphasis to whatever you're going to say. Italians often begin a sentence with it.

Ma proprio no! – you can think of this as 'no way!'.

Neanche per sogno! – in your dreams!

Su / Dai – very energetic expressions that can be used to say 'hurry up' or to express encouragement, as in 'come on'.

Va bene – just like we use 'alright' in English, as a synonym for 'ok'

GRAMMAR EXPLANATION: comparisons

Italian makes it very easy to compare things. You can describe something as 'more' or 'less', 'bigger' or 'smaller', plus a range of other comparisons using *più* and *meno*:

> VOCAB: *meno*
> Meno (less) looks a lot like 'minus' (but with very different pronunciation).

⋯⋗ **più** + adjective for 'more / -er ' → *più grande* (bigger)
⋯⋗ **meno** + adjective for 'less' → *meno bello* (less handsome)
⋯⋗ **il più** (or *la / i / le più*) + adjective for 'the most / -est'
  → *il più grande* (the biggest)
⋯⋗ **il meno** (or *la / i / le meno*) + adjective for 'the least'
  → *il meno bello* (the least handsome)

When making comparisons between two people / places / things, use **di** for 'than':

Examples: *Sono più alto **di** te.*   I am taller **than** you.
        *Sei più giovane **di** me.* You're younger **than** me.

VOCAB: *'of the'*
You'll notice that the words *in*, *di* and *a* combine with *il* as *nel*, *del*, *al*, with *i* as *nei*, *dei*, *ai* and also with *la/l'/ lo/le* by doubling the *l*, such as *nell'*, *della*, *alle*.

Vocab	Example	il più / il meno	Example
più + grande (bigger)	La tua città è più grande della mia. (Your city is bigger than mine.)	**il più** + grande (biggest)	La tua città è la più grande del paese. (Your city is the biggest in the country.)
più + interessante (more interesting)	Per me questo museo è più interessante. (I think that this museum is more interesting.)	**il più** + interessante (most interesting)	È la persona più interessante che conosco. (This person is the most interesting (one) that I have known.)
meno + esperto (less skilled)	È meno esperta di suo fratello. (She is less skilled than her brother.)	**il meno** + esperto (least skilled)	Sei la meno esperta qui. (You are the least skilled here.)

To compare amounts, you can also use *più* and *meno*:

Example: *Ci sono meno turisti al Pantheon che al Colosseo.*
    (There are fewer tourists at the Pantheon than at the Colosseum.)

Some Italian adjectives have special forms, the most important of which are *buono* (good) and *cattivo* (bad):

Adjective	'-er' form	'-est form'
buono (good)	migliore (better)	il/la migliore (best)
cattivo (bad)	peggiore (worse)	il/la peggiore (worst)

Example: *Per me questo ristorante fa la migliore pizza del mondo!*

1 Practise using the different forms of *più, meno, meglio* or *peggio*, with the phrases given.

Example: a smaller city (*città piccola*) → una città più piccola

a nicer (*simpatico*)

_____

b more charming (*affascinante*)

_____

c more books

_____

d most famous (*famoso*)

_____

e the best restaurant

_____

f a better friend

_____

g a younger man (*uomo*)

_____

h less difficult

_____

i fewer days

_____

j least expensive (*caro*)

_____

k the worst film

_____

l worse quality

_____

PRACTICE

1 Practise using *c'è / ci sono* by combining this phrase with the sentence endings given to form new sentences in Italian.

Example: There are not … (enough days in the weekend)!
Non ci sono abbastanza giorni in un weekend!

a Are there … (only three students here)?

_____

b There are some … (books at my house).

_____

c I find that there are … (fewer dogs in the park today). (*cani al parco*)

_____

2 How would you translate the following into Italian?

a Milan is bigger than Trieste.

_____

b There are fewer people (*gente*) here than at your house (*a casa tua*).

_____

c I find this restaurant too small.

_____

PUT IT TOGETHER

Quale parte del mondo vuoi visitare? Practise creating your own sentences. Recommend to a friend some things to do in a city you know or would like to visit. Use vocab you learned in Conversation 2, and any new 'me-specific' vocab that you look up on your own. Try to include:

···⟩ the places you would like to visit (*vorrei*)
···⟩ which sites or experiences you think would be the best (*migliore*)
···⟩ what for you is a 'must see' (*bisogna vedere*)
···⟩ phrases for comparison (*più, meno*)
···⟩ phrases for expressing your opinion (*secondo me*).

CONVERSATION 3

What do you recommend?

Another important dinner topic in Italy is culture. You don't need to quote Dante, but it's good to learn some phrases you can use to contribute to conversations and give your opinion about books, music, art or politics.

🔊 06.05 Now that their debate is settled, Melissa and Paola share their opinions on music and books and give one another suggestions. What phrase does Melissa use to say 'tell me'?

Melissa:	Dimmi una cosa, Paola. Vorrei sapere di più sulla musica italiana. Cosa consigli?
Paola:	È una bella domanda! Secondo me la migliore musica pop in Italia è di Laura Pausini.
Melissa:	Ah sì! Canta 'La Solitudine', no? Vorrei imparare i testi delle sue canzoni.
Paola:	Devi imparare di più sulla musica italiana. Domani ti do delle canzoni da ascoltare.
Melissa:	Grazie! Ho appena finito di leggere un libro su come la politica influenza la musica.
Paola:	Oh! Mi interessa molto la politica e mi sembra un libro interessante ma, francamente, non mi piacciono i politici!
Melissa:	Neanche a me. Secondo me parlano tanto ma in realtà dicono poco o niente.
Paola:	Ti do ragione al cento per cento. A proposito, mi puoi consigliare un libro sulla politica in inglese? Devo praticare il mio inglese.
Melissa:	Certamente! Leggo tutto il tempo. Domani ti do il libro che ho finito di leggere. Ti piace di sicuro.
Paola:	Grazie!
Melissa:	Grazie a te!
Paola:	Vediamo un po' dov'è il cameriere. Voglio chiedere il conto. Il conto per favore!
Melissa:	Offro io!

Literally 'thanks to you,' *Grazie a te* is like saying 'no, thank you!' as a reply to grazie.

FIGURE IT OUT

1 Answer the questions about the conversation with a short phrase in Italian.

    a What does Paola think is the best music in Italy?_____

    b What would Melissa like to learn? _____

    c What is Melissa going to give Paola? _____

2 Deduce the meaning of these phrases:

    a *francamente* _____   **b** *certamente* _____

3 How do you ask the following in Italian?

    a Where is the waiter? _____

    b What do you recommend? _____

    c The bill, please! _____

4 Find and circle the opinion phrases in the conversation.
    a in my opinion   **b** the best …   **c** It seems to me …

5 Recognize the familiar verbs and underline them in the conversation.
    a I would like   **b** I'm going to give you   **c** you can recommend

NOTICE

🔊 06.06 Listen to the audio and study the table.

Essential phrases for Conversation 3

Italian	Meaning
dimmi una cosa ...	tell me something ...
vorrei sapere di più	I would like to know more
cosa consigli?	what do you recommend?
è una bella domanda!	that's a good question!
la migliore è ...	the best is ...
devi imparare di più su ...	you should learn more about ...
ti do ...	I'll give you ...
... delle canzoni da ascoltare	.... some songs to listen to
ho appena finito di leggere un libro su ...	I just finished reading a book about ...
mi interessa molto la politica	I'm very interested in politics
mi sembra un libro interessante	it seems to be an interesting book
ma francamente	but frankly
non mi piacciono i politici!	I don't like politicians!
neanche a me	me neither
parlano tanto	they talk so much
ma in realtà dicono poco o niente	but in reality, they say little to nothing
ti do ragione al cento per cento	I agree with you one hundred per cent!
mi puoi consigliare ...?	can you recommend to me ...?
leggo tutto il tempo	I read all the time
... il libro che ho finito di leggere	... the book I just finished reading
ti piace di sicuro	you'll like it for sure
vediamo un po'... dov'è il cameriere	let's see ... where's the waiter?
voglio chiedere il conto	I'm going to ask for the bill
offro io	my treat! (offer I)

PRONUNCIATION:
consigli
If you remember how *-gli* is pronounced, you'd know this sounds something like 'kon-seel-yee'.

While you may be tempted to translate 'ask for' as (chiedere per), the 'for' is implied in **chiedere**. No need for it! Think of it as the way we use the word 'request' in English. The same works for aspettare, which means 'to wait for': *ti aspetto* (I'm waiting for you).

VOCAB: *offro io*
I love that 'I offer' is how you say 'it's my treat' in Italian. And notice the use of *io* here for emphasis – just in case Paola is ready to protest, Melissa makes it clear it's definitely her paying.

1 How do you say these phrases in Italian?

  a you'll like it for sure _____ b I like it _____

2 Match the correct Italian phrases with the English translations.

  a *ti do*   1 I'm sure that
  b *sono sicura che*   2 I'd like to learn
  c *secondo me la migliore*   3 I'll give you
  d *vorrei imparare*   4 I'm going to ask
  e *voglio chiedere*   5 in my opinion the best

3 Notice the phrases that can be used to ask for recommendations. Then write them out here in Italian.

  a What do you recommend? _____ c Tell me something _____

  b Can you recommend to me … _____

PRACTICE

1 Practise adapting power phrases to use in different situations.

  a Power phrase : *Voglio chiedere …* (I'm going to ask for …)

    … some water   _____
    … more time   _____
    … another drink   _____

  b Power phrase: *Vorrei sapere di più su… (qualcosa)*
    'What new places or topics would you like to learn more about?' Use this power phrase to write two sentences about them.

    _____

    _____

2 Fill in the blanks with the missing words in Italian.

  a *Adoro _____ classica. _____ _____ _____ _____*
    moderna. (I love classic **art. I like** (that) **more than** modern **art.**)

  b _____ _____*, che libro* _____ _____ *interessante?*
    (**In your opinion,** which book **is more** interesting?)

  c *Un momento,* _____ _____ _____ *nostro indirizzo!* (Hold on a minute, **I have to**
    give you our address.)

#LANGUAGEHACK:
sound more fluent with conversation connectors

As a beginner, when you're asked a question in Italian, you may be tempted to give single word answers. Do you like this book? *Sì.* How is your food? *Buono.*

While you may not be able to give as detailed replies in Italian as you'd like to (yet), you can learn versatile phrases to use instead of brief answers. Conversation connectors are power phrases that you can tack on to nearly anything you say to make your conversations flow better and feel less one-sided. For example, in Conversation 3, Melissa uses the conversation connector *è una bella domanda* during her discussion with Paola.

How to use conversation connectors

Good conversation connectors should be versatile. They don't need to add extra information to the sentence, but should expand on what could otherwise be a very short answer. For example, if someone asks you: *Hai fame?*, you could reply with:

> *A dire la verità ho molta fame, e tu?*

Here are some different conversation connectors to get you started.

for adding your opinion

francamente (frankly speaking)
a dire la verità (to tell the truth)
secondo me (in my opinion)
detto tra noi (between us)
se ho capito bene (if I understand correctly)
sfortunatamente (unfortunately)
mi sembra che (it seems to me that)

for concluding an idea

sempre più (more and more)
anche se (even if)
finalmente (finally)
per lo meno (at least)

for changing the subject

d'altra parte (on the other hand)
a proposito (by the way)

for elaborating on an idea

è per questa ragione che ... (and that's why ...)
è perché (that's because)

Example: *Be', detto tra noi, ho una fame da lupi. / A dire la verità ho una fame da lupi.*

Here are a few more examples of how to use conversation connectors:

⋯⋗ If asked, Quanti anni hai?, you could say *Ho 41 anni*
   or: *Beh ... detto tra noi ... sfortunatamente ho già 41 anni!*

⋯⋗ If asked, *Perché studi l'italiano?*, you could say, *mi piace la cultura italiana*,
   or: *A dire la verità ... mi piace la cultura italiana! È per questa ragione che studio l'italiano!*

YOUR TURN: use the hack

1 ◀⑴ **06.07** Practise getting more familiar with the sound and pronunciation of conversation connectors. Listen to the audio, and repeat each connector phrase to mimic the speaker.

2 ◀⑴ **06.08** Now practise recognizing the phrases. Listen to the audio, and write down the connector phrase you hear in Italian.

a _____   d _____

b _____   e _____

c _____   f _____

3 Use the conversation connectors suggested to practise giving more lengthy replies to common questions.

Example: *Questa casa ti sembra troppo piccola?*

A dire la verità, questa casa non mi sembra piccola!

a *Ti piace la cena?* _____

b *Dove vivi?* _____

c *Vuoi qualcosa dal supermercato?* _____

_____

d *Prendi un caffè?* _____

PUT IT TOGETHER

Imagine you have a friend who wants to have a culture-filled weekend, and asks you to recommend some worthwhile cultural endeavours. Create 'me-specific' sentences in which you:

⋯⟩ describe music, art, or books that you love
⋯⟩ use phrases for offering your opinion (*secondo me, trovo, mi piace*)
⋯⟩ include power phrases (*vorrei sapere di più su …*)
⋯⟩ use conversation connectors (*francamente, detto tra noi …*)
⋯⟩ use comparisons (*più, meno, meglio*).

> This technique will help you develop a conversational flow even if you have too few words to keep your side of the conversation very interesting for now. For beginners, **momentum helps** conversations stay alive better than more words.

COMPLETING UNIT 6

Check your understanding

🔊 06.09 Listen to the audio recordings. The first statement gives information about someone. The second statement attempts to summarize that information. Based on what you understand, circle *vero* if the summary is correct or *falso* if it's false.

Example: *Secondo Susanna, questa città è bella.*
Summary: *Le piace la città.* (vero) / *falso*

a vero / falso   d vero / falso
b vero / falso   e vero / falso
c vero / falso

Show what you know ...

Here's what you've just learned. Write or say an example for each item in the list. Then tick off the ones you know.

☐ Ask for a specific food item using 'I'll have'.
☐ Ask for a specific drink using 'I would like'.
☐ Use phrases in formal situations:
    ☐ good evening
    ☐ please (formal/informal)
    ☐ thanks to you (informal)
☐ Talk about unspecified amounts and plurals:
    ☐ some songs
    ☐ too many tourists
    ☐ so many churches
☐ Say 'I agree', 'I disagree', and 'in my opinion'.
☐ Give one phrase each for giving and asking for recommendations.
☐ Give the comparison words 'more than', 'less than', 'most' and 'better than'.
☐ Give two examples of conversation connectors.

COMPLETE YOUR MISSION

It's time to complete your mission: convince your friend to try out your favourite restaurant. You'll need to prepare phrases for giving opinions and explaining why you agree or disagree. Describe a restaurant you know and love, or research restaurants in an Italian-speaking country you want to visit.

STEP 1: build your script

Keep building your script! Use opinion phrases to:

⋯⋗ describe your favourite restaurant. Say what type of food and drinks they serve. Why do you like it so much? Which are your favourites and why?
⋯⋗ convince a friend to try it out by saying what makes it better than other restaurants in town (use comparisons!)
⋯⋗ give or ask for recommendations
⋯⋗ include power phrases and conversation connectors.

Write your script, then rehearse it until you feel confident.

LEARNING STRATEGY: 'reading online'
Read restaurant reviews in Italian online to help you form your argument. You can see how Italian speakers in real life describe their own favourite (or least favourite) restaurant experiences by reading their own words ... online! Get more details on adding this step to your mission by going online to the #LanguageHacking community.

STEP 2: it's all about me! ... *online*

When you feel good about your script, go online to find your next mission, and share your recording with the community. This time, as you're speaking and while you're thinking use conversation connectors between phrases and to help your Italian flow better. By using these phrases right away, you'll also start burning them into your muscle memory, so they are at the tip of your tongue when you need them!

STEP 3: learn from other learners

Test out your debating skills with other language hackers! **Your task is to reply in Italian to at least three different people** to tell them whether you agree or disagree with the argument they made and why.

Yes, it is! Personalize your language to talk about yourself and what's important to you! Learning a language is easier when you can talk about things that are meaningful.

STEP 4: reflect on what you've learned

What did you find easy or difficult about this unit? Did you learn any new words in the community space? After every script you write or conversation you have, you'll gain insight for what gaps you need to fill in your script.

HEY, LANGUAGE HACKER, LOOK AT YOU GO!

Now you can share opinions, talk about food, make comparisons, and keep the conversation flowing – you've come a long way. Cherish this feeling and know that things can only improve from here!

Next, let's make a huge leap forward with the range of conversations you can have – by starting to talk about the past.

Dai che ce la fai!

7 TALKING ABOUT YESTERDAY ... LAST WEEK ... A LONG TIME AGO

Your mission

Imagine this – you just joined an Italian meet-up group and you have to introduce yourself by sharing personal stories, but with a twist – it can be true or completely made up.

Your mission is to tell a true, but possibly unbelievable story or one completely made-up story in as convincing a way as possible so that the others can't guess if it's true or false. Be prepared to **describe a personal story** or **a life lesson you've learned** from **your past experiences**, whether in learning a new language, moving to a new place, or taking a big risk.

This mission will help you expand the range of conversation topics you can confidently contribute to in casual situations and allow you to start using anecdotes to spice up your Italian repertoire!

Mission prep

⋯⋗ Talk about the past in just two steps: *ho parlato ...*
⋯⋗ Answer questions about the past: *Cosa hai fatto? Sono andato ...*
⋯⋗ Say how long ago something happened using *fa* and *scorso*.
⋯⋗ Use the past tense to talk about your progress in Italian – *Ho detto bene questa parola?*

BUILDING LANGUAGE FOR RICHER CONVERSATIONS

The range of what you can discuss in Italian has focused on what's happening now or in the future. We'll expand on that now, and by the end of this unit, you'll be able to give detailed descriptions of things you did in the past, which will help you have much richer conversations. You'll also learn shortcuts for learning irregular verb forms, and for getting by in conversations even when you haven't learned all the verb forms yet.

#LANGUAGEHACK
time travel – talk about the past and future using the present tense

CONVERSATION 1

What did you do last weekend?

CULTURE TIP:
baci sulle guance –
kisses on the cheek
Since Melissa knows
Daniele already, when
she sees him again
they'll greet each other
with two *baci* – pecks/
kisses on both cheeks.
It's a typical greeting,
in Italy. Remember that
Italians start kissing on
the right cheek and
then on the left.

As you make friends with other Italian speakers, or practise with the same people regularly, a big question is 'What am I going to talk about?' Being able to use and understand the Italian past tense is a great solution to this problem. You can use it to describe personal stories about your life, which makes for endless conversation topics.

🔊 07.01 Melissa is talking again with Daniele, one of her Skype teachers. She's describing what she did over the weekend with Paola. How does Daniele ask, 'What did you do last weekend?'

The word *mostre* shows one of the few times where getting your word genders mixed up can alter your meaning! I once promised I'd visit *tutti i mostri di Londra* (all the monsters in London). .. whereas I meant to say I'd visit *tutte le mostre* (all the exhibitions)!

Daniele: Ciao Melissa! Come vanno le cose? Cosa hai fatto il fine settimana scorso?

Melissa: Sono andata a un ristorante con Paola e ho parlato con lei dei nostri programmi per il weekend. Poi, ieri, abbiamo visitato il Pantheon e abbiamo visto un sacco di posti di Roma e molte mostre!

Daniele: Non hai conosciuto Paola solo una settimana fa?

Melissa: Sì, è vero.

Daniele: Perché hai deciso di andare al Pantheon con lei? Perché non alla Cappella Sistina?

Melissa: È uno dei posti preferiti di Paola. È un'appassionata della storia di Roma antica. Che meraviglia! A dire il vero, andiamo alla Cappella Sistina domani!

Daniele: Ho visitato una volta il Pantheon a Roma quattro anni fa.

Melissa: Ti è piaciuto? Cosa ne pensi di questa basilica?

Daniele: Niente male, ma mi ricordo meglio il posto dei gelati lì vicino dove ho mangiato il migliore gelato della mia vita. Era davvero delizioso!

VOCAB: *ti è piaciuto*
You should recognize this from similar phrases you've already seen: *mi piace, ti piace*.

FIGURE IT OUT

1   What is Daniele's opinion of the Pantheon?

   a It's fun.   b It's not bad.   c It's one of his favourite places.

2   Look for these phrases in the conversation and write them out in Italian.

   a last weekend _____

   b What do you think? _____

   c I talked with her about our plans. _____

3   What do you think the phrase *Perché avete deciso di andare al Pantheon* means?

   _____

4   *Vero o falso?* Select the correct answer.

   a Paola read about a restaurant she'd like to go to.   *vero / falso*
   b Melissa spoke with Paola.   *vero / falso*
   c Yesterday, Melissa went to the Cappella Sistina.   *vero / falso*
   d Melissa met Paola one week ago.   *vero / falso*

5   Can you figure out the following Italian phrases? (Take your best guess, then check the phrase list to fill in any you missed.)

   a What did you do? *Cosa* _____ _____?
   b I ate _____ _____
   c I went _____ _____
   d we visited _____ _____
   e I talked _____ _____
   f we saw _____ _____
   g you met _____ _____
   h Did you like it? *Ti* _____ _____?

NOTICE

07.02 Listen to the audio and study the table. Repeat to try to mimic the speakers. Pay special attention to the way Melissa pronounces the phrases:

sono andata   *ho parlato*   *abbiamo visitato*   *abbiamo visto*

Essential phrases for Conversation 1

Italian	Meaning
come vanno le cose?	how's it going?
cosa hai fatto il fine settimana scorso?	what did you do last weekend?
sono andata a un ristorante con ...	I went to a restaurant with ...
ho parlato con lei di ...	I talked to her about ...
poi, ieri	then yesterday
abbiamo ... visitato il Pantheon	we ... visited the Pantheon
visto un sacco di posti	saw a bunch of places
non hai conosciuto ... ?	didn't you meet ...?
solo una settimana fa	only a week ago
perché hai deciso di ...	why did you decide to ...
è uno dei posti preferiti di Paola	it's one of Paola's favourite places
che meraviglia!	it was wonderful!
a dire il vero	to tell the truth
ho visitato una volta ...	I once visited ... (I've visited one time)
quattro anni fa	four years ago
ti è piaciuto?	did you like it? (to-you it-is pleased)
cosa ne pensi di?	what did you think? (what of-it thought you?)
niente male	it was OK
mi ricordo ...	I remember ...
vicino, dove ho mangiato il migliore gelato della mia vita!	nearby, where I ate the best ice cream of my life!
era davvero delizioso!	it was really delicious!

In English we say 'there's a bunch of stuff' or 'there's a ton of stuff' – in Italian, they use the word **sacco** (sack) exactly the same way.

GRAMMAR TIP:
word order with di
Notice the word order of the phrase **uno dei posti preferiti di Paola**. This is an example of the *di* used to describe 'the-something-of-someone' structure that you saw in Unit 5. It's necessary here because Melissa is referring to someone by name. Otherwise, she'd use **suoi**: the possessive 'her'.
Also, notice that you speak 'of ' things (*di*) rather than 'about' them in Italian.

VOCAB: *fa* – 'it makes', 'it does' or 'ago'
The word *fa* (usually 'it makes/does') can also mean 'ago' depending on context.

1 Look at the phrase list and write the Italian for these words.

a ago _____

b last _____

c once _____

d near / nearby _____

GRAMMAR EXPLANATION: forming the past in two easy steps

There are several ways to talk about the past in Italian, but let's focus on the easiest and most commonly-used one:

visito (I visit) → *ho visitato* (I visited)

Step 1: start with the present form of the verb *avere* (to have):

ho	hai	ha	abbiamo	avete	hanno
I have	you have	he/she has	we have	you (pl.) have	they have

Step 2: add the verb you want to use, but modify it slightly to become the past form, which is usually very predictable. For most verbs, just replace the last three letters of the dictionary form as follows:

Dictionary form	-are verbs	-ere verbs	-ire verbs
Past form ending	-ato	-(i)uto	-ito

Examples: *ho mangiato*   (I ate)
          ha finito   (he / she finished)

1 Try it! Use these steps to say 'I talked' in Italian.

 a Write out 'I have'. _____

 b Write out the past form of *parlare*. _____

 c Now put them together to form 'I talked'. _____

These two steps are all you'll need to use most of the time.

PRONUNCIATION: *-ciuto*
To keep the 'j' or 'ch' sound in words that have them in the dictionary form, an *i* gets added if the letter before *-ere* in the dictionary form of a verb is either *g* or *c*.

VOCAB: *ho mangiato*
Word-for-word, *ho mangiato* means 'I-have eaten', but in Italian, this is simply how you say 'I ate'.

There are of course some exceptions, and some verbs you saw in Conversation 1 don't follow this rule. I'll give you shortcuts for learning the most important exceptions later in the unit.

GRAMMAR TIP:
o/a endings
One other difference when you have a past with *essere* is that you also see an a ending for a female and o for a male (and e/i for several females or males). That's why Melissa says *Sono andata.*

Using *essere* (to be) for movement

If a verb involves movement, like:

andare (to go), arrivare (to arrive), entrare (to enter / go in), scendere (to go down / get off), tornare (to return), uscire (to exit / go out), venire (to come), etc. ...

then you'll use *essere* (to be) instead of *avere*, following the same two steps.

To translate 'Marco arrived yesterday' we follow similar steps to what we had previously, using *essere*:

(1) *Marco è ...*   (2) *arrivato*

So we would say: *Marco è arrivato ieri.*

There are some other situations where you'd use *essere* to talk in the past, but you can learn them as you come across them. For now the only other one you'll have seen is *ti è piaciuto* (you liked) – think of this as a set expression for now, and you can learn the logic behind it later.

2 Fill in the gaps using the past form of the given verbs with *avere*.

a ___ _____ i ravioli.   (I ate ...)

b ___ _____ italiano oggi.   (I studied ...)

c ___ _____ tutto.   (I understood ...)

d ___ _____ un regalo.   (I received ...)

3 Using what you've learned about *avere* and *essere*, select the correct answer in Italian to form the past tense.

a *Sono uscito / Ho uscito con i miei amici.* (I went out with my friends.)
b *Sono scelto / Ho scelto questo museo.* (I chose this museum.)
c *Elena ha visto / è visto il film la scorsa settimana.*
   (Elena watched the film last weekend.)

PRACTICE

1 Use *fa* to say how long 'ago' in a sentence that's true for you. When did you meet your best friend (*il tuo migliore amico / la tua migliore amica*) or partner?

Ho conosciuto _____ *fa.*

I met _____ ago.

2 Now practise creating full sentences in Italian.

  a You should go to the restaurant where I ate lunch two days ago.

    _____

  b I liked the film! _____

  c He has seen Anna's boyfriend.

    _____

3 Daniele also talked a little about his past during the call. Fill in the gaps, taking note of whether to use *avere* or *essere*.

  a *Tre mesi* _____, _____ _____ *in Canada.*
    (Three months **ago, I went** to Canada.)

  b _____ _____ *una ragazza molto interessante.*
    (**I met** a very interesting girl.)

  c *Questa mattina,* _____ _____ *in metro.*
    (This morning **I arrived** by metro.)

  d _____ _____ *qui per molto tempo.*
    (**They have worked** here for a long time.)

  e _____ _____ *in questo ristorante l'anno scorso.*
    (**We ate** in this restaurant last year.)

CONVERSATION STRATEGY: *guess when you're not sure!*
If you're ever not sure, can always fall back to 'Tarzan Italian', and just use the *avere* form, and people will understand you. Even though 'ho andato' is a mistake, people will recognize that you're learning and know exactly what you mean. For now, just try to be confident with verbs you know you'll use often. Your dictionary will also indicate whether the verb takes *essere* or *avere*, if you're ever in doubt.

VOCAB EXPLANATION: getting to know someone

There are three useful verbs you can use in Italian to describe your interactions with other people you know or are getting to know:

vedere	*incontrare*	*conoscere*
(to meet)	(to bump into)	(to get to know)

When you want to say you plan 'to meet' someone, use *vedere*, but if you're describing a time you 'bumped into' a friend, use *incontrare*. Or, to talk about someone you've just met and that you're 'getting to know', use *conoscere* instead!

1 Try it! Use the context of each sentence to fill in the blank with the correct form of either *vedere*, *incontrare*, or *conoscere*.

a *Ragazzi, _____ _____ vostra madre in una stazione ferroviaria quindici anni fa.* (Kids, I met your mother in a train station.)

b *Oggi _____ _____ la tua ragazza nel supermercato!* (Today I met your girlfriend in the supermarket!)

c _____ *il mio insegnante* _____ *mercoledì.* (I meet my teacher every Wednesday.)

PUT IT TOGETHER

Let's use the past tense forms you've just learned to create 'me-specific' sentences that you could use in real conversations. Be sure to make the sentences as relevant to you as possible, and look up new words in your dictionary as often as you need.

1 First, practise answering a common question in the past tense:

Come vanno le cose? Cosa hai fatto ieri / lo scorso weekend?

Answer this question in Italian with real details about your life. You might include:

⋯⋗ where you went or what you did
⋯⋗ who you talked to
⋯⋗ what you talked about

2 Now use the past tense to describe the details of a trip you took to another city. Draw from your own experiences to create sentences that are true for you, and be sure to answer these questions:

⋯⋗ *Dove sei andato? (Sono andato / andata a / in ...)*
⋯⋗ *Quanto tempo hai passato ...? (Ho passato ...)*
⋯⋗ *Perché hai deciso di visitare ...? (Ho deciso di andare a ... perché ...)*
⋯⋗ *Ti è piaciuto? Perché? (Mi è piaciuto/Non mi è piaciuto perché ...)*
⋯⋗ *Cosa hai visto in questo posto? (Ho visto ...)*

CONVERSATION 2

Did you have time to …?

Another great way to expand the scope of your Italian conversations is to learn to talk about your Italian progress, in Italian! People will definitely ask you these questions, so let's prepare you to answer them in Italian.

🔊 **07.03** Now that Melissa and Daniele have caught up, they start discussing what Melissa has been doing to improve her Italian. How does Daniele ask, 'Did you have time to …?'

VOCAB: *bravo!*
While you may think of this word mostly to exclaim praise after a good theatre or concert show, in Italy it simply means 'good job' and is used very liberally by Italians, for any and all situations. As a language learner you will hear *bravo* or *brava* (for ladies) quite frequently! The first few times it happens you may find yourself lost in thought picturing a standing ovation and roses thrown up on stage – as you should for getting your verb forms right! *Bravissimo/a* is for when you do exceptionally well!

Daniele:	Allora, hai avuto tempo di studiare italiano questa settimana?
Melissa:	Sì, ho studiato un po'. Ho imparato delle parole nuove e ho praticato delle frasi con Paola.
Daniele:	Ottimo! Hai fatto i compiti?
Melissa:	Sì, ho fatto i compiti. Sono qui.
Daniele:	È tutto chiaro? Hai bisogno di aiuto?
Melissa:	Sì, ho una domanda! Qual è la differenza tra 'ora' e 'adesso'? Ho detto bene 'ora'?
Daniele:	Non c'è nessuna differenza. E sì, l'hai detto bene. Brava, bravissima! Devo dire che sei un'ottima studentessa. Quando hai iniziato a studiare italiano?
Melissa:	Ho iniziato solo pochi mesi fa. L'estate scorsa ho deciso di viaggiare per un anno, così ho comprato un biglietto aereo e sono venuta a Roma!
Daniele:	È vero! Mi hai già raccontato tutta la storia!

FIGURE IT OUT

1 *Vero o falso?* Select the correct answer.

    a Melissa studied Italian over the weekend.   *vero / falso*
    b Melissa practised some phrases alone.   *vero / falso*
    c Melissa started learning Italian one year ago.   *vero / falso*

2 Read the conversation and answer the questions in Italian.

    a What did Melissa do with Paola to help her Italian this week?

    _____

    b When (how long ago) did Melissa start learning Italian?

    _____

    c What is the meaning of the phrase: *È vero! (Mi hai già raccontato tutta la storia?)*

    _____

3 There are 14 past forms in the conversation – highlight them.

NOTICE

🔊 07.04 Listen to the audio and study the table.

Essential phrases for Conversation 2

Italian	Meaning
hai avuto tempo di ...	have you had time to ...
studiare italiano questa settimana	study Italian this week?
ho studiato un po'	I studied a little
Ho imparato delle parole nuove	I learned some new words
ho praticato delle frasi	I practised some phrases
hai fatto i compiti?	did you do your homework?
sono qui	I have it here (they-are here)
è tutto chiaro?	is everything clear?
hai bisogno di aiuto?	do you need help?
ho una domanda!	I have a question!
qual è la differenza tra ... e ...	what is the difference between ... and ...?
ho detto bene ...?	did I say ... right?
non c'è nessuna differenza	there is no difference (no there-is none difference)
devo dire che ...	I have to say that ...
hai iniziato a ...?	did you start ...?
ho iniziato solo pochi mesi fa	I started only a few months ago
l'estate scorsa, ho deciso di ...	last summer, I decided ...
viaggiare per un anno	to travel for a year
così ho comprato ... un biglietto aereo	so I bought ... a plane ticket
sono venuta ... a Roma!	I came ... to Rome!
mi hai già raccontato!	you already told me!

1 Find the following phrases and write them out here in Italian.

    a Did you have time to …? _____

    b I have to say that … _____

    c You told me that … _____

2 Use the phrase list to help you recognize the past tense phrases in Italian. Choose the correct Italian phrase, then write it out next to its English counterpart.

> You may notice that these two past forms don't fit the rule you learned after Conversation 1. You'll learn why shortly.

ho fatto	ho deciso	ho iniziato

    a I decided _____   **c** I started _____

    b I did _____

3 Find the following past tense phrases in Italian, and fill them into the cheat sheet below in the left column (section 1). Leave the rest of the cheat sheet blank for now.

    a I studied   **c** I started   **e** I bought   **g** I did   **i** I answered

    b I practised   **d** I learned   **f** I had   **h** I decided to   **j** I said

Past tense cheat sheet

1. Past tense: regular verbs		2. Past tense: irregular verbs		3. 'me-specific'
Ho_____	I studied	Ho_____	I did	
Ho_____	I practised	Ho_____	I decided to	
Ho_____	I started	Ho_____	I answered	
Ho_____	I learned	Ho_____	I said	
Ho_____	I bought			
Ho_____	I had			

GRAMMAR EXPLANATION: top 'irregular' past verbs

In Conversation 1 you learned a simple rule for forming past sentences. As you saw in Conversation 2, there are still many exceptions to the rule, which you'll learn as you come across them. But here are a few patterns to give you a head start.

Irregular verbs: -ere verbs that don't follow the -uto pattern

Dictionary form	Past form	Meaning
decidere	deciso	to decide – decided
vedere	visto	to see – seen
chiedere	chiesto	to ask – asked
rispondere	risposto	to answer – answered
prendere	preso	to take – taken

Irregular verbs that have double letters or reduced syllables

Dictionary form	Past form	Meaning
fare	fatto	to do/make – done/made
dire	detto	to say/tell – said/told
leggere	letto	to read – read
scrivere	scritto	to write – written
venire	venuto	to come – come

1 Now complete the table with the missing Italian translations.

Italian	Meaning	Italian	Meaning
	we made		he wrote
	you wrote		I read
	I decided		we said
	he saw		I liked it
	she took		we asked
	I saw		we answered

2 Refer back to the Past tense cheat sheet, and:

    a Fill in the past tense forms for Section 2 of the cheat sheet.

    b Review the past tense verb forms you've learned to find any 'me-specific' verbs you think you'll need to use. Add them to the cheat sheet in Section 3.

PRACTICE

1 Practise rephrasing Italian sentences using the past tense. The following sentences use *da* (since / for) in the present tense. Change them to the past using *fa* (ago), while maintaining the same general meaning.

Example: ***Sono a Roma da una settimana. (arrivare)***

    → *Sono arrivata a Roma una settimana fa.*

    a *Insegno italiano da nove mesi.* (Hint: to start)

        → *Ho* _____ *a* _____ _____ *nove* _____ _____ .

    b *Sono single da tre mesi.* (Use: *lasciare*)

        → *Ho* _____ *il mio ragazzo* _____ _____ _____ .

    c *Conosco Andrea da alcuni anni.* (Hint: to meet and get to know)

        → _____ _____ *Andrea* _____ _____ _____ .

2 How would you say the following in Italian? (use *guardare*)

    a I am watching the film now. _____

    b I am going to watch the film tomorrow. _____

    c I watched the film last week. _____

VOCAB: *use the past to describe your life!*
Here are some examples of things you can say now:

...⟩ *Non ho mai letto Il Principe di Machiavelli.* (I've never read Machiavelli's 'The Prince'.)

...⟩ *Ho visto molti film.* (I've seen many films.)

...⟩ *Hai già fatto i compiti?* (Have you done your homework already?)

...⟩ *Giacomo è venuto ieri.* (Giacomo came yesterday.)

...⟩ *Abbiamo scritto cartoline tutto il giorno.* (We've written postcards all day.)

CULTURE TIP: *names*
Italians can have very interesting names, but some that take some getting used to include *Andrea* and *Luca*, which are always names for guys, not girls.

3 Fill in the blanks with the missing phrases in Italian.

    a *Vivo qui* _____ *due anni.* (I've been living here **for** two years.)

    b _____ _____, _____ _____ *a Firenze da sola.* (**Once, I** went to Florence by myself.)

    c *L'*_____ _____, _____ _____ _____ _____ *dalla Spagna all'Italia.*
       (**Last summer, I travelled by train** from Spain to Italy.)

    d _____ _____ *dei dizionari?* _____ _____ _____.
       (Do **you** need the dictionaries? **I have them here.**)

    e _____ _____ _____ *i compiti sono* _____ _____ *della* _____
       _____.
       (I have to say that the homework is **easier than last week.**)

PUT IT TOGETHER

1 Imagine you're having a conversation with someone in Italian. When you casually mention something you once did or somewhere you went, the other person says: ***Fantastico! Cosa hai fatto esattamente? (Cool! What did you do exactly?)***

At this point, you've learned quite a lot of Italian verbs, and you know how to use them in different ways. Use everything you've learned to create detailed sentences about a time in your life. You could write about somewhere you went, a film you saw, or anything else – but try to use new verbs you haven't used before. Be as detailed as you can to include:

⋯⋗ specific details of what happened – who did what? (*Hanno incontrato …*)
⋯⋗ specific details of conversations – who said what? (*La ragazza ha detto …*)
⋯⋗ say where you went and when you returned (*Sono stato …*)
⋯⋗ several past tense verbs in various forms.

CONVERSATION 3

Did you know …?

The conversation continues between Melissa and Daniele, as they use the past tense to discuss Melissa's progress in Italian.

🔊 **07.05** Pay attention to which words and phrases you recognize. What phrase does Melissa use to ask, 'Did you know …?'

Melissa: Sapevi che ho studiato italiano a scuola per un anno?

Daniele: Sul serio? Ma non eri principiante?

Melissa: Ho dimenticato tutto quello che sapevo, quindi penso di essere ancora principiante.

Daniele: Perché non hai imparato niente?

Melissa: Il mio insegnante ha insegnato solo la grammatica. Non abbiamo mai parlato davvero in italiano. Una noia mortale!

Daniele: Secondo me, è meglio provare a parlare il più possibile. ⟵

Melissa: Una volta ho provato a parlare e ho trovato la mia pronuncia orribile! Ero molto nervosa.

Daniele: Ma che dici! Non hai un accento forte. Ti fai capire benissimo! E sai dire così tante cose!

Melissa: Grazie, è gentile da parte tua!

You don't have to learn a complicated new structure to say 'as much as possible'. Il più possibile does the trick!

FIGURE IT OUT

1 Highlight the following cognates and near cognates in the conversation.

   a nervous   b my pronunciation   c accent   d grammar

2 *Vero o falso?* Select the correct answer.

a Melissa studied Italian in school for one year.   *vero* / falso

b They often spoke Italian in her class.   *vero* / *falso*

c Melissa's school teacher said her
   pronunciation was terrible.   *vero* / *falso*

NOTICE

🔊 **07.06** Listen to the audio and study the table.

Essential phrases for Conversation 3

Italian	Meaning
sapevi che ...	did you know that ...
ho studiato a scuola	I studied in school
sul serio?	really?
ma non eri ...	but were you not ...
ho dimenticato ...	I forgot ...
tutto quello che sapevo!	everything that I knew!
perché non hai imparato niente?	why didn't you learn anything? (why not you-have learned nothing)
il mio insegnante ...	my teacher ...
ha insegnato solo la grammatica	he only taught grammar
non abbiamo mai parlato davvero in italiano	we never really spoke any Italian!
una noia mortale!	it was boring!
una volta ho provato a ...	once I tried ...
ho trovato la mia pronuncia orribile!	I found my pronunciation horrible!
ero molto nervosa	I was really nervous
ma che dici!	no way! (but what you-say)
non hai un accento forte!	you don't have a strong accent!
ti fai capire benissimo!	you can be understood perfectly!

1 How would you write the following in Italian?

a It's better to learn a little every day. _____

b I forgot your name. _____

c Once I tried to study Russian. _____

VOCAB:
tutto quello che
(everything that) in
Italian has an extra
quello in the sentence,
which wouldn't be
translated in English.
Remember this phrase
as a word chunk, and
then you'll recognize it
when you see or hear it.

GRAMMAR TIP:
double negatives
Italian is a language
that loves its double
negatives! Whenever
you say *niente* (nothing)
or *nessuno* (nobody),
usually you'll go
further and make the
sentence negative: *non
capisco niente* (I don't
understand anything/I
understand nothing),
non conosco nessuno
(I don't know anybody/I
know nobody).

2 Based on how the phrase *non abbiamo mai parlato* is formed, complete the following sentences:

a *Non abbiamo* _____ .
(We haven't seen anything. / We've seen nothing.)

b *Non c'è* _____ .
(There isn't anyone here. / There's no one here.)

c *Non ho* _____ .
(I've never eaten a bruschetta.)

3 The following phrases from this conversation can be adapted for a variety of conversational situations. Find them in the phrase list and write them out here.

a Did you know that _____

b I found _____

c I tried _____

Hint: just as Italian doesn't directly translate 'do' in present tense questions, you also won't directly translate 'did' if there is another main verb.

GRAMMAR EXPLANATION: the habitual past

As you advance in Italian, you will learn to use the 'habitual past' to describe things you used to do often. For now just recognize the verbs that are most commonly used in this form.

pensare (to think)	volere (to want)	sapere (to know)	essere (to be)	avere (to have)
io pensavo	io volevo	io sapevo	io ero	io avevo
tu pensavi	tu volevi	tu sapevi	tu eri	tu avevi
lui/lei pensava	lui/lei voleva	lui/lei sapeva	lui/lei era	lui/lei aveva

Examples:

Pensavo che eri occupato.   (I thought that you were busy)

Sapevi che era qui?   (Did you know that she was here?)

PRACTICE

1 How would you say the following in Italian:

   a Cecilia had the book. _____   **b** She didn't know. _____

   c I wanted to eat with you. _____

2 Use the vocab you've learned in this unit to complete the dialogue.

   a Qual è la differenza tra _____ _____ _____?
      (What is the difference between **the two words**?)

   b _____ _____ così velocemente! Cosa _____ _____?
      (**You talked** so fast! What does that **mean**?)

   c _____ _____? (**Did you understand**?)

   d Com'è la mia _____? _____ _____ bene quella _____?
      (How is my **pronunciation**? **Did I say** that **word** right?)

   e _____ _____ di dirmi la password. (**He forgot** to tell me the password.)

   f L'altro giorno _____ _____ alla mia insegnante 'come _____ _____

      _____ _____ e lei _____ _____ 'non è male'.
      (The other day, **I asked** my teacher 'how **do you find my accent**?' and she **said** 'pretty good'.)
      (Hint: trovare)

   g _____ _____ la _____ tutta la settimana. (**I studied grammar** all week.)

   h _____ _____ stasera per quel tema. _____ _____ delle _____.
      (**I'll call** you tonight for that composition. **I wrote** some **phrases**.)

   i Mi _____ _____ molto. Grazie! (**You helped** me a lot. Thank you!)

3 Practise double negatives. How would you say these phrases?

   a You never help me! _____

   b He didn't say anything. _____

   c I don't know anyone here. _____

VOCAB EXPLANATION: time indicators

Throughout this unit, you've seen phrases that help you describe something in the past, or in the future. We'll call these phrases 'time indicators':

Past	Future	Specific days
ieri (yesterday)	domani (tomorrow)	lunedì (Monday)
la settimana scorsa (last week)	la settimana prossima (next week)	martedì (Tuesday)
il mese scorso (last month)	il mese prossimo (next month)	mercoledì (Wednesday)
l'anno scorso (last year)	l'anno prossimo (next year)	giovedì (Thursday)
mercoledì scorso / l'estate scorsa (last Wednesday / summer)	il prossimo novembre / il weekend (next November / weekend)	venerdì (Friday)
una volta (one time / once)	un giorno (one day)	sabato (Saturday)
due settimane fa (two weeks ago)	tra due settimane (in two weeks)	domenica (Sunday)

You can use time indicators to add detail to sentences.

VOCAB: tra for 'in/between'
You saw earlier that tra was used for 'between' (la differenza tra ...). When followed by a time period it simply means 'in' that amount of time from now.

1 Fill in the gaps with the past or the present form of the verb in brackets, depending on whether a past or future time is given.

a *Lunedì scorso* _____ *italiano sul mio libro. (studiare)*

b *Il prossimo anno io e mio fratello* _____ *a Roma. (andare)*

c *La prossima settimana* _____ *un libro in italiano. (leggere)*

d *La settimana scorsa io e lui* _____ *tutto il giorno. (praticare)*

e *Ieri i miei amici* _____ *tutta la torta. (mangiare)*

f *Una settimana fa mia cugina* _____ *la mia città. (visitare)*

g *Domani* _____ *al cinema. (andare)*

🔧 #LANGUAGEHACK: time travel – talk about the past and future using the present tense

Language learning is a process, and as a beginner Italian learner, it's important to re-member that you don't need to learn everything at once! One of the truly fun aspects of languages is how flexible, fluid and creative they can be! Let's explore that now, to figure out how many inventive ways you can express yourself in the past, even if you don't think you have the grammar or vocab for it yet.

1 Use 'I have' ...

This is the most common way to form the past tense in Italian, and you've seen it used throughout this unit. To form the past tense with 'I have', simply say *ho* using a past form and you're done!

Some verbs may require you to use *sono* instead of *ho* (like *sono andato* 'I went'), but to get by as a beginner, it's OK to not master this switch ... and use *ho* all the time. It can be your go-to past form while you learn.

Examples: *Ho parlato con lui ieri.*   *Hai letto il libro?*

Remember, people will see that you're a beginner, and they will forgive the error!

That said, you're not limited to just using 'I have' to talk about other times! Let's get creative. Why not ...

2 Travel to the future ... right now!

You've also seen that you can refer to a future event without learning any new verb forms. Just add a time indicator and you're done! Notice the difference between:

Parlo molto italiano. (I speak a lot of Italian)

Fra un mese, parlo molto italiano! (In a month, I will speak a lot of Italian!)

We often do the same thing in English:

Chiamo i miei genitori fra due ore. (I'm calling my parents in two hours.)

I recommend you focus on improving one major aspect of your language skills at a time. Start with the most important ones first, then fine tune from there.

3 Tell a story

Once you've learned to use time indicators, you can build on it and form the past through 'storytelling'. For example, have you ever told a story that went something like this?

> 'So, the other day, there I am ... minding my own business, when someone comes up to me, and you'll never guess what happens!'

What's unique about this form of storytelling is although it's clearly an anecdote about something that happened in the past, the entire sentence is actually told using present forms – 'there I am', 'someone comes up to me'.

You can do the same thing in Italian! To make this narrative style work, you just need to give some details that set the context of the situation, to make it clear that it's a story: say where you are, when it's happening, or what you're doing. Then simply tell what happened, using the present form!

Examples: *Allora, sono al mercato e compro dei pomodori ...*
(So, I'm at the market, and I'm buying some tomatoes ...)
Lunedì scorso, mangio la miglior focaccia di Roma ...
(Last Monday I'm eating the best focaccia in Rome ...)

4 Just say it 'Tarzan' style!

If all else fails, and your mind completely freezes up, the world won't end if all you can think of is a dictionary or other form of the verb. Though you will want to use this sparingly, people will get the gist of what you're saying even if all you can get out is something like 'Ieri ... io ... mangiare pizza'.

YOUR TURN: use the hack

While this #languagehack is very powerful, you only need to use it if you can't think of the past form introduced in this unit. Use it as a crutch until you are confident!

1 Unscramble the sentences and use time indicators to describe future actions. Be sure to change the verbs to the present form for *io*.

Example: *Stasera* _____ _____ _____ (guardare / un film)
 → *Stasera, guardo un film.*

a *Domani* _____ _____ _____ e _____ al _____.
 (preparare / dei panini / andare / al parco)

b *Lunedì prossimo* _____ e _____ a _____ _____.
 (cucinare / mangiare / casa tua)

c *La prossima settimana* _____ _____ _____ e _____
 _____ _____. (prendere / il treno / viaggiare / per l'Italia)

2 How could you tell this story if you couldn't think of the past form of the verbs:

Tre giorni fa, _____ _____ _____ e _____

_____ _____! (prendere il treno / vedere / un orso (a bear))

3 Now create 'me-specific' sentences in which you describe things you did at different time periods. Say what you did:

a a week ago _____

b last Saturday _____

c two years ago _____

d yesterday _____

4 Now say what you are going to do:

a next Wednesday _____

b in one year _____

PUT IT TOGETHER

(Maybe you were even nervous before one of your earlier missions?)

1 Think about a time you got nervous trying to speak Italian with someone. Use what you've learned in this unit to describe those moments – what you were thinking ... doing ... saying ... Use your dictionary to look up new words so that your script is as 'me-specific' as possible. Be sure to include:

⋯⟩ at least three verbs in the past (*pensare, volere, sapere, essere, avere*)
⋯⟩ a specific time indicator (*lunedì scorso ...*)
⋯⟩ what you did to overcome your nerves (*ho deciso di parlare del mio weekend ...*).

COMPLETING UNIT 7

Check your understanding

You know the drill! Listen to the audio rehearsal, which will ask you questions in Italian. Use what you've learned to answer the questions in Italian with details about yourself.

1 ◀) 07.07 Listen to this audio rehearsal first, in which an Italian speaker, Claudio, describes what he did this morning. Feel free to take notes or listen to it multiple times.

2 ◀) 07.08 Now listen to the second audio, which will ask you questions about Claudio. Answer them out loud in Italian.

Show what you know ...

Here's what you've just learned. Write or say an example for each item in the list. Then tick off the ones you know.

- ☐ Say these past tense phrases:
  - ☐ 'I thought' and 'I said'
  - ☐ 'I saw' and 'I went'
  - ☐ 'I was' and 'I learned'
- ☐ Give a sentence using *fa* to say how long ago you did something.
- ☐ Give time indicators for:
  - ☐ 'one time' and 'yesterday'
  - ☐ 'last week' and 'tomorrow'
- ☐ Write two sentences about the progress you've made in Italian.

COMPLETE YOUR MISSION

It's time to complete your mission: put on your poker face and start your story. Try to fool the language hacking community as best you can.

STEP 1: build your script

ho pensato ... sono andato ... ho imparato ...

Perhaps about an embarrassing situation when you used the wrong word in Italian, or a time when you overcame a personal struggle and felt really encouraged.

Expand on your scripts by talking about the past. Use 'me-specific' vocab to describe an important life lesson you gained from a past experience. Be sure to include:

···⟩ time indicators to describe when this happened (... fa)

···⟩ several past tense verbs in various forms to describe what you thought, what you wanted, what you learned, and more

···⟩ as many details as possible! (use the time travel #languagehack if you get stuck).

Write down your script, then repeat it until you feel confident.

Research in learning emphasizes the importance of social context in facilitating language learning.

STEP 2: don't be a wallflower. Use language in real social contexts ... *online*

If you're feeling good about your script, it's time to complete your mission! Go online to find your mission for Unit 7, and share your recording.

STEP 3: learn from other learners

What words of wisdom do the other language hackers have to offer? Which stories are real and which ones are *falso*? **Your task is to watch at least two video clips uploaded by other hackers.** Then ask three follow-up questions in Italian to see if they can keep the conversation going, to help them fill the gaps in their script, and to find out whether what they say is true or false. Make your guess.

STEP 4: reflect on what you've learned

HEY, LANGUAGE HACKER, SEE HOW THINGS HAVE CHANGED?

You just learned how to talk about anything in the past. Now you can reminisce on the long-forgotten days when you couldn't speak Italian. Next, you'll add even more detail to your conversations by describing the specific parts of your daily routine.

Ora sai dire così tante cose in italiano!

8 IT'S BEEN A WHILE!

Your mission

Imagine this – one of your Italian-speaking friends writes a blog about the daily routines of highly productive people – like you! – and you've been asked to contribute an article.

Your mission is to **prepare your best productivity advice** – in Italian – for the blog. Be prepared to **describe your daily routine** from your first morning beverage to your bedtime. Talk about what works well and what you'd like to be different.

This mission will broaden your ability to discuss your daily life, a common topic, and help you become comfortable with small talk in Italian.

Mission prep

- ⋯⟩ Talk about your hobbies, routines and daily life.
- ⋯⟩ Use versatile phrases to express your opinions and perceptions – *è importante*, *sono felice di*, *vedo che*.
- ⋯⟩ Use phrases for catching up with people you know – *quanto tempo!*, *sono felice di rivederti*.
- ⋯⟩ Build on modes of transport – *prendere la metro*.
- ⋯⟩ Talk about what you would like to do – *mi piacerebbe*.

BUILDING LANGUAGE FOR DESCRIBING DAILY LIFE

As a beginner Italian learner, it's difficult to be very detailed when you speak, so your energy is often best spent learning phrases that express a general idea of what you're trying to say.

But now you're quickly becoming an *upper-beginner* Italian learner! So it's time to learn some tricks for adding more detail to your conversations. And you can do this without having to learn a huge amount of new vocab. In this unit, you'll learn to build detail into the conversations you're likely to have, and we'll break down a typical conversation into its component parts to develop a more complex strategy for helping each part flow well.

#LANGUAGEHACK
the rephrasing technique for talking your way through complicated sentences

CONVERSATION 1

It's been a while!

When a conversation has passed the point of introduction and the other usual pleasantries, where should you go from there? You don't have to think it up on the spot – instead, prepare for these situations in advance by learning strategic phrases you can use to initiate, warm up, and continue any conversation.

Melissa and Luca are meeting for lunch at a café. Since they already know each other, they can't rely on the usual first time meet-and-greet expressions.

◀)) 08.01 What phrases do Luca and Melissa use to 'warm up' the conversation?

> **Luca:** Ciao Melissa! Sono felice di rivederti!
>
> **Melissa:** Sì, quanto tempo!
>
> **Luca:** Vedo che il tuo livello di italiano è molto migliorato. Allora dimmi, come vanno le cose?
>
> **Melissa:** Be', sono molto occupata in questo momento. Recentemente ho iniziato a cucinare. Vado a lezione!
>
> **Luca:** Davvero? Quante lezioni: di italiano, di cucina … E cosa hai imparato finora?
>
> **Melissa:** L'ultima volta abbiamo imparato a fare la parmigiana. Ma quando provo a farla da sola a casa non è mai buona.
>
> **Luca:** Forza e coraggio! Io sono un imbranato in cucina… Ma fare pratica è importante.
>
> **Melissa:** Lo so, ma imparo in fretta. La prossima volta spero di imparare a fare il tiramisù!

GRAMMAR TIP:
ri- prefix
Italian uses **the prefix** *ri-* much more than we do in English to imply 'again'. While we can't 're-see' in English, you can *rivedere* in Italian, hence *arrivederci* (goodbye) is more or less 'until-the-re-seeing!/until we see each other again'. Similarly, you can say:

⇢ *riascoltare* (to listen to again)

⇢ *riabbracciare* (to embrace again),

⇢ *riprovare* (to try again)

FIGURE IT OUT

1 Use your understanding of the conversation to fill in the rest of the sentence in English. Underline the corresponding Italian phrases in the conversation.

    a Luca thinks that Melissa's level in Italian is _____ .

    b Melissa started taking a cooking class _____ .

    c At her last class, Melissa learned to make _____ .

2 How do you say 'I'm happy to see you again!' in Italian?

    _____

3 Answer the questions, giving your answers in Italian.

    a *Cosa ha iniziato a fare Melissa recentemente?* _____

    b *Cosa fa Melissa la prossima volta?* _____

4 Find these phrases in Italian in the conversation and circle them:
    a What's new?   **b** it's been a while   **c** at the moment

5 What does *fare pratica è importante* mean in English? _____

NOTICE

🔊 08.02 Listen to the audio and study the table.

As well as 'to do', fare doubles as also meaning 'to make'. Handy!

Essential phrases for Conversation 1

Italian	Pronunciation
sono felice di rivederti!	I'm happy to see you again!
sì, quanto tempo!	yes, it's been a while!
vedo che ...	I see that ...
il tuo livello di italiano è molto migliorato	your (level of) Italian has improved a lot
be', sono molto occupata	well, I'm very busy
in questo momento	at the moment
recentemente ho iniziato a ... cucinare	recently I started ... cooking
vado a lezione!	I'm taking a class!
quante lezioni: di italiano, di cucina ...	so many (how many) lessons: Italian, cooking ...
cosa hai imparato	what have you learned
... finora?	... so far? (until now)
l'ultima volta ...	last time ...
abbiamo imparato a fare ...	we learned how to make ...
ma quando provo a farla	but when I try to make it
... da sola a casa	... myself at home
non è mai buona!	it's never good!
forza e coraggio!	keep it up! (strength and courage!)
io sono un imbranato in cucina	I'm a disaster in the kitchen
fare pratica è importante!	practice is important! (to-make practice is important)
ma imparo in fretta	I'm learning fast
la prossima volta ...	next time ...
spero di imparare a fare il tiramisù!	I hope to learn how to make tiramisu!

1 Look at the literal translations of the following phrases and notice how they are expressed differently in Italian than in English. Write the Italian phrases here.

a Keep it up! _____   b When I try to ... _____

2 Use the phrase list to fill in the gaps in each expression.

a _____ *tempo!* (It's been a while)

b _____ *hai imparato finora?* (What have you learned so far?)

c *Spero di imparare* _____ _____ ... (I hope to learn how to make ...)

CONVERSATION STRATEGY: learn set phrases for each 'stage' of a conversation

A lot of people get nervous about what to say during a conversation. If you're meeting someone for the first time, it's easy – just introduce yourself. But if you've talked before, or you've finished your greetings, you'll need to keep the conversation going, so you can keep practising your Italian!

When you understand the structure of a typical conversation, you can break it down into its component parts and prepare phrases to use at the different stages in a conversation. This way, you're never stuck wondering what to say next. Let's take a look at the stages of a typical conversation, and start preparing phrases you can learn for each one in advance.

Warm up the conversation

During the first few seconds of a conversation, you could set the stage with a simple, *Ciao, come va?,* but learning longer pleasantries will give you more time to collect your thoughts.

Examples: *Quanto tempo!*   It's been a while!
          Sono felice di rivederti!   I'm happy to see you again!

Get the conversation started

After the initial pleasantries, a conversation topic begins. Prepare some phrases you can use to get the other person talking for a few minutes:

Examples: *Dimmi, come vanno le cose?*   Tell me, what's new for you?
          Vedo che ... (non sei cambiato)   I see that ... (you haven't changed)

Lead the conversation yourself

Eventually, the other person will have answered your question, and they'll ask you a question about yourself. When it's your turn to talk, think of some phrases you can use to lead the discussion on your own and introduce a new conversation topic:

Examples: *Allora, recentemente ho iniziato a ...*   Well, recently I started to ...
          ... lavorare come segretaria ...   ... work as a secretary ...
          ... andare a lezioni di cucina, etc.   ... go to cooking class, etc.
          Ultimamente sono stato ...   Lately I have been ...

Extend the conversation

As the other person is talking, you could show your interest with filler words like *interessante!* or *davvero?* But a slightly more detailed question, prepared in advance, will urge the other person to expand on the topic, and therefore extend the conversation.

Examples: *Quindi ti piace?*   So, do you like it?

  E come lo trovi?   And how have you found it?

Add detail to your conversation

Remember – you can get more out of a conversation by expanding on a simple topic with details about when, where, or how something happened. In Conversation 1, Melissa describes her hobby, *cucinare* (cooking). But she elaborates on this by adding descriptive details (when? what?):

Examples: *L'ultima volta* (when), *abbiamo imparato ... la parmigiana* (what)

  Quando provo ... (how), *... a casa* (where)

  La prossima volta (when), *spero ... il tiramisù* (what)

Language Hacker A	Language Hacker B
Conversational warmers	**Conversational warmers**
quanto tempo!	grazie mille...!
sono felice di rivederti!	
Conversational starters	**Starting replies**
dimmi, come vanno le cose?	non ho molto da raccontare
vedo che... non sei cambiato	faccio... le solite cose
... ora hai la ragazza	**Conversation leads**
parlami di te	allora, recentemente ho iniziato a...
	... lavorare come segretaria
	... andare a lezione di cucina.
	in questo momento, io...
	l'ultima volta che abbiamo parlato...
Conversation extensions	**Conversation details**
quindi ti piace?	l'ultima volta (when) ho imparato ... la parmigiana (what)
e come lo trovi?	quando provo ... (how) ... a casa (where)
	La prossima volta (when) spero ... il tiramisù (what)

PRACTICE

1 Look back at the phrase list. Underline the following conversation components:

    a two conversational warmers   c one conversation lead

    b two conversational starters

2 Now create some conversation starters using the verbs *sapere* or *vedere* in the correct form.

    a I know that … _____

    b Do you know if …? _____

    c Have you seen …? _____

3 What is your hobby? Pick a hobby or something you like to do that you would discuss in a conversation. Use the phrases *Recentemente ho iniziato a …* or *In questo momento io…* along with vocab you look up on your own, to create two of your own conversation leads.

PUT IT TOGETHER

Create a script in which you describe your hobby to a friend. Start with a conversational lead, but then add details about the same topic.

Try to include:
- details about why/when you started it (*recentemente, ho iniziato, fa*)
- details of what you do (*l'ultima volta, quando provo …*)
- what you've learned or achieved so far (*finora*)
- what you hope to learn or achieve (*spero che … sono contento … è interessante*)

CONVERSATION 2

Your daily routine

Let's prepare for more conversation topics by learning to talk about your typical routine. What do you normally do in a day? In a week?

🔊 08.03 Melissa and Luca are talking about the things they do on a regular basis. How does Melissa say 'it was strange at first'? What helped her get into the swing of things?

VOCAB:
'how often?'
You can express repetition using words like *ogni* (each) followed by a singular version of the word, or *tutti i/ tutte le* (every) followed by a plural: *ogni giorno* (each day) and *tutte le settimane* (every week). You can also use any number + *volta/e* (times) to describe 'how often':
una volta, due volte, molte volte

Luca: Mi sembra che ti trovi bene qui a Roma.

Melissa: Sì, grazie. All'inizio era strano, ma ora mi sono ambientata e ho una routine. Ogni mattina prima del lavoro vado a fare una passeggiata per la città.

Luca: Anch'io. Di solito la mattina porto fuori il mio cane e ogni tanto vado a fare un giro in bici per prendere un po' d'aria fresca.

Melissa: Io vado in bicicletta ovunque! Non prendo la metro.

Luca: Neanche io, o raramente, perché spesso vado al lavoro in macchina.

Melissa: E a pranzo mangio sempre nello stesso ristorante – hanno i migliori spaghetti all'amatriciana.

Luca: Io a volte vengo in questa trattoria per pranzo, ma normalmente cucino a casa.

Melissa: Non sono mai stata prima in questa trattoria. Vuoi prendere qualcosa?

FIGURE IT OUT

1 Each of the statements about the conversation is *falso*. Circle the
incorrect part in English and write out the correct Italian word(s).

   a At first, Melissa loved living in Rome. But now, she misses home.

   _____

   b Melissa takes the metro.

   _____

   c Luca rarely goes to work by car.

   _____

   d Melissa eats at a restaurant that has the worst spaghetti
   all'amatriciana.

   _____

   e Luca normally has lunch at a café.

   _____

2 Is everything going well for Melissa in Rome? Fill in the blanks with
words in English that correctly describe the conversation.

   At first it was _____, but now _____.

3 Which phrase means 'It seems to me that …'? Write it out here in
Italian. Would you use this as a conversation starter, warmer or an
extension?

   _____

4 Find and circle each of the following:

   a two sets of opposite phrases:

      1 _____ (me too)   3 _____ (rarely)

      2 _____ (me neither)   4 _____ (normally)

   b two different modes of transport

   _____   _____

NOTICE

1 Listen to the audio and study the table.

Essential phrases for Conversation 2

Italian	Meaning
mi sembra che ...	it seems to me that ...
ti trovi bene qui a Roma	you are doing well here in Rome
all'inizio era strano, ma ora ...	it was strange at first ... but now ...
mi sono ambientata e ho una routine	I'm settled in and have a routine
ogni mattina ... prima del lavoro ...	every morning ... before work ...
vado a fare una passeggiata per la città	I go for a walk around the city
anch'io	me too
di solito ... la mattina ...	usually in the mornings ...
porto fuori il mio cane	I walk my dog
ogni tanto ...	from time to time ...
vado a fare un giro in bici	I go for a bike ride
... per prendere un po' d'aria fresca	... to get some fresh air
io vado in bicicletta ovunque!	I ride my bike everywhere!
non prendo la metro	I never take the metro
neanche io, o raramente	me neither, or rarely
spesso ...	often ...
vado al lavoro in macchina	I go to work by car
mangio sempre nello stesso ristorante	I always eat at the same restaurant
hanno i migliori ...	they have the best ...
io a volte ...	sometimes I ...
vengo in questa trattoria per pranzo	come to this restaurant for lunch
ma normalmente ...	but normally ...
cucino a casa	I cook at home
non sono mai stata prima in questa trattoria!	I've never been to this café before!

In Italian you don't 'take' a walk, you 'do' a walk.

VOCAB: *guidare / andare* **to drive / to go by car**
'To drive' can be *guidare* when you talk about driving in general, but when you want to talk about the mode of transport to get you somewhere, it's more common to say *andare in macchina* (go by car).

GRAMMAR TIP:
stesso/stessa
The translation used for 'same' works in a similar way to words like *molto* or *tanto* and changes with gender and number: *le stesse sorelle* (the same sisters), *la stessa casa* (the same house).

2 Use the conversation to fill in the table with 'detail phrases' you could use to answer the questions: When? How often? Why / How? Where?

Conversation details chart

When?	How often?	Where?
1 before work	4 usually di solito	11 through the city
2 in the morning la mattina	5 from time to time	12 outside fuori
3 at lunch time	6 rarely	13 everywhere
	7 often	14 to (the) work
	8 always	15 in the same (restaurant)
	9 sometimes	16 at home
	10 never	

In English, to say 'in the mornings', we add an 's'. In Italian, the singular is most commonly used to show repeated periods of time. That gives *il pomeriggio* (in the afternoons), *la sera* (in the evenings), *la mattina* (in the mornings), *il lunedì* (Mondays) ...

3 Describe what you typically do during the week, using *di solito* ...

Example: Il mercoledì sera di solito, vedo il mio programma preferito alla TV.

a *Il sabato pomeriggio* _____

b *La domenica mattina* _____

c *Il venerdì dopo il lavoro* _____

d *Il giovedì dopo pranzo* _____

e *Il martedì prima di dormire* _____

PRACTICE

1 What activities do you do in your own life? Do you build things? Jog every day? Sing, dance, code, or body build? Look up the 'me-specific' verbs that describe how you spend your time.

Example: Suono il violino. _____

_____   _____

2 Now let's practise adding detail to basic phrases to expand on an idea.

    a *Cosa ti piace fare?* Use the phrase *All'inizio era ..., ma ora ...* to describe one of your hobbies.

Example: <u>All'inizio era difficile, ma ora mi diverto molto!</u>

_____

    b *Qual è il tuo posto preferito?* Think about one of your favourite places and write a simple sentence about it in Italian. Then use the phrase *Vado in ... perché* to say why you go there or how often.

Example: <u>Mi piace andare in biblioteca. Vado spesso in</u>
<u>biblioteca perché ci sono molti libri.</u>

_____

_____

    c *Sei stato in qualche posto interessante?* Now use the phrase *Non sono mai stato ...* to say somewhere you've never been before, but would like to go one day.

Example: <u>*Non sono mai stato al teatro di Broadway!*</u>

_____

PUT IT TOGETHER

1 Write a script that describes the different parts of your normal routine. Be sure to build on basic phrases to give more detailed descriptions of your daily life. You might include:

⋯⟶ what makes up your daily routine (ex: how you get to work/school every day)
⋯⟶ your hobbies, interests, or other activities
⋯⟶ details of how often, when, where, why, or how.

CONVERSATION 3

Going out at night

The last component of any conversation is, of course, the goodbye. You already know essential phrases like *presto* and *prossimo*. Let's expand on that with phrases for making plans for next time.

🔊 08.05 Melissa and Luca start talking about what they could do this evening. How does Luca ask 'What are you doing after this?'

Luca: Cosa fai dopo? Io spero di andare al parco con alcuni amici a giocare a calcio. Ti va di venire?

Melissa: Mi piacerebbe molto, ma purtroppo ho già in programma di andare a fare shopping con un'amica e poi ho lezione di cucina alle quattro. Ho del tempo libero più tardi se vuoi!

Luca: Sarebbe perfetto! Organizzo una piccola festa con degli amici a casa mia stasera. Perché non vieni?

Melissa: Fantastico! Cosa devo portare? E a che ora?

Luca: Alle nove. Manca solo il dolce. Magari puoi portare il tiramisù che prepari questo pomeriggio, no?

Melissa: Che bella idea! Prometto di farlo bene … non un disastro come la mia parmigiana. E dove vivi?

Luca: Non è lontano. Il mio appartamento si trova accanto alla stazione.

Melissa: Puoi scrivermi il tuo indirizzo?

Luca: Certamente! E se hai il cellulare, te lo mostro sulla mappa!

GRAMMAR TIP: *te lo*
You've seen that objects for 'me' and 'you' are usually *mi* and *ti*, but if there are two objects in the one phrase, these change to *me* and *te* before 'it': *te lo do* (I'll give it to you), *Me la racconti?* (Will you tell it (*la storia*) to me?)

FIGURE IT OUT

1 *Vero o falso?* Select the correct answer.

    a After this, Luca is going to get a drink with his brother.   *vero / falso*

    b Luca invites Melissa to play football with him, and then
       to a get-together.   *vero / falso*

    c Melissa has already planned to go shopping with a friend.   *vero / falso*

    d Melissa's Italian class starts at 4 p.m.   *vero / falso*

2 Highlight the following conversation components:

    a First underline the routine Luca describes about going to the park.

    b Now circle the details. (Why?) (With who?)

    c Underline the phrase in which Melissa says she has other plans.

    d Now circle the detail. (With whom?)

VOCAB EXPLANATION: time in Italy

Italian doesn't use a.m. and p.m. to indicate time of day. Instead, say:

di mattina	in the morning	*sette di mattina*	7.00 a.m.
del pomeriggio	in the afternoon	*due del pomeriggio*	2.00 p.m.
di sera	in the evening	*undici di sera*	11.00 p.m.
di notte	at night	*due di notte*	2.00 a.m.

The 'o'clock' part of the time is represented by saying *alle*: *alle otto di mattina* (at 8 a.m.).

There is just an exception: *all'una* (at 1 o'clock).

The 24-hour clock is also used but it is more formal (e.g. for opening hours and timetables).
Example: *Il treno parte alle sedici.* (The train is leaving at 16:00.)

NOTICE

🔊 08.06 Listen to the audio and study the table.

Essential phrases for Conversation 3

Italian	Meaning
cosa fai dopo?	what are you going to do after this?
Io spero di ...	I hope to ...
... andare al parco con alcuni amici a	... to go to the park with some friends
... giocare a calcio	... to play football
ti va di venire?	would you like to come? (to-you it-goes of to-come?)
mi piacerebbe molto	I'd love to
... ma purtroppo ho già in programma	... but unfortunately I already have plans
di andare a fare shopping con un'amica	to go shopping with a friend
e poi ho lezione di cucina	then I have cooking class
... alle quattro	... at four
ho del tempo libero più tardi se vuoi!	I have free time later if you want!
sarebbe perfetto!	that would be great!
organizzo una piccola festa con degli amici	I'm having a get-together (organizing a small party) with some friends
... a casa mia stasera	... at my house tonight
perché non vieni?	why don't you come?
cosa devo portare?	what should I bring?
e a che ora?	and at what time?
alle nove	at 9 (at-the nine)
manca solo il dolce	a cake is the only thing missing
non è lontano	it's not far
il mio appartamento si trova accanto alla stazione	my apartment is (finds itself / one finds it) beside the train station
puoi scrivermi il tuo indirizzo?	could you write down the address?
te lo mostro sulla mappa!	I can show you on the map!

GRAMMAR EXPLANATION: 'it would...' – the conditional form

GRAMMAR TIP:
sarebbe

This form has its own irregulars, and one is *essere* 'to be' changed to *sarebbe* 'it would be'. Despite how different it is, learning this form will be worth your while in all that you'll be able to say. The *e* is dropped from *potere* and *dovere* in *potrebbe* and *dovrebbe*.

When talking about a possible future in Italian, replace the final *-e* of dictionary forms of verbs with *-ebbe* for '*he/she/it would*'. Verbs that end in *-are* will change to *-erebbe*. The -are verbs change the -are ending to -erebbe, for example:

> *cantare* → *canterebbe* (he/she would sing)
> *scrivere* → *scriverebbe* (he/she would write)
> *partire* → *partirebbe* (he/she would leave)

There are other forms to learn (*io, tu, loro*, etc.) that we won't get into here, but you can say a lot with just this one, such as:

⋯⟩ what would be true:
   Sarebbe impossibile senza di lui.   (It would be impossible without him.)
⋯⟩ what you would like to do:
   Mi piacerebbe uscire stasera.   (I would like to go out this evening.)
⋯⟩ what someone could or should do:
   Potrebbe dormire qui se vuole.   (He could sleep here if he wants.)
   Dovrebbe mangiare meno.   (He should eat less.)
⋯⟩ to be more polite and say anything using *Lei*:
   Lo venderebbe per 50€?   (Would you sell it for €50?)
   Potrebbe ripeterlo per favore?   (Could you repeat it please?)

Now it's coming in very handy that this is literally 'it would be pleasing', since you don't need to learn a new form thanks to using mi. Similarly, *ti piacerebbe* is 'you would like'.

CULTURE TIP: *currency*
Currency symbols usually come after the number in Italy (and all across Europe). As well as this, commas and decimals get swapped, so '€2,200.22' becomes 2.200,22 € in Italian!

CONVERSATION STRATEGY: 'Tarzan' conditional

Until you learn the other endings for the conditional, a temporary workaround is to use the he / she / it form you just learned, even for the wrong person. So if I wanted to say:

> I **would buy** chocolate, but I'm on a diet

I could try:

> '*Io ... comprerebbe cioccolata', ma sono a dieta.*

This gets the point across and lets you get more spoken practice without worrying about knowing all the right endings.

1 Fill in the gaps to form the conditional in the following phrases:

a Tua sorella _____ vivere in Italia! (adorare)

b _____ troppo caro per me. (essere)

c Ti _____ guardare un film con me? (piacere)

d Credi che il mio ragazzo _____ in pubblico? (parlare)

2 Find phrases for getting the specifics. Find the following phrases in the phrase list and write them out.

a What should I bring? _____

b At what time? _____

c Can you write down the address? _____

d I can show it to you on the map. _____

3 Now, use those phrases as templates to mix and match the vocab from this conversation to create new sentences in Italian.

a What time does it end? (to end = finire; it ends: finisce)

_____

b Do you know the address? _____

c Where is the apartment? _____

d When should I arrive? _____

e Can I bring some wine? (vino) _____

CULTURE EXPLANATION:
what to bring
When you're invited over for dinner in Italy, you shouldn't show up empty-handed! *Non andare mai a mani vuote* – as Italians say. Common gifts include a bottle of wine, champagne or the Italian *spumante*, some flowers or a plant (especially if your host will have been cooking for you). An alternative is to bring some dessert (either self-made or bought, for example ice cream in the summer, or a box of chocolates), but it is always nice to check with the host to see if they've already prepared something. If you don't know what's best, you can always ask!

PRACTICE

1 Mix and match phrases for inviting someone to do something. Select from the English suggestions given to complete the original sentence in Italian in two different ways.

Example: *Mangiamo in un ristorante cinese* (this evening) (Monday) (later) (at 7 p.m.) (next week)?

   Mangiamo in un ristorante cinese questa sera?

a *Cosa fai* (after this) (later) (at 5 p.m.) (tonight) (tomorrow)?

_____

_____

b *Ho tempo libero* _____ *per andare al concerto. Vieni?*
(after this) (later) (at 5 p.m.) (tonight) (tomorrow)

_____

_____

2 Mix and match phrases for accepting or turning down an invitation. Select from the English suggestions given to complete the original sentence in Italian in two different ways.

a *Sarebbe* (cool) (perfect) (amazing) (fun) (impossible) (too late)

_____

_____

b *Mi piacerebbe, ma* (unfortunately …) (I already have plans) (I'm busy)

_____

_____

3 How would you say the following in Italian?

a Would you like to learn Italian with me?

_____

b Would you like to go shopping this weekend?

_____

PUT IT TOGETHER

1 You bump into an elderly Italian tourist in your home town, and once he discovers that you speak Italian, he can't wait to pick your brain. Give him your local know-how and tell him what an ideal day would look like for him to get the best out of his visit. Try to include the following (remembering to use *Lei* – the formal 'you'):

⋯⋗ the first thing that he would do
   (Per cominciare potrebbe mangiare ...)
⋯⋗ the best place for him and why
   (Il posto migliore da visitare sarebbe ...)
⋯⋗ what activities he would do
   (Potrebbe prendere un taxi per andare a ...)
⋯⋗ other insider tips *(Dopo le cinque*
   il biglietto sarebbe meno caro ...).

2 An old friend from school wants to hang out, but you have plans to go to your next Italian language event this evening. You know if you invite him, he'll speak English all evening and you'll get no practice, so when he suggests something less interesting, you have to think of an excuse quick! To get you in the right frame of mind, say in Italian what you might come up with:

⋯⋗ First, say that you would really like to *(Mi piacerebbe molto – mi sembra ...)*.
⋯⋗ But then say how it's not possible *(Ma purtroppo ...)*.
⋯⋗ And give inventive excuses for what you would be doing that you know he wouldn't want to join you in *(Ho già in programma di ...)*.

#LANGUAGEHACK: the rephrasing technique for talking your way through complicated sentences

You're used to expressing yourself with a lot of complexity and nuance when you speak in your native language, but when you're learning a new language, you can't do this right away. Getting used to (and comfortable with) this shift is a big part of being a successful language learner. So how do you convey your more complex thoughts and feelings when you are still only working with the very basics of the language?

Expressing yourself with even limited language skills is largely a matter of skillful rephrasing. You'll need to simplify your sentences to use words and phrases you are more comfortable with.
Here's how to break it down.

Figure out the core idea

⋯⫶ First, recognize that the rules of expressing yourself as an eloquent native do not (usually) apply to you as a beginner Italian learner. The nuanced language you search for in your head and the desire to know how to say what you want and how to convey the right tone and courtesy … Sometimes, you have to just let that go.

'Excuse me … I'm sorry … I just overheard you speaking Italian … I've actually been studying it for a while … do you mind if I practise a few phrases with you? … I hope I'm not bothering you …'

⋯⫶ Next, figure out the one core idea you're most trying to express.

'You speak Italian? Me too! Let's talk.'

⋯⫶ Finally,translate your simpler concept, or 'piggy-back' your idea off another expression that works just as well.

Parli italiano? Anch'io! Parliamo!

Back to the basics

The gist of what you're trying to say is very often quite simple.

⋯⋗ Instead of trying to say,

'Would you like to dance with me?' you can say, 'Dance with me!' – *Balla con me!*

⋯⋗ Instead of trying to say, 'I should avoid eating fish as much as possible due to a medical condition that I have', you can say, 'I can't eat fish because I have an allergy' (or in Tarzan Italian, 'no fish' – *no pesce*).

⋯⋗ Instead of trying to say, 'I'm looking for a flatmate that speaks Italian and wants to rent the room for at least 12 months', you can say something like 'I need a flatmate to practise my Italian with for a year'.

⋯⋗ Instead of trying to say 'Would you like to dance with me?' you can say, 'Dance with me!' – *Balla con me!*

⋯⋗ Instead of trying to say 'I should avoid eating fish as much as possible due to a medical condition that I have', you can say, 'I can't eat fish because I have an allergy' (or in 'Tarzan Italian', 'no fish' – *no pesce*).

⋯⋗ Instead of trying to say 'I'm looking for a flatmate that speaks Italian and wants to rent the room for at least 12 months', you can say something like 'I need a flatmate to practise my Italian with for a year'.

YOUR TURN: use the hack

1 Practise this rephrasing skill now. For each of the lines given, write an alternative (shorter) translation in Italian that conveys a similar meaning as the original, but avoids any complicated grammar. There may be a variety of ways to say each one – just try to get the idea across as best and simply as you can.

Remember, this is a skill, which means that practice is the key to getting better.

Example: I'm probably not going to be able to go out with you.

→ <u>Non posso uscire con te</u>. (I can't go out with you.)

a I'm not sure if they will be able to win (*vincere*).

_____

b i'm so happy that we were able to come to the restaurant together.

_____

c I would really love it if you would be willing to dance with me.

_____

d I'd rather go to the supermarket later.

_____

COMPLETING UNIT 8

Check your understanding

1   ◀》 08.07 Listen to the audio rehearsal in which an Italian speaker describes his routine, as well as things he wishes he could do. Feel free to take notes or listen to it again.

2   ◀》 08.08 Now listen to questions about what you've just heard, and answer them out loud in Italian.

Show what you know ...

Here's what you've just learned. Write or say an example for each item in the list. Then tick off the ones you know.

- ☐ Write a sentence that describes a hobby.
- ☐ Say when you started it, and what you've achieved so far.
- ☐ Give two different details about your hobby.
- ☐ Give three phrases that describe your normal routine using:
  - ☐ 'often'
  - ☐ 'usually'
  - ☐ 'sometimes'
- ☐ Say 'it would be' and 'he could' in Italian.

COMPLETE YOUR MISSION

It's time to complete your mission: give your best productivity advice to be published on your friend's blog. To do this, you might need to observe yourself and keep track of the things you do regularly. You could even read some Italian blogs about productivity and mindfulness to help you.

STEP 1: build your script

Keep building your script by using the phrases you've learned in this unit combined with 'me-specific' vocabulary to answer common questions about yourself. Be sure to:

····} talk about different parts of your life and weekly routine
····} describe where you go, how you get there and what you do
····} include details of how often, when, where, why or how
····} describe something else you would love to do but haven't done yet
····} describe what you like about your routines and what could be better.

Write down your script, then repeat it until you feel confident. This time, incorporate conversation starters, leads or extensions to help get the conversation flowing, e.g. vedo che ... (I see that you ...)

STEP 2: learn from your mistakes, and others' ... *online*

When learning a new language, mistakes are inevitable. Part of the charm of speaking a second language is realizing that people are much less critical than you imagine!

It's time to complete your mission. Share your productivity advice with the rest of the community! And in return, enjoy some free advice about how you can be more effective in your life. So go online to find your mission for Unit 8, and use the community space to find out how you can make learning Italian part of your daily routine.

To complete this mission, research blogs on 'routines' or 'productivity' in Italian. Try searching online for **produttività personale**, or **essere più produttivo**. Go online to the #LanguageHacking community for help finding them!

The key is that if you're making mistakes, you're learning. And if you speak, you can even notice them more easily and fix them yourself. **Added bonus**: you can learn from the mistakes of other language hackers too. So look at the corrections and comments people leave – you'll find that your common mistakes are most likely shared.

STEP 3: learn from other learners

What productivity tips can you gain from other language hackers? After you've uploaded your own clip, check out what the other people in the community have to say about their routines. **Your task is to let at least three different people know what you thought was most useful about their routine.**

This time, incorporate conversation starters, leads or extensions to help get the conversation flowing, e.g. *vedo che* ... (I see that you ...)

STEP 4: reflect on what you've learned

HEY, LANGUAGE HACKER, YOU'RE ALMOST THERE!

In this unit we talked a lot about the strategy behind preparing for the kinds of conversations you're likely to be having. All the scripts you've been building are preparing you for this ultimate goal.

With the strategies you'll learn next in Missions 9 and 10, you will be amazed at how well your first conversation goes ...

Manca poco!

9 DESCRIBE IT!

Your mission

Imagine this ... you're applying to be a tour guide in an Italian-speaking city. You have to prove your ability to describe a place in detail and give recommendations for where to hang out and what to do.

Your mission is to pretend you're a local by **describing a city that you know** (or want to know!) well. Be prepared to do your research and give a short description of the highlights of what to do and see.

But here's the twist – don't say the name of the city. See if others can guess where you're describing! **Describe the best places, explain their characteristics,** and explain how it might suit **different personalities.**

This mission will enable you to communicate more creatively by explaining the characteristics of people, places and things in the world around you in more detail.

Mission prep

- ⋯⟩ Describe places and where you live – *vivo in campagna*.
- ⋯⟩ Describe the weather and environment – *fa caldo*.
- ⋯⟩ Describe people and their personalities – *Lei è avventurosa*.
- ⋯⟩ Describe what someone or something looks like – *mi sembra*.
- ⋯⟩ Learn shopping phrases – *il più economico, pagare in contanti*.

BUILDING LANGUAGE FOR DESCRIBING PEOPLE, PLACES AND THINGS

As you're getting closer to your conversation in Italian, let's start filling in some of the most important gaps. In this unit you'll learn how to describe personalities and characteristics of other people, and you'll also be able to express your thoughts more creatively in Italian. When you can't think of a word you need, you can try to describe it instead!

#LANGUAGEHACK
use your hidden moments to get Italian immersion for the long-term

CONVERSATION 1

Describing the city

Melissa is getting ready to fly back to the United States, and she's thinking about what she misses about home. She describes her home town to her friend Luca as they hang out by the *Tevere* on a sunny day.

🔊 09.01 What word does Melissa use to say she's 'going back' home?

When you start talking to people from other countries, they're going to show interest in where you're from, and how it's different from where they're from. Prepare your answers now!

Melissa: Presto ritorno negli Stati Uniti. È la mia ultima settimana a Roma!

Luca: Che peccato! Sei felice di tornare a casa?

Melissa: Amo Roma, ma sai che io vivo in campagna? Mi mancano le montagne e anche il lago e la foresta vicino a casa mia. Comunque ... se penso che presto parto, Roma già mi manca un po'!

Luca: Me lo immagino! Senti, ho un'idea ... perché non compri alcuni regali per la tua famiglia e per ricordare il tempo che hai passato qui?

Melissa: È una buona idea. Adoro fare shopping! Dove posso andare a comprarli?

Luca: Hmmm ... Dipende. Sei già stata a Via dei Condotti? È più carina dei centri commerciali e la via è piena di negozi. C'è così tanto da vedere!

Melissa: Non lo so ... Oggi fa bel tempo, ma muoio di caldo. Non posso stare tutto il pomeriggio al sole. Mi stanco!

Luca: A dire il vero, a quest'ora del giorno la via è all'ombra, quindi fa fresco.

Melissa: In questo caso, sì! Andiamo!

FIGURE IT OUT

LEARNING STRATEGY:
Actively take notes
By now you have a great base of Italian vocabulary. At this point, it's a good idea to **actively take note** of any new verbs or words you come across, to add to your script or your study materials.

1 Underline the word(s) that make each of these sentences *falso*, and write out the corresponding word(s) that are *vero* in Italian.

a It's Melissa's last day in Rome. _____

b Melissa and Luca are planning to go dancing. _____

c The street has a lot to eat. _____

2 Use your understanding of the conversation to figure out the meaning of:

    a *Presto ritorno negli Stati Uniti* _____

    b *Che peccato!* _____

    c *Dipende.* _____

3 Find the following phrases in the conversation and write them in Italian.

    a in the countryside _____   **d** near my house _____

    b the mountains _____   **e** under the sun _____

    c the lake and the forest _____

NOTICE

◀)) 09.02 Listen to the audio and study the table. Repeat out loud to mimic the speakers.

Essential phrases for Conversation 1

Italian	Meaning
presto ritorno negli Stati Uniti	soon I'll be back in the US
che peccato!	that's a pity!
sei felice tornare a casa?	are you happy to go home?
in campagna	in the countryside
mi mancano le montagne	I miss the mountains
e anche il lago e la foresta	as well as the lake and the forest
Roma mi manca già un po'!	I already miss Rome a little!
perché non compri dei regali per la tua famiglia...	why don't you buy some gifts for your family ...
per ricordare il tempo che hai passato qui!	to remember your time here!
dove posso andare a comprarli?	where should I go to buy them?
è più carina dei ...	it's nicer than ...
la via è piena di negozi	the street is full of shops
c'è così tanto da vedere!	there is so much to see!
oggi fa bel tempo	it's nice out today (today it-does beautiful weather)
la via è all'ombra, quindi fa fresco	the street is shaded, so it's cool

1 Review the phrase list to answer questions in Italian about the conversation.

Example: Che cosa manca a Melissa?

Melissa *mancano le montagne, il lago e la foresta.*

a Quando ritorna negli Stati Uniti?
Melissa _____

b Cosa compra Melissa per la sua famiglia?
Melissa _____

c Dove li compra? Melissa li _____

VOCAB: *ricordare* 'to remember' / 'to remind'
In Italian, *ricordare* can mean both 'to remember' and 'to remind'! *Non mi ricordo il suo nome* (I don't remember her name), *Puoi ricordarmi il tuo indirizzo?* (Could you remind me what your address is?)

2 How would you say each of the following in Italian? Fill in the gaps to complete each sentence.

a You need to remind me of ... *Devi* _____.

b I'm going to remind you tomorrow. *Te lo* _____ *domani.*

c He reminded me of my appointment.
_____ *il mio appuntamento.*

3 Match the Italian phrases from the conversation to the English expressions closest in meaning. Notice that some of the Italian expressions can have more than one meaning in English. Notice that some of the Italian expressions can have more than one meaning in English.

As a beginner, it's good to know how to rephrase your words to more easily convey your thoughts.

a in questo caso
b che peccato!
c dipende

1 when you put it that way
2 there are two ways to look at it
3 that's a shame

4 A good memory technique is to learn vocab in 'clusters' – learning words of a similar category together. Use the phrase list to fill in this vocab cluster with words describing places.

Nature and landscape vocab

Italian	Meaning	Italian	Meaning
	the countryside		the forest
	the mountains		the sun
	the lake		the shade
la città	the city		

5 Use the nature and landscape vocabulary you've learned along with different ways of saying 'in' from the phrase list to answer the following questions about yourself in Italian.

a Do you live in the countryside, or in a city?

Vivo _____.

b Do you prefer to stay in the sun, or in the shade?

Preferisco stare _____.

c Which place do you prefer to spend a quiet week, the lake, the forest, or the mountains?

Preferisco _____

per passare una settimana tranquilla.

PRACTICE

1 Look up new words to describe where you live or the landscape in your area. Do you live near the sea? In the suburbs? In a studio apartment? Add your 'me-specific' vocab to the list.

2 Now use the vocab you just looked up to create sentences in Italian that are true for you.

a I live ...

_____

b Near my house, there is / there are ...

_____

VOCAB EXPLANATION: *mancare* for 'to miss'

GRAMMAR TIP:
mancare for 'to miss'
We've mostly talked
about *mi/ti piace*, but
you can also use *ci* (us),
gli (him), *le* (her) and *vi*
(you-plural). Otherwise,
use a followed by the
person's name (e.g. *a
Melissa manca la città*).

Conversation 1 uses two examples of the verb 'to miss':

Mi mancano le montagne.   *Roma mi manca già un po'!*

Notice that the word order in these sentences is very similar to the way
we use *mi piace*:

Mi piace Roma.   *Mi mancano le montagne.*
(I like Rome.)   (I miss the mountains.)
(lit. 'to-me, is-pleasing Rome') (lit. 'to-me are-missing the mountains')

We use *mancano* with the *-ano* ending ('they' form) when we say that 'the
mountains' plural are missed.

Examples: *Ti mancano le montagne.*   (You miss the mountains.)
Ci mancano le montagne.   (We miss the mountains.)

1 Use either *manca* or *mancano* to write each sentence in Italian.

a I miss my dog. ————————————————

b I miss the seven cats. ————————————————

c We miss Rome. ————————————————

d Francesco misses Italian coffee.

————————————————————————

e Do you miss your home town?

————————————————————————

f Why don't you miss the parties?

————————————————————————

VOCAB EXPLANATION: talking about weather

Che tempo fa? (How's the weather?)

When you want to describe the weather in Italian, you'll often use the
verb *fare* in the phrase '*fa ...* '

Fa caldo may mean
'it's hot' to describe
the day in general,
or your environment,
but if you want to
describe how you
feel, you'd use *avere*
(*ho caldo* 'I'm hot',
ho freddo 'I'm cold').

Italian	Meaning	Italian	Meaning
Fa bel tempo / è bello	It's nice	C'è il sole	It's sunny
Fa brutto tempo	It's bad	C'è vento	It's windy
Fa caldo	It's hot	Piove	It's raining
Fa freddo	It's cold	È nuvoloso	It's cloudy

1 Practise creating new sentences to describe the weather in Italian.

a It's nice out. _____

c Is it raining tomorrow? _____

b The weather is bad. What a pity! _____

2 Use *fa* or *c'è* to give two sentences describing the weather where you are right now.

_____

_____

3 Refer back to the phrase list from Conversation 1. Find the adjectives in the list and write them out here in their masculine (singular) and feminine (singular) forms.

a nice   _____(m)   _____(f)

b full   _____(m)   _____(f)

c good   _____(m)   _____(f)

PUT IT TOGETHER

You now have a greater ability to talk about your environment, so let's put that into action! Create a script in which you describe where you live, or a place that you love to visit, in as much detail as possible. Be sure to include descriptive words (adjectives and nouns) and answer these questions:

⋯⟶ What's the landscape like?
⋯⟶ What is the weather usually like? Sometimes like?
⋯⟶ What do you miss most about it? / What would you miss if you were to leave?

Normalmente vivo ...

CONVERSATION 2

What would you buy for someone who is ...?

You've learned how to describe places – now let's focus on a new set of descriptive words you can use to talk about people and their personalities.

Melissa and Luca have made it to the *Via dei Condotti* to go shopping, and they're discussing what gifts Melissa should get for her family based on their personalities.

🔊 09.03 What words does Melissa use to describe her sister, brother and parents?

CULTURE TIP: haggling and street markets
While the *città vaticana* is gorgeous to visit, my favourite spot for shopping is actually the flea market at Porta Portese. I love to *trattare il prezzo* (haggle) to get a good deal there. It's more fun than when you know the price is standard, and excellent for Italian practice!

Melissa:	Questa via è straordinaria! Ci sono così tanti negozi!
Luca:	Sai già cosa vuoi comprare?
Melissa:	Voglio comprarmi un sacco di cose. Ma per la mia famiglia … non ho la minima idea!
Luca:	Com'è la tua famiglia?
Melissa:	È difficile descriverla – per esempio, mia sorella è avventurosa e vuole veramente venire in Italia un giorno. Magari alcuni souvenir tipici di Roma per lei?
Luca:	O un vestito … La moda italiana è famosissima!
Melissa:	Perché no! … Mio fratello è giovane e troverebbe noiosi i souvenir. Cosa compreresti a una persona timida?
Luca:	Non hai bisogno di comprare qualcosa di italiano. Sai che alcuni prodotti tecnologici sono più economici qui?
Melissa:	Ah sì, ora ricordo – le sue cuffie sono piuttosto vecchie e non funzionano bene. Ha bisogno di cuffie nuove!
Luca:	E i tuoi genitori? Non puoi dimenticarti di comprare qualcosa anche per loro!
Melissa:	I miei sono più tradizionali e mi hanno già detto che vogliono un buon vino italiano.
Luca:	Problema risolto! So già dove comprarlo! Qui all'angolo della strada c'è un'enoteca. Dobbiamo assolutamente prendere una bottiglia anche per noi, solo per provarla!

GRAMMAR TIP:
adjectives first
You'll usually see adjectives follow nouns, but there are some cases where they can come before, with a subtle change in meaning. When this happens, you can see that *buono* gets shortened to *buon*.

FIGURE IT OUT

1 *Vero o falso?* Select the correct answer.

    a Melissa is shopping for her friends.   *vero / falso*

    b Melissa's brother doesn't like souvenirs.   *vero / falso*

    c Melissa knows exactly what to buy.   *vero / falso*

2 Answer these questions about the conversation.

    a What is Melissa going to get her sister?   *Alcuni* _____

    b Why? How does Melissa describe her?   *Lei è* _____

    c How does Melissa describe her brother?   *Lui è* _____

    d How do Melissa and Luca describe   *Sono* _____

        Melissa's parents?

    e What does Luca say about   *Sono* _____

        technology (products) in Italy?

3 Highlight the adjectives in the conversation, then write them out.

    a impressive _____   e old _____

    b really famous _____   f shy _____

    c typical _____   g traditional _____

    d boring _____   h new _____

4 Find the following phrases in the conversation and underline them. Then, write out the word in bold.

    a that **reminds** me _____

    b she **really** wants _____

    c he'd **find** souvenirs _____

    d they are **quite** old _____

    e they **already** told me _____

NOTICE

🔊 09.04 Listen to the audio and study the table.

Essential phrases for Conversation 2

Italian	Meaning
questa via è straordinaria!	this street is impressive!
voglio comprarmi	I want to buy myself
non ho la minima idea	I've no idea
com'è la tua famiglia?	how is your family?
è difficile descriverla	it's hard to describe them (la famiglia – the family)
mia sorella è avventurosa	my sister is adventurous
souvenir tipici	typical souvenirs
mio fratello è giovane	my brother is young
troverebbe ...	he would find ...
cosa compreresti a una persona ...?	what would you buy a ... person?
alcuni prodotti tecnologici sono più economici qui	some technology is cheaper here
ora ricordo	now I remember
le sue cuffie sono piuttosto vecchie	his headphones are quite old
non funzionano bene	they don't work well
ha bisogno di ...	he needs.....
e i tuoi genitori?	what about your parents?
più tradizionali	more traditional
un buon vino italiano	a good Italian wine
all'angolo della strada	at the corner of the street
solo per provarla	just to try it

1 Find the following phrases and write them out in Italian.

a now I remember _____

b what would you buy _____

c my parents are more traditional _____

2 Another effective memory technique is to learn words in pairs with their opposites. Use the adjectives from the phrase list, or a dictionary, to complete the sentences.

You may know how to form many masculine and feminine adjectives, but when you're speaking spontaneously, you shouldn't stress over getting these forms right. If you use whichever form you remember, the person you're speaking to will understand you.

a *Non è* _____, *è* _____. (It's not **easy**, it's **hard**.)

b *Non è* _____, *è* _____. (It's not **unique**, it's **typical**.)

c *Non sono* _____, *sono* _____.
(They aren't **stupid**, they're **wise**.)

d *Non sono* _____, *sono* _____.
(They aren't **modern**, they are **traditional**.)

e *Non è* _____, *è* _____. (She's not **adventurous**, she's **shy**.)

f *Non è* _____, *è* _____. (He's not **old**, he's **young**.)

3 Use the different forms given to create sentences. Be sure to use the correct word order and gender / plural agreement. Use each form in the box only once.

mio fratello	è	aperto
i miei fratelli	sono	aperti
mia sorella	era	alto
le mie sorelle		alta
il negozio		alti
i negozi		alte

a The shop is open. _____

b The shops are open. _____

c The shop was open. _____

d My brother is tall. _____

e My brothers are tall. _____

f My sister is tall. _____

g My sisters are tall. _____

PRACTICE

1 How would you say 'it's the cheapest' in Italian? _____

2 Practise forming the adjectives you've learned according to gender. Fill in the missing words in the table, which are grouped by opposites. Be sure to include both the masculine and feminine forms (if they are different). Use your dictionary to look them up if you need to.

Describing people

Italian (m / f)	Meaning	Italian (m / f)	Meaning
	shy / timid	avventuroso(a)	
	ugly	bello(a)	
vecchio(a)			young
strano(a)			typical
	unpleasant	simpatico(a)	
	pessimistic	ottimista	
	proud	modesto(a)	
	funny	serio(a)	

A lot of Italian adjectives are cognates of English, which means that when you're speaking Italian naturally in a conversation, you can often guess the Italian form of an English adjective you know – just be sure to say it with Italian pronunciation. Try it!

3 🔊 09.05 Look at the English adjectives given, which are all cognates of Italian. How do you think you would pronounce them in Italian? Listen to the audio to check your answers.

a interesting
b attentive
c creative
d curious

e honest
f intelligent
g sincere
h tolerant

i ignorant
j impatient

4 Practise using adjectives to describe yourself and people around you. Complete the sentences with words that are true for you (look up words if you need to), and try to use the correct genders.

a Sono _____.

b Il mio lavoro è _____.

c Mio padre/il mio amico/mio fratello è _____.

d La sua casa è _____.

e Mia madre/la mia amica/mia sorella _____.

PUT IT TOGETHER

1 When you meet someone new, they'll very likely ask you about the people in your life. Prepare for these questions with a script that describes the personalities of at least two important people in your life. Make your script as 'me-specific' as possible by looking up any new descriptive words now, so you'll have them ready during your conversations.

⋯⋗ Describe two different people in your life.
⋯⋗ Use adjectives to describe their personalities.
⋯⋗ Be sure that your adjectives agree with the person in gender and number.

CONVERSATION 3

It looks like …

By knowing how to describe things in Italian, you'll have a handy new trick up your sleeve to use in Italian conversations. When you can't think of a particular word for something, you can just *describe it* instead!

🔊 09.06 Melissa is looking for that headset for her brother and asks Luca for advice. Which phrase does she use to ask, 'Is this one OK?'

> **Melissa:** Questo negozio vende cuffie, mi sembra.
>
> **Luca:** Per che cosa usa le cuffie tuo fratello?
>
> **Melissa:** Gioca ai videogiochi online. Queste vanno bene?
>
> **Luca:** No, quelle nere sono per fare jogging. Il regalo migliore per lui sarebbe questo … le cuffie verdi.
> In più sono anche di una qualità migliore.
>
> **Melissa:** Come lo sai?
>
> **Luca:** Conosco la marca. Sono un po' care, ma oggi sono in offerta, a metà prezzo! A tuo fratello piacciono di sicuro!
>
> **Melissa:** Perfetto! Quanto costano? … Hmm, con questo prezzo non posso pagarle in contanti. Devo usare la mia carta di credito.
>
> **Luca:** La accettano sicuramente. Andiamo a pagare alla cassa. Devo dire che sei la migliore sorella del mondo.

FIGURE IT OUT

1 The following statements about the conversation are *falso*. Underline the word(s) that make each one incorrect, and write the correct word(s) in Italian.

   a Melissa's brother needs a new headset because he lost them. _____

   b The headset is not expensive. _____

   c Melissa is going to pay in cash. _____

2 Highlight the two ways of paying mentioned in the conversation. What do you think the word *cassa* means? _____

3 Use your understanding of the conversation to answer the questions:

   a Which headset is better for jogging? *Quelle* _____

   b Which headset is better for Melissa's brother? *Quelle* _____

4 Find the Italian phrase for 'would be' and highlight it.

NOTICE

🔊 09.07 Listen to the audio and study the table.

Essential phrases for Conversation 3

VOCAB: 'this'
The word for 'this'
changes depending
on the next word, but
don't worry about trying
to master it for now.
questo/a/e/i means
'this' or 'these'. You can
also use *quello/quella/
quelli/quelle (which
can mean 'that one/
those ones')...* to mean
'one(s)' as in *quelle
verdi* (the green ones).

Italian	Meaning
questo negozio vende cuffie, mi sembra	this shop looks like it sells headphones
per che cosa usa le cuffie tuo fratello?	what does your brother use the headphones for?
gioca ai videogiochi online	he plays video games online
queste vanno bene?	are these ones OK?
quelle nere / verdi	the black / green ones
il regalo migliore per lui sarebbe ...	the best present for him would be ...
in più	besides
sono anche di una qualità migliore	they're also better quality
conosco la marca	I recognize the brand
sono un po' care	they're a little expensive
sono in offerta	they're on offer
... a metà prezzo	... at half price
quanto costano?	how much do they cost?
... pagare in contanti	... to pay in cash
... usare la mia carta di credito	... to use my credit card
la accettano sicuramente	they will accept it
andiamo a pagare alla cassa	let's go to the register
Devo dire che sei la migliore sorella del mondo.	I have to say that you're the best sister in the world

The best way to ask if something is 'OK' is to ask if it 'goes well' – *va bene?*

You learned to describe people and places in Conversations 1 and 2. Now, notice the new vocab you can use to describe things.

1 What phrases could you use to say:

a what something looks like? _____

b what you use something for? _____

2 Can you find two uses of the verb *usare* in the phrase list?

3 If you needed to describe an item you wanted to a shopkeeper, you could use the following phrases. Write them out in Italian.

a that one _____

c the small one _____

b the black ones _____

d the new ones _____

4 If you don't know the word for the item, you could also just say the name of *la marca* (the brand). Which international brands could you use to ask the questions …

You'll recognize a lot of familiar brands in Italy, and you can use this to your advantage when you're trying to describe what you want. In case you don't remember the word, don't worry: Italians also use the English word 'brand'.

a *Vendete _____? (shoe brand)*

b *Vorrei una scatola di _____. (tissue brand)*

c *Bevo una _____. (cola brand)*

d *Vorrei comprare un _____. (computer brand)*

e *Posso andare a lavorare con la tua _____? (car brand)*

5 How would you say the following expressions related to purchases?

a a little expensive _____

b pay in cash _____

c use my credit card _____

d the till _____

PRACTICE

1 Practise creating new questions you could use to ask about things.

a How much does this one (fem.) cost (*costa*)? _____

b How is the quality? _____

c Do you (*Lei* form) accept credit cards? _____

d I can only pay in cash. _____

2   Fill in the blanks with the missing words in Italian.

    a   *Non conosco* _____ _____. (I don't know that brand.)

    b   *Pago alla* _____. (I'll pay at the cash register.)

    c   *Mi piace* _____ _____ _____ *a sinistra*. (I like the big computer on the left.)

3   Fill in any missing translations in the table with words for describing things.

Italian	Meaning	Italian	Meaning
largo(a)		giallo(a)	yellow
corto(a)	short	rosso(a)	red
	full	blu	blue
di cattiva qualità		bianco(a)	white
			green
		nero(a)	

PUT IT TOGETHER

1   *Cosa cerchi?* (What are you looking for?) Build sentences you could use to describe something you were looking for, wanted to buy, or lost. Think of an item to describe, then write out:

⋯⋙ what it looks like / what you use it for

⋯⋙ what brand or colour it is

⋯⋙ a description using 'this' or 'that' one

⋯⋙ any other descriptive words you know!

#LANGUAGEHACK: use your hidden moments to get Italian immersion for the long-term

Rather than thinking about how many months or years it may take to learn Italian, a more effective learning strategy is to focus instead on the *minutes* that it takes.

Don't overlook the value of these short periods of time. They really add up, and more importantly, they're a great way to consistently keep up momentum in your learning.

Not everyone has a few hours every day to devote to Italian. But everyone has a few minutes. Even if you live a busy lifestyle, you can still find 'hidden moments' throughout your day for Italian practice. Standing in line in the supermarket, waiting for the lift, sitting on a bus, train or taxi, waiting for a tardy friend ... all of these are perfect moments for squeezing Italian practice into your daily life.

Italian immersion – from anywhere

As you've followed Melissa's story, perhaps you've thought, 'Well, she's quite lucky to go to Italy to improve her Italian through immersion!' But in fact, *you* can also create an Italian immersion environment, from anywhere in the world, no matter where you live – thanks to technology. When you have bigger windows of time to practise Italian, you can create an at-home immersion environment in loads of different ways:

LEARNING STRATEGY: study on the go When I'm in language-learning mode, I use a vocab study app on the go, whenever I have to wait somewhere. Since my smartphone is with me anyway, I use it to learn what I can, when I can, even if it's just a word or two. See our Resources for some suggestions!

···➔ You can connect with other learners (like you've been doing with our online community!) to get practice with them through regular video / audio calls.
···➔ You can listen to live streaming radio or watch streaming video from Italy online.
···➔ Do you play *videogiochi*? You could change the language settings to Italian!
···➔ You could also change the language of websites and even your operating system.

YOUR TURN: use the hack

1 Pick a few apps and tools from our Resources, and add them to your computer or smartphone now so they are ready and waiting for you during your quiet moments.
2 Look at the websites, apps, games, browsers and even the operating system you use the most, and see if they have an option to change the language to Italian. Since you're already used to where you'd normally click or tap, why not change the language?

You'll see it's not that bad, and you can always change it back if you find it too hard. Usually, you'll just need to look for 'lingua' somewhere in your settings.

COMPLETING UNIT 9

Check your understanding

1 ◀》 09.08 Listen to someone describing their environment and people around them in Italian. Feel free to take notes or listen to it multiple times.
2 ◀》 09.09 Then listen to questions in Italian about the audio rehearsal you just heard and try to answer the questions out loud in Italian.

Show what you know ...

Here's what you've just learned. Write or say an example for each item in the list. Then tick off the ones you know.

- ☐ Say something you miss using *mancare*.
- ☐ Give two sentences describing where you live.
- ☐ Say 'it's hot' 'it's cold' and 'it's raining'.
- ☐ Give a sentence that uses an adjective to describe a family member's personality. Put the adjective in the right word order and gender.
- ☐ Use three different adjectives to describe your interests – your favourite clothes, digital devices, games?, etc. – in Italian. Put the adjectives in the right word order and gender.
- ☐ Ask the questions:
  - ☐ Can I pay in cash?
  - ☐ Can I pay with a credit card?

COMPLETE YOUR MISSION

It's time to complete your mission: pass for a local and use your descriptive language to point out the best places in town to a foreigner. To do this, you'll need to describe the details and characteristics of different places, people, and things.

STEP 1: build your script

Think about your favourite city. What does it look like? How is the landscape? How would you describe the buildings, the atmosphere, and the people? Build a script to help you give more detailed descriptions of places, people and things. Be sure to:

⋯❯ describe what it's like in your favourite city
⋯❯ say what type of landscape is nearby
⋯❯ say what the weather is usually like
⋯❯ explain what the houses, apartments or neighbourhoods look like
⋯❯ describe the personalities of people living there
⋯❯ match adjectives to the gender and number of the objects they describe.

Write down your script, then repeat it until you feel confident.

STEP 2: a little goes a long way ... *online*

This is your last dress rehearsal before you speak one-on-one with a native speaker!

If you're feeling good about your script, go ahead and give it another go! Go online, find your Unit 9 mission, and share your recording with the community for feedback and encouragement.

STEP 3: learn from other learners

How did other hackers describe their city? After you've uploaded your own clip, check out what the other people in the community have to say. What city are they describing? Would you hire them as a tour guide? Ask them two more questions about the city.

Learn every day, even if it's just a little. You will learn more if you distribute your practice.

STEP 4: reflect on what you've learned

Did you learn any new words or phrases in the community space? Did you find a new place to add to your bucket list? What did you learn about the gaps in your scripts?

HEY, LANGUAGE HACKER, ARE YOU READY?

You've just learned how to describe pretty much anything, as well as how to work around any gaps you may have in your Italian. I know that you're ready for the ultimate mission – do you?

Pronti, partenza ... via!

10 HAVING YOUR FIRST CONVERSATION

Your mission

You've worked hard. You've kept at it. And now, you're armed with a solid base in the Italian language. More importantly, you know how to use clever #languagehacks and conversation strategies to make the Italian phrases you know stretch even further for you.

Your mission is to have a one-on-one conversation – online with video – with a native Italian speaker.

This mission will set you up with the phrases, the confidence, and an insider look at how to have your first conversation in Italian – even if you don't think you're ready.

Mission prep

⋯⋗ Apply what you've learned in the context of a first conversation.
⋯⋗ Prepare the essential phrases you need to have a conversation.
⋯⋗ Develop the mindset: overcome nerves; don't worry about the grammar.
⋯⋗ Find a language partner, and schedule your first conversation!

BUILDING LANGUAGE FOR HAVING A CONVERSATION

Here's where all of the vocabulary – and just as importantly – all of the conversation strategies you've learned over the past nine units come into play. You're going to have your first 'face-to-face' conversation with another Italian speaker! Face-to-face conversations with a native Italian speaker can be intimidating. That's why I like to 'cheat' – by having my first few conversations in a new language with a partner online. This takes off the pressure, and you have the added luxury of being able to quickly search for words or phrases with online translators and dictionaries. Let's take a look at how you can strategize your own first conversations!

#LANGUAGEHACK
develop a cheat sheet and go into 'autopilot' during your first conversation

YOUR FIRST CONVERSATION

**HACK IT:
'Groundhog-Day'**
Through the beauty of
the internet, you can
**have the same 'first
conversation' over
again** with different
language partners until
you feel comfortable
with it. Then start
speaking with the same
people again and again
to push yourself into
new territories.

I suggest you use
this phrase even if
you already know
the name of your
language partner
in advance. After
all, the point of
this conversation is
to practise using
the phrases you
know!

🔊 **10.01** Listen to this sample 'first' conversation between a language
hacker and his Italian conversation partner, Claudio. As you listen,
underline any words or phrases you'd like to use in your own first
conversation with a native speaker.

Claudio:	Ciao!
Language hacker:	Ciao, come ti chiami?
Claudio:	Mi chiamo Claudio, e tu?
Language hacker:	Mi chiamo Benny.
Claudio:	Piacere di conoscerti, Benny. Dimmi, vivi qui?
Language hacker:	Sono irlandese ma ora vivo a New York.
Claudio:	Ah, che interessante! L'Irlanda. Non sono mai stato in Irlanda ma ho visitato New York una volta, a 20 anni. Sei stato in Italia?
Language hacker:	No … non ancora. Un giorno spero … Scusa, vado a lezione di italiano solo da alcune settimane. Puoi parlare più piano?
Claudio:	Oh, certo!
Language hacker:	Sei molto paziente. Grazie che parli con me. Quindi, da quando insegni italiano?

PUT YOUR CONVERSATION STRATEGIES INTO ACTION

What should I say?

Every conversation has a certain 'formula' – phrases you can expect the conversation to include. We've talked a lot about this throughout this course. You can use the expected nature of conversations to your advantage.

Imagine that you're talking with our native Italian speaker, Claudio, for your own first conversation in Italian. In this case, the conversation will flow in a different way. Use the prompts given to practise applying the phrases you know, and fill in the gaps in the conversation.

Claudio: Ciao, piacere …

Language hacker: _____

(Greet your language partner.)

Claudio: Mi chiamo Claudio. E tu?

Language hacker: _____

(Give your name and ask if you can speak in the *tu* form.)

Claudio: Sì, certo!

Language hacker: _____

(Thank him for talking with you today.)

Claudio: Nessun problema, è un piacere. Perché studi italiano?

Language hacker: _____

(Answer his question about why you're learning Italian.)

Claudio: Benissimo! Vuoi parlare altre lingue?

Language hacker: _____

(Say whether or not you want to speak any other languages.)

Claudio: Il mio studente canadese dice che questa lingua è molto difficile!

Language hacker: _____

(Say that you couldn't understand what he said. Ask her to write it out.)

Claudio: Certo. Il mio studente del Canada, Eric, dice che questa lingua non è facile.

Don't take corrections personally. Your language partner knows the reason you're there is to improve your Italian. By correcting you, they're helping you do that!

Now that you've seen two examples of a first conversation in action, let's start preparing you for the real thing.

#LANGUAGEHACK: develop a cheat sheet to go into 'autopilot' during your first conversation

Here's how I know you can handle this conversation, even if you think you're not ready: because you're going to 'cheat', so to speak.

There is no shame in 'cheating here. This isn't an exam. This is a conversation. The way I like to prepare for my conversations online is to make up a cheat sheet of the words and phrases I plan to use during the conversation – and because I'm having my first conversation online, I can have my cheat sheet right in front of me (on paper, another window, or another device), the whole time.

We'll do the same thing for you. You're going to have your own phrases ready, planned out, and written out in front of you, so you'll be able to glance at them while you're speaking Italian. This way, it doesn't matter if your mind goes blank. You'll just take a breath, and look at your cheat sheet.

Consider your cheat sheet as a crutch. It will help you make the transition from studying Italian to *speaking* Italian. Using a cheat sheet now, gives you momentum so that you become a lot more experienced at speaking over less time.

Let's get to work preparing your cheat sheet. I like to separate mine into four parts:

1 Essential phrases
2 Survival phrases
3 Questions I plan to ask
4 'Me-specific' phrases.

ESSENTIAL PHRASES

My essential phrases are the words and phrases I know I'll need to use in every conversation. These are usually greetings and sign-off words, as well as questions I expect to be asked and my planned answers.

I've started you off with some suggestions. Write out the ones you plan to use in Italian, and then add some new ones of your own.

Consider your cheat sheet as stabilizers. It will help you make th transition from studying Italian to speaking Italian. Using a cheat shee now, gives you momentum so that you become a lot more experienced at speaking over less time.

Don't worry about thinking up every possible word or phrase you might need. Instead, let the language tell you what you need to learn. Use the language you know now in natural conversation– however much or little it may be – and you'll quickly learn the 'me-specific' phrases that you haven't (yet!) added to your script.

Essential phrases

(Refer to Units 1–3 for inspiration.)

Greetings	Sign offs
ciao! come va?	alla prossima!
grazie che parli con me	bene, devo andare

(Refer to Units 1–6 for inspiration.)

Typical questions	Prepared answers
come ti chiami?	
di dove sei?/dove vivi?	
dove lavori?	
perché studi italiano?	
parli altre lingue?	

SURVIVAL PHRASES

Don't be afraid of making mistakes in Italian. Instead, expect them. Prepare for them. Have a plan for dealing with difficult moments. Even if you forget every word you know or can't understand a single word the other person is saying, you can still have a conversation if you've prepared your survival phrases.

I've started you off with some suggestions. Add some new ones of your own.

Survival phrases for when I need help

(Refer to Unit 3 for inspiration.)

Full phrases	Or shorten them!
puoi aspettare un momento?	un momento
puoi scriverlo?	scritto, per favore
puoi ripetere?	ancora?
più piano, per favore	piano?
non capisco	cosa?
puoi dirlo di nuovo?	ancora?
_____	_____
_____	_____
_____	_____
_____	_____
_____	_____

While ideally we'd always form full, grammatically correct sentences, in the heat of the moment there is a lot to think about. Don't worry about saying single words to get your point across. You can always add a per favore to the end to make sure your partner knows you don't mean to be impolite!

QUESTIONS I PLAN TO ASK

Plan out a few questions that you can ask the other person. You can use them to take the pressure off, while the other person talks for a while. And they are great to have ready for when there's a lull in the conversation.

I've started you off with a few good options, but make sure you add some more of your own.

···⊁ questions about life in the other person's country (*Fa freddo a Torino?*)
···⊁ questions about the Italian language (*Cosa significa 'quotidiano'?*)
···⊁ questions about the other person's life, work or hobbies (*Cosa vuoi fare il weekend?*).

Speaking Italian with a new person gives you an opportunity to learn about that person's life, language, and culture! I make sure I prepare in advance if there's anything in particular I'm curious to know.

Prepared questions

(Refer to Units 2–9 for inspiration.)

fa caldo a _____ ?

da quanto tempo _____ ?

sai parlare _____ ?

come si dice in italiano _____ ?

mi aiuti a _____ ?

cosa ne pensi di _____ ?

_____ ?

_____ ?

_____ ?

_____ ?

_____ ?

_____ ?

'ME-SPECIFIC' PHRASES I WANT TO PRACTISE

These are the conversation topics specific to me that I want to practise talking about. Things like my interests, what I've been doing lately, what my upcoming plans are, and the people in my life.

In your first conversation, if you've practised your essential phrases and your survival phrases, everything from there is just a bonus!

In my online conversations, I like to create a goal of a few new phrases I want to practise during each conversation. But keep it to just a few (2–5 phrases) which is plenty to accomplish in your first conversation. You could prepare to talk about:

···⟩ what you're interested in (*Adoro la fantascienza!*)
···⟩ what you've been doing today or lately (*Ho letto un articolo sui treni in Italia.*)
···⟩ what your upcoming plans are (*Voglio ballare questo weekend.*)
···⟩ the people in your life (*La mia ragazza parla un po' di italiano.*).

Me-specific phrases

mi piace (molto) ...

voglio ...

il mio amico (la mia amica) ...

_____

_____

_____

_____

_____

_____

_____

_____

GETTING READY FOR YOUR FIRST CONVERSATION

I highly suggest having your first few conversations online with video enabled. Technology really is your friend in this situation. In an online chat, you can easily refer to your notes, and you can even look up words on the spot or put phrases you need into an online translator – right in the middle of the conversation.

Know this: if all else fails, you can have an entire conversation in Italian even if you only know these three phrases: *Non capisco. Puoi scriverlo? Un momento*. Don't believe me? Envision it. Worst case scenario:

···⟩ Your conversation partner says *ciao*, you say *ciao* (success!). But then she says, @yego^3*8ham#3pt9ane1&? And your mind goes blank.

···⟩ You reply with *Non capisco. Puoi scriverlo*, per favore?

···⟩ She types out what she said and sends it to you via chat. You select what she wrote, copy and paste it and quickly find a translation. Ah, you think, I understand! But now it's your turn to respond, and your mind, again, goes blank.

···⟩ You say, *Un momento*. She waits patiently while you type what you want to say in English into your online translator. You hit enter and get a translation in Italian. You read out the words in your best Italian accent.

···⟩ Rinse and repeat.

Is this scenario ideal? No. But is it better than not having a conversation at all? *Absolutely*.

Luckily, you've already been preparing for this moment for the past nine missions. So you're ready – even if you think you're not. Trust me on this. Here's how I suggest you set yourself up for your conversation:

···⟩ Open up your cheat sheet and keep it within easy view.

···⟩ Have your translation tool ready. (See our Resources!)

···⟩ Get ready to connect the call.

···⟩ Just before your conversation, practise listening to and repeating some Italian audio.

In fact, you'd be surprised by how much you'd learn even in this worst-case scenario. Even if you forgot every single phrase you learned in Italian except these three, you could have a conversation (of sorts) in Italian with another person. And you would learn loads of Italian by the end of it.

Automatic translation is never a replacement for language learning, but it works as a crutch at a pinch!

This will get your ears and your tongue 'warmed up' for the conversation. We've provided one for you at the end of this unit. (Additional audio resources are recommended in our Resources).

WHAT TO EXPECT

The first conversation is always the hardest, and it's always the most nerve-wracking. But it's a completely crucial first step towards becoming comfortable as a beginner Italian learner. Beginners make mistakes. And as a beginner Italian learner, you shouldn't expect to know all (or most) of the words. You should expect the opposite. During this conversation, don't focus on saying things perfectly. Focus on getting your point across. Being understood – communicating with another human being – is the main goal here. Don't stress about knowing all the grammar, using precisely the right word, or having a perfect accent.

Let's review some of the skills you've learned throughout this course. They'll come in handy in your first conversation!

···> **Rephrasing** – Remember, you'll need to take many of the phrases you want to say, and rephrase them so that they're much more basic (but still convey the same idea). Rephrasing your thoughts into simpler forms is an essential skill for language hackers.

···> **'Tarzan Italian'** – Don't be afraid to speak in 'Tarzan Italian'! If you know how to say something right, say it right. But if you know how to say something kind of wrong, then say it wrong! Your language partner will help you figure out the wording you need.

···> **Learn from your gaps** – Despite rephrasing, you'll realize that there's still a lot you don't yet know how to say. And as you talk, you'll realize you've been pronouncing some words wrong. Your partner may correct you. Good! This is valuable information. Take note of the phrases you wish you knew. You can learn it in advance for next time.

···> **When in doubt, guess!** – Finally, if you're not sure what your conversation partner just said, guess! Use context – facial expressions in the video feed and whatever words you do understand – to infer the meaning of the entire phrase.

Talking one-on-one with another person is the best language practice you can get. If there's one secret to #languagehacking, this is it.

Enjoy your first conversation, and the many others to come!

HANDLING YOUR NERVES
It's typical for a beginner learner to expect to be judged by another speaker. If you find yourself staring at the screen, afraid to push that Call button – and we've all been there – have a friend nearby to boost your confidence (and maybe give you that extra push to get started!). The other person is probably just as nervous as you! If you are doing a language exchange and plan to also help your partner with their English, then they may be worried more about how their English sounds than how you sound speaking Italian. If you are starting with a new teacher, he or she may be hoping to make a good first impression.

COMPLETING UNIT 10

One mission left to go! Review the phrases and conversation strategies from the unit one more time. When you're feeling confident, listen to the audio rehearsal, which will help you practise your listening, pronunciation and speaking skills.

1 Practise answering common questions.

🔊 **10.02** Listen to the audio rehearsal, which will ask you questions in Italian.

⋯⋗ Give spoken answers in Italian that are true for you.
⋯⋗ Pause or replay the audio as often as you need.

2 🔊 **10.03** In this audio rehearsal, an Italian speaker talks casually about herself. Listen to the audio, and after each clip, use what you understand (or can infer) to answer questions about the speaker.

⋯⋗ What is her name? _____
⋯⋗ Where is she from? _____
⋯⋗ Where does she live now? _____
⋯⋗ How long has she been teaching Italian? _____
⋯⋗ Does she speak any other languages? If so, which ones? _____
_____

⋯⋗ What are some of the things she is interested in? _____
_____

Show what you know ...

Are you ready for your final mission? Before you move on, make sure to:

☐ Write up the essential phrases you'll need into your cheat sheet.
☐ Write up survival phrases and add them to your cheat sheet.
☐ Prepare 2–5 'me-specific' phrases you want to practise. Add them to your cheat sheet.
☐ Prepare at least three questions you plan to ask. Add them to your cheat sheet.

CONVERSATION STRATEGY: *warm up before your first conversation!* Practising with audio is one of the best ways to prepare for a conversation. An hour or two before your Italian conversation begins, come back to these exercises and replay them to help you get into the flow of Italian.

HACK IT: *focus on the skills you need now* This is exactly what you'll be doing in your first conversation – listening to your partner's end of the conversation and using a combination of your new #languagehacking skills and, as well as context to help you even through the tricky parts.

Remember that perfectionism is your enemy. If you guess right, the conversation will advance, and if you guess wrong, the earth won't open up and swallow you whole. In fact, you'll have had an opportunity to learn something new. That's what this is all about, after all!

Don't forget, you can always **ask for specific help** ... whether it's learning new phrases, or improving your pronunciation, it's always OK to ask for the help you need!

LEARNING STRATEGY:
My partner Lauren likes to set up a 'conversation bingo' for herself when she's practising a language online. She writes out a few phrases she wants to practise during the call (either by speaking them or hearing them), and tries to cross off as many as she can.

WHAT ARE YOUR GOALS?

One more thing. It helps to know before you set up your first chat what you want to accomplish or what phrases you'd like to practise. Be realistic, but ambitious! And be flexible – you never know where a conversation will take you, and that's a very good thing for language learners.

Write out a few notes on what you want to practise during your first conversation, or create your own bingo sheet! Then, find your language partner.

COMPLETE YOUR MISSION

It's time to complete your mission: having a one-on-one conversation with a native ... online. To do this, you'll need to prepare to:

···▷ say hello and use essential greeting vocabulary
···▷ say goodbye or set up a time to talk again
···▷ ask at least three questions
···▷ give your answers to commonly asked questions
···▷ use survival phrases when you can't understand or need help.

STEP 1: find your conversation partner and schedule your first conversation

Follow our Resources guide to find a conversation partner online and schedule your first chat with them now.

When you're setting up your first conversation online, the first thing to do is send out a few messages to the exchange partners or teachers who look like a good fit for you. Break the ice and send them a message (in Italian of course!) to set up your first chat. A good icebreaker tells the other person:

···❭ your name
···❭ your language level
···❭ what you'd like to practise or discuss during the conversation.

Example:

Ciao! Mi chiamo Melissa. Voglio parlare italiano con te. Voglio dire frasi semplici. Per esempio, il mio nome e il mio paese. Sono principiante, quindi grazie per la tua pazienza!

Be friendly, and give a short intro about yourself and explain what you want to practise – but don't say too much. Save some phrases for the conversation! Write out your own icebreaker now.

HACK IT: *pressure is your friend.* Schedule your conversation for tomorrow or the earliest possible slot. Don't give yourself a long window to get ready – overthinking this step can lead to procrastination later. Make a request for the next time slot, and don't look back!

STEP 2: go all the way ... *online*

The first time might be scary, but it will get easier! So go online and have your first conversation in Italian for an authentic and good time!

Here's what to do during your conversation:

···❭ Practise rephrasing your thoughts into simple forms.
···❭ Speak 'Tarzan Italian' if you have to – it's better than nothing!
···❭ Take note of any 'gaps' in your Italian vocabulary.
···❭ Write down any phrases or words you want to say, but don't know yet.
···❭ Write down new words or phrases you want to review later.

Remember, your first conversation is just that – a first conversation. The only way to get to your 50th conversation is to get the first one out of the way, then keep going from there.

STEP 3: learn from other learners, and share your experience!

Tell the community how it went! (Or, if you're nervous, head over to see how other people's first conversations went.) **Your task is to ask or answer at least three questions from other learners:**

···⟩ Were you nervous? How did you handle your nerves?

···⟩ What was your teacher or exchange partner like?

···⟩ What went well? what didn't? What would you do differently next time?

STEP 4: reflect on what you've learned

After your first conversation, it's easy to focus on the words you didn't know or the things you couldn't say. But it's much more productive to focus on your successes instead. Were you 'only' able to give your name, your job, and say that you live with your cat? Those are huge wins! Don't overlook those achievements.

···⟩ What were your wins? What phrases were you able to say or understand?

···⟩ Review the notes you took during your conversation. What words did you need that you didn't know yet? What new words did you learn?

HEY, LANGUAGE HACKER, YOU JUST HAD A CONVERSATION IN ITALIAN

Or at least I hope so!

You just broke one of the biggest barriers in language learning! Now that you've crossed the threshold, you're on a fast track to fluency in Italian that most people only ever dream about. Enjoy this milestone.

And remember – your second conversation will be even better than your first. Your third will be even better than that. Schedule your next spoken lesson now – don't put it off – that ticking clock is a powerful motivator for language hackers.

Your next mission: *continua così!* keep it up!

ANSWER KEY

UNIT 1

CONVERSATION 1

Figure it out **1** I am. **2** Ciao (Hello!) e benvenuta a Roma. (and welcome to Rome.) **3** E tu?
4 a. giornalista b. americana c. Roma

Notice 1 a. sono b. vivo a c. E tu? d. Sono italiano. **2** Parlami di te!

Practice 1 b. Examples: Giappone, Germania, Brasile (countries); giapponese, tedesco, brasiliano
(nationalities); ingegnere, professore, traduttore (professions), videogiochi, pesca, pallacanestro
(interests) **2** a. Example: Sono Richard. b. Example: Sono inglese. c. Example: Sono (un) dentista.
d. Example: Vivo a Londra.

Put it together Examples: Sono Richard. Sono inglese. Sono (un) dentista. Vivo a Londra.

CONVERSATION 2

Figure it out **1** Cosa ti piace? **2** a. la pizza b. Non mi piace la bruschetta. c. dormire
3 a. letteratura b. adoro c. musei d. visitare **4** Examples: pizza pizza, cinema cinema, attivo active,
tennis tennis, sport sport, preferito preferred

Notice **1** Italian literally translates to: 'to-me it-pleases' (Mi piace). **2** a. musei b. mi piace
c. amo d. adoro e. non mi piace f. letteratura g. visitare

Practice **1** Example: La pallacanestro (Il basket) è il mio sport preferito. **2** Examples:
a. La pasta è il mio cibo preferito. b. *Titanic* è il mio film preferito. c. La Galleria Nazionale è il mio
museo preferito

Your turn: use the hack **2** Examples: americana, giornalista, studiare, ovviamente, pizza,
cinema, letteratura, attivo, visitare, musei, adoro, tennis, sport, preferito **3** Examples: geografia,
organizzazione, taxista, possibilità, influenza, discussione, divisione

Grammar explanation: verb + noun 1 Examples: a. Amo/Adoro il caffè. b. Mi piace la
televisione. c. Non mi piace parlare inglese.

Put it together Example: Mi piace parlare italiano. Voglio un caffè. Amo la musica italiana. Mi
piace dormire. Non amo lo sport. Non mi piace visitare i musei.

...it out **1** Perché? = Why? Perché ... = Because ... **2** voglio parlare una bella lingua; ...o capire la cultura italiana; voglio vivere e lavorare in Italia; la musica italiana è molto ...teressante **3** a. Italian culture b. classical music or pop music c. in Italy **4** Example: cultura, interessante **5** Voglio is the io (I) form. Vuoi is the tu (you) form.

Conversation strategy **1** a. o b. ma c. e d. perché **2** a. Il cinema è interessante. b. La cultura è differente qui. **3** imparare, parlare, capire, vivere, lavorare **4** a. Voglio imparare b. Amo parlare c. Adoro vivere **5** a. cultura b. lingua c. musica d. interessante e. classica f. pop

Practice **1** a. Trovo b. Voglio vivere c. Mi piace imparare d. Visito e. Voglio f. Mi piace mangiare g. Voglio studiare h. Voglio capire **2** a. Amo parlare italiano. b. Non mi piace visitare i musei. c. Mi piace imparare le lingue. d. Voglio visitare l'Italia. **3** Examples: a. Mi piace la pasta e mi piace il caffè. b. Mi piace il tennis ma non mi piace il rugby. c. Ti piace la musica classica o ti piace la musica pop? d. Mi piace il cinema perché è interessante.

Put it together Example: Voglio imparare l'italiano perché è una bella lingua e visito presto l'Italia. Mi piace la musica classica ma non mi piace la musica pop. Voglio conoscere gli italiani e la cultura italiana. Amo studiare le lingue ma non il giapponese.

COMPLETE YOUR MISSION

Build your script Example: Sono Richard e sono un insegnante. Sono americano e vivo in Italia a Roma. Visito l'Italia perché mi piace la cultura e perché lavoro qui in una scuola di lingue. Voglio imparare l'italiano perché mi piace parlare le lingue.

UNIT 2

CONVERSATION 1

Figure it out **1** a. Due (Two) b. Sì c. No **2** a. falso b. falso c. vero **3** Sì, certo/Sì davvero. **4** You add 'non' before the verb. The word is non. **5** a. Non voglio imparare lo spagnolo. b. Non vivo a Milano. c. Non amo l'arte moderna. d. Non mi piace viaggiare.

Notice **1** bene, un po' **2** a. Parlo solo italiano. b. Amo solo la musica classica.

Grammar explanation: 'don't' a. Sì, mangio carne. No, non mangio carne. b. Sì, lavoro in ospedale. No, non lavoro in ospedale. c. Sì, voglio venire alla festa. No, non voglio venire alla festa.

Practice **1** a. Parlo solo inglese b. Imparo un po' di russo c. Imparo tanto italiano qui a Roma. d. Davvero! Non parlo italiano! e. Oggi studio (lo) spagnolo! **2** a. R b. R c. D d. D e. D f. R **3** a. Alessandro vive a Roma? b. Parli spagnolo? c. Marco impara l'italiano?

Put it together   **1** a. tedesco b. francese c. cinese d. Example: spagnolo. e. Example: russo   **2** a. Example: Sì parlo francese, tedesco e un po' di cinese. Example: No, non parlo altre lingue. Parlo solo inglese. b. Example: Sì, voglio imparare il russo. Example: No, non voglio imparare altre lingue.

CONVERSATION 2

Figure it out   **1** a. solo due settimane (for only two weeks) b. tre lingue: l'inglese, il giapponese e l'arabo c. il giapponese – perché mi piace la cultura giapponese   **2** a. 3 b. 2 c. 4 d. 1
3 a. especially b. difficult   **4** Parli molto bene italiano.   **5** a. Prego b. Da quando c. Quante

Notice   **1** Da quando, 'when'   **2** a. Melissa studia italiano da due settimane. b. Luca spera di imparare l'inglese, il giapponese e l'arabo.   **3** a. è vero b. La cultura è interessante.   **4** a. Quante b. Studio la lingua da febbraio c. Parlo due lingue. d. Da quando

Practice   **1** quanti, qui   **2** a. cinque giorni b. tre anni c. otto mesi d. quattro settimane. e. Vivo in Italia da Capodanno. f. Studio italiano da nove settimane. **4** Example: Studio italiano da 2 mesi.

Put it together
4 a. Da quando vivi in Italia? b. Da quando insegni l'italiano?

CONVERSATION 3

Figure it out   **1** What are you doing? How do you do (that)?   **2** ogni settimana, ogni giorno
3 a. Ogni settimana b. Ogni giorno   **4** a. è facile, è vero b. allora, ah, be' c. vocaboli, lezione, idea, Internet, interessante   **5** a. vero b. falso c. vero d. falso

Notice   a. Mi sembra b. Sono d'accordo c. Devo d. Semplice! e. Quello aiuta!

Practice   **1** a. parli b. visiti c. vedi d. rispondi e. senti   **2** amo – ami, imparo – impari, mangio – mangi, dormo – dormi, scrivo – scrivi, lavoro – lavori, decido – decidi   **3** a. Vivi b. Voglio c. Studio d. Faccio e. Voglio   **4** a. Cosa, fare b. Studi, vocaboli c. faccio d. Lavoro, settimana e. Imparo, ogni giorno   **5** a. Mi piace parlare italiano. b. Devi mangiare qui. c. Sai che imparo italiano da due settimane. d. Ami/Adori parlare italiano.

Put it together   Examples: Voglio parlare quattro lingue. Vado spesso in Italia. Devo parlare con tanti italiani. Ora studio il giapponese.

COMPLETE YOUR MISSION

Build your script   Example: Da quando vivi qui? Cosa ti piace fare il fine settimana? Parlo tre lingue. Parlo bene il francese e il tedesco e parlo un po' d'italiano. Spero di imparare il russo, faccio lezione su Internet ogni giorno. Imparo l'italiano da due settimane

UNIT 3

CONVERSATION 1

Figure it out **1** a. vero b. falso c. vero **2** a. grazie b. prego c. per favore **3** a. no problem b. What's your name? **4** What city are you in? (In which city are you?)

Notice **1** Più piano, per favore. **2** a. È un piacere conoscerti. b. Tutto bene. c. Adesso sono a Londra. d. Dove ti trovi? **3** a. to meet/know you b. you are (in a location / lit. you find yourself) c. my name's

Practice **2** a. 3 b. 6 c. 4 d. 1 e. 5 f. 2 **3** a. molto, oggi b. è, tutto c. Dove, adesso d. Devi insegnarmi

Grammar explanation: word order with objects **1** Column 4: dirmi, aiutarti, darti, inviarti, scriverti, chiamarti; non mangiarlo **2** a. Ti do. b. Non lo vedo. c. Puoi aiutarmi? d. Non ti sento. **3** a. Lo capisco. b. Puoi scriverlo? c. Mi vedi? d. Voglio dirti … **4** a. Non voglio disturbarti. b. Puoi dirmi? c. Voglio inviarlo. d. Non posso chiamarti.

Put it together Examples: a. Sono a Milano. b. Adesso studio italiano con il mio insegnante. c. Vedo un film in italiano. d. Visito i musei di Milano.

CONVERSATION 2

Figure it out
1 a. vero b. falso c. falso
2 a. interesting b. repeat c. reason d. moment **3** a. Do you live in another city? b. Can you repeat (that)? c. I can't hear you well. d. Can you hear me?

Notice **1** a. vivo, vivi b. sono, sei c. puoi, dici d. lavoro, sento e. capisco, non capisco

Conversation strategy: survival phrases **1** Più piano, per favore (Conv A), Mi dispiace (Conv B), Non capisco (Conv B), Puoi ripetere? (Conv B), Un momento (Conv B), Non ti sento (Conv B) **2** Examples: a. Non capisco. Puoi aiutarmi? b. Imparo italiano solo da un mese. Puoi parlare più piano?

Practice **1** Examples: a. Dove vivi? b. Cosa dici? c. In quale altra città vuoi vivere? d. Perché vuoi lavorare a Roma? e. Lavori in un'università? Ho capito bene? **2** b. Why? Perché?, Where? Dove?, When? Quando?, Who? Chi?, How many? Quanti? Quante?, Can you? Puoi? **3** a. Quando? b. Quanti? c. Chi? d. Dove? e. Perché?

Put it together Example: Sono americano, ma adesso vivo a Pisa. Vivo a Pisa da un anno. Vivo a Pisa perché mi piace l'arte italiana e mi piace parlare italiano. Lavoro in una scuola da sei mesi, insegno inglese.

CONVERSATION 3

Figure it out   **1** a. deactivate b. install c. connection   **2** a. vero b. vero c. falso d. vero
3 a. nuovo b. Mi dispiace c. A presto, Alla prossima d. Ho bisogno di   **4** a. tranquilla/o b. va bene
c. non è la mia/il mio d. forse e. sai   **5** settimana; it's feminine, because it ends in -a   **6** 'la mia'
means my

Conversation strategy: use 'Tarzan Italian'   a. Più piano, per favore. b. Quanto (costa)?
c. Supermercato, dove?

Conversation strategy: memorize the power nouns   a. luogo dei libri b. persona
del ristorante

Notice   **1** a. ho b. posso c. mi senti d. chiamare e. credo   **2** certo, tranquilla/tranquillo   **3** non
ricordo la parola

Practice
1 a. Penso che / Credo che funziona b. Pensi che posso c. Posso dire d. Puoi chiamare e. Devo
lavorare f. Devo avere g. Devi parlare **2** a. Puoi installare, nuovo b. Se vuoi, posso aiutare c. prossima,
spero di avere d. Non, dove è. e. ti sento, Puoi ripetere?

Grammar explanation: mio / mia / miei / mie (my)   a. mio b. tua c. tue

Your turn: use the hack   **1** a. un popolo b. una città c. una commedia d. un organismo e. un
appartamento f. una differenza g. un teatro h. una pace i. una religione j. un telefono k. un vino
l. una libreria m. un peperone n. un poema o. un'azione   **2** a. il popolo b. la città c. la commedia
d. l'organismo e. l'appartamento f. la differenza g. il teatro h. la pace i. la religione j. il telefono
k. il vino l. la libreria m. il peperone n. il poema o. l'azione   **3** Mascolinità ends in -à, femminismo
ends in -o.

Put it together   Example: Forse il nuovo smartphone funziona bene. Ho un portatile e uno
smartphone. Ho bisogno di (comprare) un computer nuovo.

COMPLETE YOUR MISSION

Build your script È una persona famosa. Lavora nel cinema. È un uomo molto famoso in Italia.
È un pirata pazzo. Dice sempre… dove rum?

UNIT 4

CONVERSATION 1

Figure it out

1 a. vero b. falso, Melissa asks Paola to sit next to her c. falso, Paola is very patient. 2 a. Sono di Milano. b. Scusa, parli italiano? c. Ti dispiace se pratico il mio italiano con te? d. sono ancora principiante 3 a. italiani b. paziente c. principiante 4 a. Parliamo! b. Non ti preoccupare!

Notice
1 a. Parli italiano? Ti dispiace se pratico il mio italiano con te? b. Ti dispiace se…?
2 a. ancora b. già c. tanto d. ancora e. già f. tanto

Practice
1 a. Impariamo parole nuove ogni giorno. b. Parliamo più piano con i principianti.
c. Vediamo insieme lo spettacolo. d. Ascoltiamo la radio.

Put it together
1 Ti dispiace se parlo con te? Ti dispiace se apro la finestra? 2 Example 1: ah, parli italiano!; Sono ancora un/a principiante; Imparo … solo da … Example 2: Per me è una bella lingua!; E un giorno spero di andare in Italia. Example 3: Ti dispiace se … parlo con te?/… tocco il tuo cane?/… mi siedo qui?/.. .apro la finestra?

CONVERSATION 2

Figure it out
1 a. Milano b. Assisi c. avere – ho 2 a. Quanto tempo resti a Roma? b. per alcuni mesi 3 Masculine; we see *il* before it, as well as 'o' ending adjective *prossimo*. 4 a. maybe next month b. you mean c. there's a lot to do 5 a. 6 b. 3 c. 4 d. 1 e. 2 f. 5

Notice
1 a. perché non visiti b. Voglio dire c. Vuoi dire 2 per alcuni mesi 3 a. 4 b. 1 c. 5 d. 3 e. 6 f. 2 4 a. Viaggi molto? b. Vediamo la Cappella Sistina domani. c. Voglio visitare Milan.
d. Prendo un taxi in città.

Practice
1 a. prendere b. prendo c. prendi 2 a. Prendo il treno b. Vado in macchina. c. Vado in aereo a Londra. 3 a. il weekend b. questo weekend c. il prossimo weekend d. ogni weekend 4 a. vai, per vedere b. visitare, come, e c. per andare, devi d. andare in treno, andare in macchina e. ci sono, ragioni

Put it together
1 Examples: a. Vado a Parigi. b. Per dieci giorni. c. Vado il prossimo mese.
d. Vado in aereo.

CONVERSATION 3

Figure it out
1 a. falso She wants to see the Colosseum b. vero c. vero d. falso Paola thinks this. e. vero 2 a. Per i suoi fantastici ristoranti. b. bere 3 a. The favourite place of D'Annunzio b. You will be busy (You have a lot to do). 4 a. Cosa vuoi fare a Roma? b. Voglio fare le stesse cose.

Notice **1** a. per cominciare b. poi c. per finire **2** a. voglio vedere b. vuoi **3** a. Ecco il mio numero di telefono, Ecco il mio indirizzo email b. Puoi darmi il tuo numero? Puoi darmi il tuo indirizzo email?

Practice **1** a. 4 b. 6 c. 5 d. 2 e. 3 f. 1 **2** a. Un momento, ti do il mio numero di telefono. b. Stasera ho molto da fare, ma domani sono libero. c. Non lo vedo ancora … aspetta … eccolo. d. Non so se posso. e. Vado al bar con tutti. Vuoi venire con me? f. Andiamo in treno insieme, d'accordo? **3** a. Voglio viaggiare in Italia. b. Dove posso passare il tempo? c. Non lo sai già? d. No… Non pensi di potermi aiutare? e. Certo. Per cominciare puoi sederti con me. f. Mangiamo e ti dico come scoprire il mio posto preferito.

Your turn: use the hack **1** a. Ho molto da fare domani! b. Faccio molto stasera. c. Mi chiami domani? d. Mangi al ristorante questa settimana? e. Non vado a Venezia la prossima settimana. **2** a. Voglio nuotare/Vado a nuotare nel mare b. Vogliamo/Possiamo parlare italiano insieme. c. Ti piace bere il caffè? **3** a. Non hai molto da fare. b. Sei molto occupato (domani). c. Parli italiano stasera? d. Vogliamo andare a Roma.

Put it together **1** Example: Per cominciare, voglio visitare la città. Poi voglio vedere la mia amica Annamaria. Voglio visitare i musei. Per mangiare vado al ristorante. Voglio vedere tanti negozi. **2** Example: Ecco qui il numero del mio cellulare e il mio indirizzo email. Puoi mandarmi un messaggio o un'email domani?

COMPLETE YOUR MISSION

Build your script Vado in Italia. Voglio visitare il Colosseo e i Musei Vaticani. Voglio mangiare le lasagne e i gelati. Per cominciare vado a vedere 'Piazza di Spagna'. Vado in giugno perché non fa troppo caldo. Vado in aereo e poi visito la città in autobus. Non viaggio da solo. Viaggio con mio fratello e mia sorella.

UNIT 5

CONVERSATION 1

Figure it out **1** a. Who is she? b. What is her name? **2** a. vero b. falso, 'a lawyer'– ingegnere c. falso, 'has been in Rome for only a week' – conosce Melissa per una settimana d. vero e. falso, 'This weekend' – prossimo weekend **3** a. questa b. il prossimo c. domani d. poi e. ogni estate **4** a. Cosa mi dici di nuovo? b. Chi è? c. la mia studentessa preferita d. infatti e. Sono contenta di

Notice

1 a. di vedere il film. b. di essere qui. c. di dire che posso viaggiare. d. di questo lavoro.
e. di questo ristorante. **2** è, si chiama, si chiama, è, è, resta, resta, è
3 a. (Lui) è b. visitiamo c. esco d. passiamo e. (Lei) è f. vogliamo andare **4** a. passo (del) tempo
b. abbiamo in programma c. passiamo il weekend
5 a. La conosco da (I have known her since). In English 'her' is placed after the verb, in Italian 'la' is
placed before. b. La vedo.

Practice

2 a. Hai fratelli o sorelle? b. È vicino? c. Io e il mio amico Jim vogliamo cominciare/
iniziare/avviare un'attività insieme. d. Mia mamma è una dottoressa. Lavora in un ospedale. e. Amo
passare il weekend con i miei figli. f. Parlo con mio fratello tutto il tempo e lo vedo spesso. g. Io e la
mia famiglia passiamo sempre l'estate insieme. h. Dove lavora (lui)? i. La mia ragazza fa jogging ogni
giorno. **3** a. Examples: Il mio miglior amico si chiama Michele. b. Lo conosco da dodici anni. c. Fa il
meccanico.

Your turn: use the hack

a. Non mi piace il gelato qui. Vuoi andare in un altro posto? (I don't
like the ice-cream here. Do you want to go to another place?) b. Voglio vedere il film stasera, e tu?
(I want to watch the film tonight, and you?)

Put it together

Example: La mia persona preferita è la mia migliore amica. Si chiama Jenny e
vive a Londra da sola. Non lavora, ma ha molti interessi. La conosco da dieci anni. Le piace l'arte e le
piace soprattutto visitare i musei e parchi di questa città.

CONVERSATION 2

Figure it out

1 a. molto tempo/20 anni. b. casa di Giacomo. c. (Melissa) è single.
2 a. sposata b. single c. coinquillino. **3** Feminine **4** a. Quando ritorno. b. Vuoi dire. c. Per esempio

Notice

1 si chiama, conosce, rompe **2** Il cane di mio fratello

Vocab explanation: sapere and conoscere

a. Conosco b. Sai c. Conosciamo d. sa

Practice

1 Example: a. Sono sposata, da molto tempo. b. Sì, ho due figli, un maschio e una
femmina. c. Vivo con mio marito. **2** a. Da dove vieni? b. Con chi vai? c. A che ora comincia la
lezione? **3** a. Vuoi dire ...? b. Vuol dire ... c. Vuol dire ... d. Vogliamo dire ... **4** a. Conosco il mio
migliore amico da cinque anni. Siamo molto simili. b. Oggi è il compleanno di mia madre.

Put it together

Example: Conosco mio marito da tanti anni. Lui è di una città in Essex, io sono
di Torino. Stiamo insieme da trent'anni e abbiamo un figlio e una figlia. La mia famiglia parla inglese
ma sa anche parlare un po' d'italiano. Vogliamo imparare il tedesco perché abbiamo amici tedeschi.

CONVERSATION 3

Figure it out 1 a. Four. (Siamo in quattro). b. She doesn't know. (Non lo sa). c. Non sono il mio tipo. 2 a. We have two children. b. How do you say in Italian? c. Italian men 3 a. si chiamano b. Che nomi splendidi! c. non si sa mai

Grammar explanation: loro (they) 1 a. vogliono b. parlano c. mangiano d. sperano c. viaggiano

2

Dictionary form	Io form	Tu form	Lui/ lei form	Noi form	Loro form
volere	voglio	vuoi	vuole	vogliamo	vogliono
essere	sono	sei	è	siamo	sono
andare	vado	vai	va	andiamo	vanno
conoscere	conosco	conosci	conosce	conosciamo	conoscono
capire	capisco	capisci	capisce	capiamo	capiscono

Practice 1 Non è possibile! 2 a. 6 b. 3 c. 4 d. 5 e. 1 f. 2 3 a. è. b. sono. c. vuole viaggiare d. vogliono

Put it together Example: Nella mia famiglia siamo in tre e viviamo a Manchester. I miei genitori si chiamano Jack e Claire. Lui ha 56 anni e lei 55. Mio padre è professore e mia madre lavora come segretaria. Ho sei buoni amici dell'università e lavoriamo insieme in una società informatica. Non ho un cane, ma io e la mia ragazza vogliamo comprare un gatto.

COMPLETE YOUR MISSION

Build your script La persona più importante della mia vita è la mia ragazza. È molto importante per me perché mi aiuta ogni giorno. La mia ragazza è una persona molto determinata, ottimista e molto simpatica. La conosco da 7 anni e stiamo insieme da 6 anni. La mia ragazza è professoressa e lavora all'università. È una persona molto speciale.

UNIT 6

CONVERSATION 1

Figure it out 1 gnocchi; un bicchiere di vino bianco 2 are you ready? (have you decided?) 3 you-plural: fate, avete deciso. formal you: Lei, mi può portare?, E per Lei? 4 a. per me, gli gnocchi, b. io prendo i ravioli, c. vorrei un bicchiere di vino bianco, mi può portare del vino rosso e ancora un po' d'acqua? 5 a. E da bere?, b. Cosa prendi? c. Abbiamo già deciso.

Notice   1 The literal Italian translation is 'I-have hunger', not 'I'm hungry'.   2 a. Ci porta dell'acqua frizzante?/Mi può portare ancora un po' d'acqua? b. Vorrei un bicchiere di vino bianco./Mi può portare …   3 a. prendo … b. Per me … c. Prendiamo … d. Mi può portare … e. Vorrei …
4 a. 4 b. 1 c. 2 d. 3

Practice   1 a. mangiare b. bere c. leggere   2 a. Abbiamo b. un po' c. vino, lei prende, bicchiere d. familiar tu: Cosa desideri; formal Lei: Cosa desidera e. già fame   3 Examples: a. some, del b. a, un c. some, dell'

Put it together   1 Examples: Sì, prendo gli asparagi./Come primo vorrei le fettuccine con olio e basilico./Un vino rosso e un bicchiere d'acqua naturale./Scusi?/Sì, e ho già deciso per il dolce./Un sorbetto al limone.   2 Example: Voglio mangiare gli spaghetti all'olio, aglio, peperoncino rosso. Devo comprare gli spaghetti e il peperoncino, gli altri ingredienti li ho già in casa. Vorrei bere un buon bicchiere di vino rosso e acqua naturale. Di solito, cucino a casa.

CONVERSATION 2

Figure it out   1 a. Cappella Sistina, Pantheon. b. Cappella Sistina. c. non è così interessante. d. troviamo un compromesso, d'accordo, ci sto   2 a. quello con più turisti b. ci sono molti turisti c. c'è meno gente d. ci sono meno turisti e. Se per te   3 a. Dobbiamo vedere il Mar Mediterraneo. b. Perché la spiaggia è più rilassante.   4 a. ovviamente b. sono d'accordo c. non sono d'accordo d. non è vero!   5 a. better than. b. less/fewer. c. find/consider

Notice   1 hai ragione (you have reason), ho fame (I have hunger)   2 a. il/la più. b. meglio. c. meno
3 a. lo/la trovo b. so che c. sai che d. so che ci sono e. sai che ci sono f. è unico   4 a. 3 b. 4 c. 2 d. 1 e. 6 f. 5

Grammar explanation: a. più simpatico b. più affascinante c. più libri d. più famoso e. il ristorante migliore/il miglior ristorante f. un amico migliore g. un uomo più giovane h. meno difficile i. meno giorni j. meno caro k. il film peggiore/il peggior film l. qualità peggiore

Practice   1 a. Ci sono solo tre studenti qui? b. Ci sono dei libri in casa mia. c. Trovo che ci sono meno cani al parco oggi.   2 a. Milano è più grande di Trieste. b. C'è meno gente qui che a casa tua. c. Trovo questo ristorante troppo piccolo.

Put it together   Example: Ci sono tanti posti in Australia che vorrei visitare. Le cose migliori che posso fare lì sono il surf, andare al mare e visitare il deserto. Bisogna assolutamente vedere Sydney. Melbourne è meno grande, ma più carina di Canberra, la capitale. Secondo me bisogna rimanere almeno un mese in Australia.

CONVERSATION 3

Figure it out   1 a. La musica (pop) di Laura Pausini. b. I testi delle sue canzoni. c. Un libro sulla politica in inglese.   2 a. frankly. b. certainly.   3 a. Dov'è il cameriere? b. Che cosa consiglia (lei)? c. Il conto, per favore.   4 a. secondo me b. la migliore. c. mi sembra   5 a. vorrei
b. ti do c. mi puoi consigliare

Notice   1 a. ti piace di sicuro. b. mi piace.   2 a. 3 b. 1 c. 5 d. 2 e. 4   3 a. Che cosa consigli?
b. Mi puoi consigliare ... c. Dimmi una cosa.

Practice   1 a. Voglio chiedere un po' d'acqua... più tempo... un'altra bibita b. Examples:
Vorrei sapere di più su come preparare un tiramisù. Vorrei sapere di più su quali posti visitare a Roma.   2 a. l'arte, Mi piace di più dell'arte moderna. b. Secondo te, è più. c. devo darti il

Your turn: use the hack   1 a. sfortunatamente mi sembra che ... b. secondo me c. detto tra noi d. è per questa ragione   2 a. Mi sembra che non capisco, b. Secondo me. c. È per questa ragione. d. Detto tra noi. e. Sfortunatamente. f. A dire la verità.   3 Examples: a. Detto tra noi, non credo di conoscere una persona che cucina meglio di te. b. Vivo a Milano, in un appartamento, francamente, troppo piccolo. c. Mi sembra che non ho bisogno di niente, ma grazie comunque.
d. A dire la verità non mi piace il caffè qui.

Put it together   Example: Il mio museo preferito di Roma sono i Musei Vaticani. Secondo me, è molto più grande e interessante degli altri. La mia opera d'arte preferita lì è ovviamente il Giudizio Universale di Michelangelo. Vorrei sapere di più su questa opera. Cosa c'è di più meraviglioso?

COMPLETING UNIT 6

Check your understanding   a. falso b. vero c. vero d. vero e. vero.

COMPLETE YOUR MISSION

Build your script   Domani vado a mangiare alla mia trattoria preferita di Roma. Lì fanno i migliori spaghetti alla carbonara di tutta Italia, con uova, pecorino e pepe. Mmm... buonissimi! Altri piatti tipici che puoi mangiare lì e che ti consiglio sono i carciofi alla romana. Sono carciofi fritti ed è una specialità di Roma. Questa trattoria fa dei piatti molto grandi e sono anche più economici degli altri ristoranti. Secondo me, è il migliore anche perché non è un posto turistico e solo i romani lo conoscono. Hanno una birra e dei vini della casa buonissimi! Ti consiglio il vino rosso e di andare a piedi poi! Ahah! C'è molta scelta di dolci, come la zuppa inglese, la panna cotta e la torta di mele. Quale mi consigli? Sono indeciso!

UNIT 7

CONVERSATION 1

Figure it out   **1** b   **2** a. Il fine settimana scorso b. Cosa ne pensi? c. Ho parlato con lei dei nostri programmi.   **3** 'Why did you decide to go to the Pantheon?'   **4** a. falso b. vero c. falso d. vero
5 a. Cosa hai fatto? b. Ho mangiato c. Sono andato/a d. Abbiamo visitato e. Ho parlato
f. Abbiamo visto g. Hai conosciuto h. Ti è piacuto?

Notice   **1** a. fa b. scorso c. una volta d. lì vicino

Grammar explanation   **1** a. ho b. parlato c. ho parlato   **2** a. Ho mangiato b. Ho studiato
c. Ho capito d. Ho ricevuto   **3** a. Sono uscito b. Ho scelto c. ha visto

Practice   **1** Example: Ho conosciuto la mia migliore amica otto anni fa. (I met my best friend
8 years ago.)   **2** a. Devi andare al ristorante dove ho pranzato due giorni fa. b. Mi è piaciuto il film.
c. Ha visto il ragazzo di Anna.   **3** a. fa, sono andato b. Ho conosciuto c. sono arrivato d. Hanno
lavorato e. Abbiamo mangiato

Vocab explanation: getting to know someone   a. ho conosciuto b. ho incontrato
c. Vedo, ogni

Put it together   **1** Example: Il fine settimana scorso sono andato a Torino. Ho tanti amici lì.
Sabato sera siamo andati al ristorante e abbiamo passato due ore a parlare di tante cose: il lavoro,
le vacanze, la famiglia. Mi è piaciuto molto questo tipo di weekend.   **2** Example: Sono andato in
Australia. Ho passato un mese lì. Ho deciso di andare a Sydney perché è un posto interessante e mi
è piaciuto tanto. Ho visto molti monumenti di Sydney: l'Opera House, il famoso ponte, e i negozi. Ho
comprato regali per tutta la mia famiglia.

CONVERSATION 2

Figure it out   **1** a. vero b. falso c. falso   **2** a. Ha praticato alcune frasi. b. Ha iniziato solo pochi
mesi fa. c. That's right!   **3** hai avuto, ho studiato, ho imparato, ho praticato, hai fatto, ho fatto, ho
detto, hai detto, hai iniziato, ho iniziato, ho deciso, ho comprato, sono venuta, hai raccontato

Notice   **1** a. Hai avuto tempo di …? b. Devo dire che … c. Mi hai raccontato che …   **2** a. ho deciso
b. ho fatto c. ho iniziato   **3** a. ho studiato b. ho praticato c. ho iniziato d. ho imparato
e. ho comprato f. ho avuto

Grammar explanation: top 'irregular' past verbs

1
Italian	Meaning	Italian	Meaning
abbiamo fatto	we made	ha scritto	he wrote
hai scritto	you wrote	ho letto	I read
ho deciso	I decided	abbiamo detto	we said

ha visto	he saw	mi è piaciuto	I liked it (it pleased me)
ha preso	she took	abbiamo chiesto	we asked
ho visto	I saw	abbiamo risposto	we answered

2 Past tense: irregular verbs   g. fatto h. deciso i. ho risposto j. ho detto

Practice   **1** a. Ho iniziato a insegnare italiano nove mesi fa. b. Ho lasciato il mio ragazzo tre mesi fa. c. Ho conosciuto Andrea alcuni anni fa.   **2** a. Guardo il film adesso. b. Guardo il film domani. c. Ho guardato il film la settimana scorsa.   **3** a. da b. Una volta, sono andato/a c. L'estate scorsa, ho viaggiato in treno d. Hai bisogno, Li ho qui. e. Devo dire che, più facili, settimana scorsa

Put it together   Example: Il giorno del mio compleanno, sono stato a casa la mattina. Ho ricevuto tanti regali da mio fratello, mio padre e mia madre. Abbiamo pranzato al ristorante, poi siamo andati al cinema. Alla sera sono uscito con gli amici e con la mia ragazza.

CONVERSATION 3

Figure it out   **1** a. nervosa b. la mia pronuncia c. accento d. grammatica   **2** a. vero b. falso c. falso

Notice   **1** a. È meglio imparare un po'/poco ogni giorno. b. Ho dimenticato il tuo nome. c. Una volta ho provato a studiare il russo. **2** a. Non abbiamo visto niente. b. Non c'è nessuno qui. c. Non ho mai mangiato la bruschetta.   **3** a. Sapevi che b. Ho trovato c. Ho provato

Practice   **1** a. Cecilia aveva il libro. b. Non sapeva c. Volevo mangiare con te.   **2** a. le due parole b. Hai parlato, vuol dire c. Hai capito? d. pronuncia, ho detto, parola e. Ha dimenticato f. ho chiesto, 'trovi il mio accento', ha detto g. Ho studiato, grammatica h. Ti chiamo, ho scritto, frasi i. hai aiutato   **3** a. Non mi aiuti mai! b. Non ha detto niente. c. Non conosco nessuno qui.

Vocab explanation: time indicators   **1** a. ho studiato b. andiamo c. leggo d. abbiamo praticato e. hanno mangiato f. ha visitato g. andiamo

Your turn: use the hack   **1** a. Domani preparo dei panini e vado al parco. b. Lunedì prossimo cucino e mangio a casa tua. c. La prossima settimana prendo il treno e viaggio per l'Italia.   **2** Tre giorni fa, 'prendo' un treno e 'vedo' un orso.   **3** Examples: a. Una settimana fa ho visto un bel film. b. Sabato scorso ho fatto vacanza. c. Due anni fa sono andata in Canada. d. Ieri ho lavorato al computer.   **4** Examples: a. Mercoledì prossimo vado al mercato. b. Tra un anno visito/voglio visitare la Cina.

Put it together   Example: Due settimane fa ho conosciuto un ragazzo italiano. Volevo parlare italiano con lui e l'ho invitato al bar a prendere un caffè. Ma non sapevo cosa dire, la situazione era molto imbarazzante. Dopo due o tre minuti lui mi ha chiesto perché ero in Italia. Allora ho deciso di parlare delle mie lezioni di italiano online. È stata un'esperienza divertente.

COMPLETE YOUR MISSION

Build your script   Un'anno fa sono andato a Milano per lavoro, ma non sapevo parlare italiano. Non era importante per il lavoro perché tutti parlavano inglese in ufficio, ma per la strada era un vero problema. Volevo andare a vedere la famosa Galleria con i suoi negozi molto eleganti. Quando sono arrivato, ho deciso di entrare in un negozio e comprare un regalo per la mia ragazza. Ma era tutto troppo caro! Ero molto imbarazzato: come si dice in italiano 'Have you got something cheaper?' Alla fine ho indicato un oggetto e ho detto 'quello ... poco caro'. Mi hanno capito benissimo.

UNIT 8

CONVERSATION 1

Figure it out   **1** a. a lot better (molto migliorato). b. recently (recentemente). c. parmigiana **2** Sono felice di rivederti.   **3** a. Ha iniziato a cucinare. b. Spera di imparare a fare il tiramisù. **4** a. Come vanno le cose? b. Quanto tempo! c. In questo momento.   **5** It's important to practise.

Notice   **1** a. Forza e coraggio! b. Quando provo a ...   **2** a. Quanto. b. Cosa c. a fare

Practice   **1** a. Quanto tempo! Sono felice di rivederti. b. Dimmi, come vanno le cose? Vedo che… c. Allora, recentemente ...   **2** a. So che … b. Sai se …? c. Hai visto che …?   **3** Example: Recentemente ho cominciato a cucinare. Al momento solo so fare poche ricette, ma vorrei migliorare e imparare di più.

Put it together   Example: Recentemente mi sono iscritta a un corso di cucina perché mi piace molto fare le torte, ma non so fare il risotto. L'ultima volta che ho provato a farlo, non mi è venuto bene. Finora l'ho sempre dovuto buttar via. Sono davvero imbranata, ma spero di migliorare e imparare di più.

CONVERSATION 2

Figure it out   **1** a. loved - era strano, misses home - ha una routine. b. takes the metro - va in bicicletta. c. rarely - spesso. d. the worst - i migliori. e. at a café - a casa   **2** weird, I have a routine   **3** (Mi) sembra che ... You can use this for all three: a conversation starter, a warmer or extension. **4** a. 1 anch'io 2 neanch'io 3 raramente 4 di solito. b. in bici, in auto

Notice   **2** **1**. prima del lavoro **3** a pranzo **5** ogni tanto **6** raramente **7** spesso **8** sempre **9** a volte **10** mai **11** per la città **13** ovunque **14** al lavoro **15** nello stesso **16** a casa **3** a. Il sabato pomeriggio di solito, porto il cane a fare una passeggiata. b. La domenica mattina di solito, dormo un'ora in più. c. Il venerdì dopo il lavoro di solito, vado al cinema. d. Il giovedì dopo pranzo di solito, vado a lezione di russo. e. Il martedì prima di dormire di solito, guardo un film alla televisione.

Practice   1 Examples: Vado a correre. Imparo nuove lingue. Faccio danza.   2 Examples: a. Tutti i giorni prima di fare colazione, mi piace andare a correre con il mio ragazzo vicino a casa. All'inizio era noioso e faticoso, ma ora mi diverto molto e sono in forma. b. Mi piace andare al mare e guardare il tramonto. Vado spesso in spiaggia perché mi rilassa. c. Vado spesso in centro perché mi piace fare shopping. c. Non sono mai stato ai Caraibi, ma spero di andarci un giorno.

Put it together   Example: Tutti i giorni mi sveglio alle 6 e prima di fare colazione, vado a correre mezz'ora con il mio ragazzo vicino a casa. Spesso il pomeriggio scatto fotografie splendide del tramonto del sole sulla spiaggia, della mia famiglia e dei miei amici. Poi mi piace anche imparare ogni giorno nuove parole in italiano. Dopo cena adoro guardare le mie serie preferite in italiano per migliorare ancora di più.

CONVERSATION 3

Figure it out   1 a. falso b. vero c. vero d. falso   2 a. spero di andare al parco b. con alcuni amici a giocare a calcio. c. purtroppo ho già in programma di andare a fare shopping d. con un'amica

Notice   1 a. adorerebbe b. sarebbe c. piacerebbe d. parlerebbe   2 a. Cosa devo portare? b. A che ora? c. Puoi scrivermi il tuo indirizzo? d. Te lo mostro sulla mappa!   3 a. A che ora finisce? b. Sai l'indirizzo? c. Dov'è l'appartamento? d. A che ora devo arrivare? e. Posso portare del vino?

Practice   1 a. Examples: Cosa fai stasera/ domani? b. Ho tempo libero più tardi/alle cinque per andare al concerto. Vieni?   2 a. Examples: Sarebbe meraviglioso/perfetto. b. Mi piacerebbe, ma sfortunatamente ho già altri programmi/sono occupata.   3 a. Ti piacerebbe imparare l'italiano con me? b. Ti piacerebbe andare a fare shopping questo weekend?

Put it together   1 Example: Per cominciare potrebbe mangiare in questo ristorante: fanno piatti tipici della mia città. Il posto migliore da visitare sarebbe senza dubbio la costa. Potrebbe prendere un taxi per andare alla spiaggia più bella. Può anche andare in autobus e dopo le cinque di pomeriggio il biglietto sarebbe meno caro. Ma dovrebbero avere prezzi ridotti per gli anziani tutto il giorno. Buon divertimento!   2 Mi piacerebbe molto andare al cinema con te stasera. Il film mi sembra interessante, ma purtroppo ho già in programma di cenare con mia nonna. Non la vedo da molto tempo e se non vado da lei, si arrabbia. Sei invitato se vuoi, ma non è un piano molto divertente.

Your turn: use the hack   a. Example: Non vinciamo, credo. b. Example: Sono felice di mangiare insieme. c. Example: Mi piacerebbe molto ballare con te d. Example: Vado al supermercato più tardi, è meglio.

COMPLETE YOUR MISSION

Build your script   Mi piace molto la fotografia e scattare la foto perfetta. La gente pensa che dipende solo dalla macchina fotografica, ma non è facile. Mi è sempre piaciuto fare le fotografie e ho questa macchina fotografica da cinque anni. Finora ho vinto sei concorsi di fotografia negli Stati Uniti. Ma non la uso spesso di giorno, perché lavoro dalle nove alle tre di pomeriggio. Poi torno a casa e mangio con la mia famiglia. Di pomeriggio vado normalmente a fare la spesa o vado in palestra.

Ogni weekend mi piace andare con mio marito al mare, che è vicino a casa mia. Vado in macchina e mi rilassa molto. Lì prendo il sole e faccio il bagno. Un'altra cosa che mi piace molto è fare colazione con calma la mattina. È il momento della giornata che preferisco. Per questo, mi sveglio almeno un'ora prima di uscire. Il caffè deve fare effetto, sennò non mi ricordo come mi chiamo!

UNIT 9

CONVERSATION 1

Figure it out   **1** a. last day – ultima settimana. b. dancing – fare shopping. c. a lot to eat – piena di negozi   **2** a. Soon I'll go back to the US b. What a pity! c. It depends.   **3** a. in campagna b. le montagne c. il lago e la foresta d. vicino a casa mia e. al sole

Notice   **1** a. torna negli Stati Uniti tra una settimana. b. compra alcuni regali. c. compra in Via dei Condotti.   **2** a. ricordarmi di … b. ricordo c. Mi ha ricordato   **3** a. 1 b. 3 c. 2   **4** Left column: la campagna, le montagne, il lago. Right column: la foresta, il sole, l'ombra   **5** Examples: a. in una città. b. all'ombra. c. il lago.

Practice   **1** Examples: al mare, in periferia, in collina, in una valle, vicino a un bosco, vicino all'oceano.   **2** Examples: a. Vivo in un paese vicino al mare. b. Vicino a casa mia c'è un parco/ci sono molti negozi …

Vocab explanation: mancare for miss   **1** a. Mi manca il mio cane. b. Mi mancano i sette gatti. c. Ci manca Roma d. A Francesco manca il caffè italiano. e. Ti manca la tua città? f. Perché non ti mancano le feste?

Vocab explanation: talking about the weather   **1** a. Fa bel tempo. b. Fa brutto tempo. Che peccato! c. Piove domani?   **2** Example: Fa brutto tempo, c'è vento e piove. Ma non fa molto freddo.   **3** a. carino, carina b. pieno, piena c. bello, bella

Put it together   Example: La mia città è molto bella. Si trova vicino alle montagne e per questa ragione fa sempre fresco, anche in estate. Ci sono molti parchi e negozi. In estate ci sono sempre molti turisti e quindi non è molto tranquilla. Si vado via, mi mancano sempre le montagne.

CONVERSATION 2

Figure it out   **1** a. falso b. vero c. falso   **2** a. souvenir tipici di Roma b. avventurosa c. giovane e una persona timida d. più tradizionali e. più economica   **3** a. straordinaria b. famosissima c. tipici d. noiosi e. vecchie f. timida g. tradizionali h. nuove   **4** a. ricordo b. vuole veramente c. troverebbe d. piuttosto e. già

Notice   **1** a. Ora ricordo b. Cosa compreresti c. I miei genitori sono più tradizionali **2** a. facile, difficile b. unico, tipico c. stupidi, saggi d. moderni, tradizionali e. avventurosa, timida f. vecchio, giovane   **3** a. Il negozio è aperto. b. I negozi sono aperti c. Il negozio era aperto. d. Mio fratello è alto. e. I miei fratelli sono alti. f. Mia sorella è alta. g. Le mie sorelle sono alte.

Practice 1 È il più economico. 2 timido(a) – adventurous; brutto(a) – beautiful; old – giovane; strange – tipico(a); antipatico(a) – pleasant; pessimista – optimist; orgoglioso(a) – modest; divertente – serious 3 a. interessante b. attento c. creativo d. curioso e. onesto f. intelligente g. sincero h. tollerante i. ignorante j. impaziente 4 Examples: a. Sono molto simpatico e sincero. b. Il mio lavoro è molto interessante e imparo cose nuove ogni giorno. c. Mio fratello è una persona molto ironica e gentile. d. La sua casa è molto bella ed elegante. e. La mia amica è bionda, molto alta ed è la persona migliore che conosco.

Put it together Example: Mia madre e mio padre sono persone molto interessanti. Mio padre è molto ottimista e determinato, mia madre invece è un po' pessimista, ma anche dolce e socievole...

CONVERSATION 3

Figure it out 1 a. he lost them – le sue sono piuttosto vecchie. b. not – sono un po' care c. in cash – con la carta di credito 2 In contanti, con la carta di credito. Till. 3 a. nere b. verdi 4 sarebbe

Notice 1 a. mi sembra b. si usa per 2 Per che cosa usa le cuffie tuo fratello? ... usare la mia carta di credito. 3 a. quello b. quelle nere c. quello piccolo d. quelle nuove 4 Examples: a. le Nike b. Kleenex c. Pepsi d. Mac e. Fiat 5 a. un po' caro b. pagare in contanti c. usare la mia carta di credito d. la cassa

Practice 1 a. Quanto costa questa? b. Com'è la qualità? c. Accetta carte di credito? d. Posso solo pagare in contanti. 2 a. quella marca b. cassa c. il computer grande 3 First column: pieno(a), Second column: wide, bad quality, Third column: verde, Fourth column: black

Put it together Example: Cerco una borsa di pelle molto grande, per viaggiare. Magari di colore rosso e di marca ...

COMPLETE YOUR MISSION

Build your script La città dove sono cresciuto è molto piccola e non c'è molto da fare o da vedere. Per questo non la raccomando ai turisti. Però c'è il mare con una bella spiaggia pulita! Dietro la città ci sono colline e montagne con molti uliveti. Il clima è mite e d'inverno non fa tanto freddo e naturalmente non nevica. La casa dei miei è grande, ha tre piani e un giardino. Le persone più importanti della mia vita sono i miei genitori e mio fratello. Mio fratello ha venticinque anni ed è laureato in fisica. Ecco una foto dove siamo tutti insieme durante una vacanza in montagna.

UNIT 10

COMPLETE YOUR MISSION Sono felice di parlare con te oggi. Mi chiamo Benny. Voglio imparare l'italiano per il mio lavoro. Quanti studenti hai? Da quando insegni? Non voglio parlare di grammatica. Possiamo parlare di computer? Grazie mille per il tuo tempo oggi. Ci vediamo la prossima volta!

ACKNOWLEDGEMENTS

Though my name and face may be on the cover, there are so many people whose voices and ideas are in these pages.

I was fortunate to meet many native Italian speakers who encouraged me when I was a struggling beginner, from my first Italian friends, *Francesco* who showed me around the south and *Daniele* who welcomed me to his home and invited me to Easter dinner with four generations of his family.

There aren't enough praises I can sing about my editor *Sarah Cole*, who first reached out to me with the exciting prospect of collaborating with Teach Yourself. She worked with me over two years with unwavering support and passion for my vision of a modern language course. I cannot imagine that any other publisher could have brought so much life to these courses.

Melissa Baker worked behind the scenes to juggle timetables and perform more than a few miracles to ensure all the pieces of this publishing puzzle came together. I am grateful to the rest of the *Teach Yourself* team in both the UK and US, who showed incredible enthusiasm in creating a totally new kind of language course.

Paola Tite worked with me over many months to make large and small improvements to each chapter. The other members of my 'mini team' *Michela* and *Alessandra* brought fun Italian expressions and slang to the conversations, often staying up very late to help me get them just right.

I owe a huge thank-you to the brilliant people at Team FI3M: Bálint, David, Kittichai, Dávid, Joe, Ingo, Joseph, Adam, Holly and LC, who kept my website, Fluent in 3 Months, running while I was busy writing these courses and made sure we continued to do innovative work. Thank you all.

Finally, my partner *Lauren*, without whom this course never could have come to light. She is the Pepper Potts to my Tony Stark – she makes sure my crazy ideas run smoothly and professionally, and she came up with many of the cleverest concepts that you see in these pages. Her perfectionism and academic background turned my ideas for a good course, into a truly great one.